First World War
and Army of Occupation
War Diary
France, Belgium and Germany

46 DIVISION
Divisional Troops
Royal Army Medical Corps
1/2 North Midland Field Ambulance
1 December 1915 - 31 May 1919

WO95/2680/2

The Naval & Military Press Ltd
www.nmarchive.com
Published in association with The National Archives

Published by

The Naval & Military Press Ltd

Unit 10 Ridgewood Industrial Park,
Uckfield, East Sussex,
TN22 5QE England
Tel: +44 (0) 1825 749494

www.naval-military-press.com

www.nmarchive.com

This diary has been reprinted in facsimile from the original. Any imperfections are inevitably reproduced and the quality may fall short of modern type and cartographic standards.

© **Crown Copyright**
Images reproduced by permission of The National Archives, London, England, 2015.

Contents

Document type	Place/Title	Date From	Date To
Heading	WO95/2680/2		
Heading	46th Division Medical 1/2nd Nth Midland Fd Amb. Mar 1915-1919 May		
Heading	121/5022 March 1915 1/2nd North Midland Field Ambulance		
Miscellaneous	1/2nd North Midland Field Ambulance R.A.M.C.T Summary of War Diary for March 1915	01/04/1915	01/04/1915
Miscellaneous	2nd N. Mid. Fd. Ambulance.		
Operation(al) Order(s)	Operation Order No. 3 by Brigadier General W.R. Clifford Commanding 1/1st Lincoln & Leicester Brigade	14/03/1915	14/03/1915
Operation(al) Order(s)	Operation Order No. 4. by Brigadier-General W.R. Clifford Commanding Lincoln & Leicester Infantry Brigade T.F.		
Miscellaneous	Operation Orders By Brig Gen A.J. Clifford Commanding Lincs-Leic Bde T.F.	22/03/1915	22/03/1915
Operation(al) Order(s)	Operation Order No. 5 By Brigadier General W.R. Clifford Commanding 1/1st Lincs. & Leics. Infty. Bde. T.F.	25/03/1915	25/03/1915
Heading	121/5320 April 1915 1/2 N.M. Field Ambulance Vol II		
Heading	War Diary of 1st/2nd North Midland Field Ambulance R.A.M.C.T. Lincoln and Leicester Brigade North Midland Division From April 1st to April 30th 1915		
Miscellaneous	2nd North Midland Field Ambulance R.A.M.C.T. Summary of War diary for April 1915	00/04/1915	00/04/1915
Miscellaneous	War Diary-2nd N. Mid. Field Ambulance	01/04/1915	01/04/1915
Heading	46th Division 1/2nd N.M. Field Ambulance Vol III 121/5617 May 1915		
Miscellaneous	Summary of War Diary of the 2nd North Midland Field Ambulance R.A.M.C.T. 138th Brigade 46th Division	01/06/1915	01/06/1915
Miscellaneous	Dranoutre		
Miscellaneous	Dranoutre	05/05/1915	05/05/1915
Miscellaneous	Dranoutre.	08/05/1915	08/05/1915
Miscellaneous	Senr War Diary for April to A.G. Base. Dranoutre	10/05/1915	10/05/1915
Miscellaneous	Dranoutre	12/05/1915	12/05/1915
Miscellaneous	Dranoutre	14/05/1915	14/05/1915
Miscellaneous	Dranoutre	22/05/1915	22/05/1915
Miscellaneous	Dranoutre	24/05/1915	24/05/1915
Miscellaneous	Dranoutre	29/05/1915	29/05/1915
Heading	46th Division 121/6390 1/2 N.M. Field Ambulance Vol III June 15		
Miscellaneous	Dranoutre	30/06/1915	30/06/1915
Heading	46th Division 121/6439 2nd North Midland Field Ambulance Vol V From 1st to 31st July 1915		
Miscellaneous	Abstract from War Diary of 2nd North Midland Field Ambulance R.A.M.C. 138th Brigade-26 Division in the field. for the month of July 1915	00/07/1915	00/07/1915
Heading	War Diary for July 1915 of the 2nd North Midland Field Ambulance R.A.M.C. 138 Brigade 46th Division		
Miscellaneous	Wippenhoek Farm-Poperinghe		

Heading	46th Division 1/2nd N.M. Field Ambulance Vol VI August 15		
Miscellaneous	Abstract from War Diary of 2nd N. Mid. F.A. R.A.M.C.T. 138th Brigade 46th Division in the field For the month of August 1915	00/08/1915	00/08/1915
Miscellaneous	Wippenhoek Farm-Poperinghe		
Miscellaneous	Poperinghe		
Heading	46th Division 1/2 N.M. Fd. Ambulance. Sep Vol VII Sept 15		
Heading	War Diary of 1/2nd N. Mid. F. amb R.A.M.C. September 1915 Sep-Oct 15		
Miscellaneous	Poperinghe		
Heading	War Diary 1/2nd North Midland F.A. October 1915		
Heading	War Diary of 1/2nd. N. Mid. F. Ambulance. R.A.M.C. October 1915		
Miscellaneous	Rheninghelst		
Miscellaneous	Gonnehem-France	04/10/1915	04/10/1915
Miscellaneous	Reninghelst		
Miscellaneous	Fouquieres		
Heading	46th Division 1/2nd N.M Fd amb Nov Vol VIII Nov 1915		
Miscellaneous	Oct 31st Verquin		
Heading	1/2nd. N. Mid. F Ambulance. R.A.M.C Y. December 1915 Vol IX		
War Diary	Mesplaux Farm	01/12/1915	04/12/1915
War Diary	Calonne	05/12/1915	18/12/1915
War Diary	Neufpre	19/12/1915	31/12/1915
Heading	War Diary of 1/2nd N. Mid Field Ambulance R.A.M.C.Y January 1916 Vol X		
War Diary	Neufpre	01/01/1916	04/01/1916
War Diary	In the train	05/01/1916	06/01/1916
War Diary	Parc Borely Marseilles	07/01/1916	09/01/1916
War Diary	Parc Borely	10/01/1916	20/01/1916
War Diary	S.S. Andania	21/01/1916	21/01/1916
War Diary	Parc Borely	22/01/1916	26/01/1916
War Diary	In the train	27/01/1916	28/01/1916
War Diary	Pont Remy	29/01/1916	31/01/1916
Heading	46th Div. 1/2 N U Field amb March 1916		
War Diary	Beauval-France	01/03/1916	01/03/1916
War Diary	Houvin Houvigneul France	06/03/1916	06/03/1916
War Diary	Villers-Chatel France	09/03/1916	28/03/1916
Heading	46th Div 1/2 P M. F. amb April 1916		
Heading	46 1/2 N.M. Fa amb Vol 14		
War Diary	Villers Chatel	01/04/1916	04/04/1916
War Diary	A.C.Q.	07/04/1916	14/04/1916
War Diary	Maisnil-St-Pol	21/04/1916	26/04/1916
Heading	War Diary of 2nd North Midland Field Ambulance R.A.M.C.T. 26 Division from April 1st to April 30th 1916 In the Field.		
Heading	46th Div 2nd P.M.F. amb May 1916		
War Diary	Maisnil-St-Pol France	01/05/1916	08/05/1916
War Diary	Le Souich France	09/05/1916	31/05/1916
Heading	46th Division 1/2 N. Midland Field Ambulance June 1916		
War Diary	Le Souich	01/06/1916	25/06/1916
War Diary	Gaudiempre	26/06/1916	30/06/1916

Heading	46th Division 1/2 N.M. Field Ambulance July 1916		
War Diary	Souastre	01/07/1916	01/07/1916
War Diary	Gaudiempre	02/07/1916	03/07/1916
War Diary	Larbret	04/07/1916	05/07/1916
War Diary	Couturelle	06/07/1916	06/07/1916
War Diary	Gaudiempre	03/07/1916	03/07/1916
War Diary	Larbret	04/07/1916	05/07/1916
War Diary	Couturelle	06/07/1916	31/07/1916
Heading	1/2nd N.M.F.A Aug 1916		
Miscellaneous	A.D.M.S. 46th Div	01/09/1916	01/09/1916
Miscellaneous	A.D.M.S. 46th Div	31/08/1916	31/08/1916
War Diary	Couturelle	02/08/1916	31/08/1916
Heading	46th Div 1/2nd N.M. Field Ambulance Sept. 1916		
War Diary	Couturelle France	01/09/1916	19/09/1916
War Diary	Mondicourt France	20/09/1916	30/09/1916
Heading	46th Div 2nd N.M. Field Ambulance Oct 1916		
War Diary	Mondicourt France	01/10/1916	01/10/1916
War Diary	Gouy-En-Artois France	02/10/1916	21/10/1916
War Diary	Couturelle France	22/10/1916	29/10/1916
War Diary	Grenas France	30/10/1916	31/10/1916
Heading	46th Div 1/2nd N.M. Field Ambulance No. 1916		
War Diary	Wavans France	01/11/1916	01/11/1916
War Diary	Maison-Ponthieu	02/11/1916	02/11/1916
War Diary	Le Plessiel	03/11/1916	07/11/1916
War Diary	Froyelles	08/11/1916	09/11/1916
War Diary	Ouville	11/11/1916	15/11/1916
War Diary	Ouville France	18/11/1916	21/11/1916
War Diary	Ribaudcourt	22/11/1916	22/11/1916
War Diary	Villers L'Hopital	23/11/1916	23/11/1916
War Diary	Caumesnil	25/11/1916	27/11/1916
War Diary	Caumesnil France	27/11/1916	29/11/1916
Heading	War Diary for November 1916 of 2nd North Mid. F. Ambulance R.A.M.C.T.		
Heading	46th Div 1/2nd N.M. Field Ambulance Dec.1916		
Heading	War Diary for December 1916 of 1/2nd. N.M.F.amb. R.A.M.C (T.F) Vol 22		
War Diary	Caumesnil	01/12/1916	05/12/1916
War Diary	Gaudiempre	06/12/1916	31/12/1916
Heading	46th Div. 2nd N.M. Field Ambulance Jan 1917		
War Diary	Gaudiempre	01/01/1917	31/01/1917
Heading	46th Div 1/2nd N.M. Field Ambulance Feb.1917		
War Diary	Gaidiempre	01/02/1917	02/02/1917
War Diary	St Amand	03/02/1917	27/02/1917
War Diary	Fonque-Villiers	28/02/1917	28/02/1917
Heading	46th Div 1/2nd N.M. Field Ambulance Mar.1917		
Miscellaneous	To A.D.M.S., 46th Division	01/04/1917	01/04/1917
War Diary	Fonque-Villiers	01/03/1917	19/03/1917
War Diary	Vauchelles	20/03/1917	23/03/1917
War Diary	Septonville	24/03/1917	24/03/1917
War Diary	Petit Cagny	26/03/1917	26/03/1917
War Diary	Vers	27/03/1917	27/03/1917
War Diary	In The Train	28/03/1917	28/03/1917
War Diary	Livossart	29/03/1917	31/03/1917
Heading	46th Div 1/2nd North Midland F.A. April 1917		
War Diary	Livossart France	01/04/1917	12/04/1917
War Diary	Busnes France	13/04/1917	20/04/1917

War Diary	La Beuvriere France	22/04/1917	30/04/1917
Heading	B.E.F. Summary Of Medical War Diaries For 1/2nd N. Mid. F.A. 46th Divn. 2nd Corps. 1st Corps 22/4/17 1st Army Western Front April-May. '17		
Miscellaneous	1/2nd N. Mid. F.A. 46th Divn. 2nd Corps.	22/04/1917	22/04/1917
Miscellaneous	B.e.f		
Miscellaneous	1/2nd N. Mid. F.A. 46th Divn. 2nd Corps	22/04/1917	22/04/1917
Heading	1/2nd North Midland F.A. May. 1917		
War Diary	La Beuvriere Ref France 1/40000 Bethune (Combined Sheet)	01/05/1917	09/05/1917
War Diary	La Beuvriere France	10/05/1917	16/05/1917
War Diary	La Beuvriere	17/05/1917	25/05/1917
War Diary	Aixnoulette	26/05/1917	31/05/1917
Heading	War Diary of 1/2 North Mid. Field Amb R.A.M.C.T. from May 1 to May 31 1917		
Heading	B.E.F. Summary Of Medical War Diaries For 1/2nd N. Mid. F.A. 46th Divn. 2nd Corps 1st Corps 22/4/17. 1st Army. Western Front April-May. '17		
Map	Buildings Inhabited By Civilians		
Miscellaneous	1/2nd N. Mid. F.A. 46th Divn. 1st Corps	00/05/1917	00/05/1917
Heading	1/2nd North Midland F.A. June. 1917		
War Diary	Aixnoulette France	01/06/1917	18/06/1917
War Diary	Aixnoulette	18/06/1917	30/06/1917
War Diary	Aixnoulette France	30/06/1917	30/06/1917
Heading	War Diary of 1/2nd N. Mid. Field Ambu R.A.M.C.T. 46th Division B.E.F. From June 1. 1917 To June 30 1917		
Heading	1/2nd N.M. Field Ambulance July 1917		
War Diary	Aix Noulette France	01/07/1917	01/07/1917
War Diary	Houdain France	02/07/1917	02/07/1917
War Diary	Monchy-Le-Breton France	03/07/1917	09/07/1917
War Diary	Monchy. Breton France	13/07/1917	22/07/1917
War Diary	Bethune	23/07/1917	30/07/1917
Heading	1/2nd North Midland F.A. Aug 1917		
War Diary	Bethune France	01/08/1917	23/08/1917
War Diary	Fouqieres France	24/08/1917	31/08/1917
Heading	War Diary Of 1/2nd North Midland Field Ambulance R.A.M.C.T.F. 46' Division B.E.F. France from August 1. 1917 to August 31. 1917		
Heading	1/2nd North Midland F.A. Sept 1917		
War Diary	Fouquieres (Rest Station 1 Corps) France	01/09/1917	29/09/1917
Heading	War Diary of 1/2 N Mid Field Amb R.A.M.C.T.F 46 Division from September 1st 1917 to September 30 1917		
Heading	1/2nd North Midland F.A. Oct 1917		
War Diary	Fouquieres	01/10/1917	31/10/1917
Heading	1/2nd North Midland F.A. Nov. 1917		
War Diary	Fouquieres	01/11/1917	12/11/1917
War Diary	Labourse	13/11/1917	30/11/1917
Heading	1/2nd N.M. F.A Dec 1917		
War Diary	Labourse	01/12/1917	31/12/1917
Heading	1/2nd North Midland F.A. Jan. 1918		
War Diary	Labourse	01/01/1918	24/01/1918
War Diary	Cantrainne	24/01/1918	31/01/1918
Heading	1/2nd N.M. F.A. Feb 1918		
War Diary	Cantrainne	01/02/1918	08/02/1918

War Diary	Nedonchelle	08/02/1918	09/02/1918
War Diary	Audincthun	09/02/1918	28/02/1918
Heading	1/2 Nth Mid. F. Ambulance March 1918		
War Diary	Audincthun	01/03/1918	01/03/1918
War Diary	Cuhem	02/03/1918	02/03/1918
War Diary	Le Cornet Bourdois	03/03/1918	03/03/1918
War Diary	Bethune	04/03/1918	26/03/1918
War Diary	Pt. Sains (Fosse 10)	28/03/1918	30/03/1918
Heading	1/2 N.M. Field Ambulance Apr 1918		
War Diary	P. Sains (Fosse. 10)	01/04/1918	13/04/1918
War Diary	Barlin	13/04/1918	22/04/1918
War Diary	Labeuvriere	24/04/1918	28/04/1918
Heading	Appendix I has been detached and field under Wars "Rest Stations"		
Miscellaneous			
Heading	1/2 Nth. Mid. F.a. May 1918		
War Diary	Labeuvriere	01/05/1918	31/05/1918
War Diary	Wavrans	31/05/1918	31/05/1918
Heading	War Diary Of The 1/2 North. Midland. Field Ambulance For June 1918 Vol 40		
War Diary	Wavrans	01/06/1918	30/06/1918
Heading	War Diary Of 1/2 North Midland Field Ambulance From 1/7/18. to 31/7/18. Vol 41		
War Diary	Wavrans	01/07/1918	03/07/1918
War Diary	Bruay	05/07/1918	31/07/1918
Heading	War Diary of 1/2 North Midland Field Ambulance From 1/8/18 to 31/8/18 Vol 42		
War Diary	Bruay	01/08/1918	31/08/1918
Heading	War Diary Of 1/2 North Midland Field Ambulance For Month ending 30/9/18 Vol 43		
War Diary	Bruay	01/09/1918	12/09/1918
War Diary	Corbie	12/09/1918	12/09/1918
War Diary	Franvillers	12/09/1918	18/09/1918
War Diary	Poeuilly	19/09/1918	21/09/1918
War Diary	Hancourt	23/09/1918	23/09/1918
War Diary	Vendelles	24/09/1918	24/09/1918
War Diary	Hancourt	25/09/1918	25/09/1918
War Diary	Vadencourt	28/09/1918	30/09/1918
Heading	War Diary Of 1/2 North Midland Field Ambulance for the Month of October. 1918 Vol 44		
War Diary	Hancourt	01/10/1918	01/10/1918
War Diary	Vaden Court	02/10/1918	08/10/1918
War Diary	Levergies	09/10/1918	10/10/1918
War Diary	Fresnoy-Le-Grand	12/10/1918	16/10/1918
War Diary	Bohain	17/10/1918	18/10/1918
War Diary	Fresnoy	19/10/1918	31/10/1918
Heading	From November 1st. 1918 to November 31st. 1918 O.C. 1/2nd N.M. Field Ambulance Vol 45		
War Diary	Busigny	01/11/1918	04/11/1918
War Diary	L'Arbre De Guise	04/11/1918	04/11/1918
War Diary	Catillon	05/11/1918	06/11/1918
War Diary	Mezier	06/11/1918	06/11/1918
War Diary	Cartignies	07/11/1918	09/11/1918
War Diary	Sains Du Nord	09/11/1918	13/11/1918
War Diary	Avesnes	14/11/1918	16/11/1918
War Diary	Bousies	18/11/1918	30/11/1918

Heading	War Diary Of 1/2nd N.M. Field Ambulance 1st December 1918 to 31st December 1918 Vol 46		
War Diary	Bousies	01/12/1918	29/12/1918
Heading	46 2 N M Fd amb Vol XIII		
Heading	War Diary Of 1/2nd North Midland Field Ambulance (T.F.) Jan 1st to Jan 31st 1919 Vol 47		
War Diary	Bousies	05/01/1919	29/01/1919
Heading	War Diary Of 1/2nd N.M. Field Ambulance 1/2/19. To 28/2/19 Vol 48		
War Diary	Bousies	01/02/1919	23/02/1919
War Diary	Solesmes	24/02/1919	28/02/1919
Heading	1/2nd North Midland F.A. Mar. 1919		
War Diary	Solesmes	01/03/1919	09/03/1919
War Diary	St Hilaire	10/03/1919	31/03/1919
Heading	1/2 Nth Mid F.a. Apr 1919		
War Diary	St Hilaire	03/04/1919	03/04/1919
War Diary	Inchy	07/04/1919	29/04/1919
Heading	1/2nd North Mid F.A May 1919		
War Diary	Inchy	06/05/1919	31/05/1919

W0951268019

46TH DIVISION
MEDICAL

1/2ND NTH MIDLAND FD AMB.

MAR 1915 - ~~DEC 1918~~

1919 MAY

121/5022
March 1915

1/2nd Notts & Derby Field Ambulance

1/2nd North Midland Field Ambulance:
R A M C T.
Summary of War Diary for March 1915.
_____

Except for a few days in Belgium, the unit has spent this month in France. The Unit left HAVRE on March 3, proceeding by train to:
March 4: CASSEL (ZEMERZELE)., and (ZUITPEN)
" 9: STRAZELLES. by route march
" 11: SAILLY. by route march
" 12: BEC-ST-MAURE. by road.
" 16: VERRIER (SALOMÉ-LA-NOIRE FARM) Route March
" 18: STEENWERKE (AYMARDS FARM). Route March

WORK OF UNIT:
ZUITPEN: Hospital Established
BEC-ST-MAUR: Hospital Established
SAILLY: Hospital Established
AYMARDS FARM: Hospital Established.

In some cases, notably at AYMARDS FARM, the accommodation was totally inadequate for running as Hospital. At the latter place, the room used for Hospital was also the Orderly Room, and sleeping room for the Clerks. Beds were not to be obtained; and the floor was of slate.
Two motor ambulances were attached to the unit towards the end of the month, and

by this means the cases admitted were quickly evacuated to MERRIS or HAZEBROUCK, and I was able to keep the Hospital from becoming choked up. Bathing accommodation has been difficult to obtain, especially in cases of Bivouacs or Billets: but latterly, large tubs from Farms have been obtained, and things have gone better.

After every Brigade or Divisional march, a number of men were either left behind in billets, or fell out on the roadside, unfit to proceed. At first, much confusion occurred, owing to R.M.O.'s failing to notify me that this had been done, and in some cases considerable difficulty was experienced in collecting these derelicts. Latterly, however, this fault has been mended, and the R.M.O.s send in a list of men unfit to march, and their billets: these men are collected by my Motor Ambulances, and conveyed to their new billeting Area.

There is still a considerable number of men unable to do even a moderately long march. Many of these men have been sent from the reserve units, to which they were originally transferred from the Imperial Service Unit. This practice should be absolutely stopped. The Imperial Service Unit is not a dumping ground for the lame ducks of the Home unit; many men are fit for Home Service, but unfit for Service abroad.

With regard to equipment, the Unit is now well fitted out, both Medical equipment and Clothing. One mistake I think was made, in serving out boots to the men several sizes too large; the result was sore and blistered feet. Another factor is the very marked "Cambre" of the roads here, necessitating the men on the flank, especially the right Flank, of the section of fours, walking with his ankles more or less twisted — a very tiring process. It would be a good thing to change the flank and centre men over every hour, at the hourly Halt. There has been little serious illness in the Brigade: a few of the common Zymotic diseases. Nearly every man has been inoculated. In this Unit 97%. — a necessary precaution, seeing the quality of the Water in Northern France. Drinking Water for this Unit, is kept boiling in the Field Cooker. This Unit has undertaken during the month many inoculations for the Battalions and other details. All wounds are treated with Anti-tetanic Serum as soon as possible.

Training of Unit

In addition to physical drill and Route Marches to keep the men fit, practical training was given to 2 Officers and 6 Sergeants, who were attached to the 12th Field Ambulance at STEENWERKE from March 5th to March 8th inclusive; and to 6 Officers and 160 men, who were attached to the 10th and 11th Field Ambulances at BOHAIN and ARMENTIERES respectively, from March 26th March 31st, gaining practical experience in Advance Dressing Station and Dressing Station Work.

The weather during the first half of the month was wet and cold, but latterly it has cleared, and though frosty at night, is bright during the day.

The Discipline has been good.

I still require one Officer to complete Establishment

R. M. West
Major
O/C 1/2 N.M.F.A. B.M.E.T.

STEENWERKE
1.4.15

2nd N. Mid. Fd. Amb c

March 1. 1915
HAVRE. SANVIC rest Camp N° 2.
Under canvas. Visit from ADMS.
North Midland Division Casualty Clearing Station (Col. Seake)
in Camp.
Have no news as yet of 30 men of B Section who were
transferred from the S.S. BLACKWELL at S'AMPTON.

March 2. 1915
HAVRE. SANVIC rest Camp N° 2.
Made good deficiencies in mens Kit.
Orders received at 10 P.M. to entrain tomorrow at 8.30 AM,
for some destination unknown. Made out orders, issued
rations, and organized details — 1 party to proceed to station
at 7 AM to take over forage and rations; one party to pack
wagons; and Captain TURNER to act as entraining
Officer.

March 3. 1915
IN TRAIN
Reveille 4 AM. Completed wagon packing, returned
spare blankets to store. Marched to GARE DES MARCHANDISES
Entrained wagons and horses in good time. The Horses
packed 8 in each Van, parallel to the
lines of rail, in fours, facing one
another, with saddles and forage in
space between, and 2 Transport men in
each Van

The men travelled in Vans, 40 in each Van, with straw to lie on.

Left HAVRE at 11.59 AM, en route for ROUEN and ABBEVILLE.

March 4th 1915
ZEMERZELE, FRANCE

Arrived at CASSEL at 8 AM. Detrained and marched to ZEMERZELE, where unit is billeted. Sent in marching in state to Div! Headquarters. At 10 PM, orders from ADMS to proceed, with 1 Officer and 6 Sergeants, tomorrow to a certain place to undergo 4 days instruction.
The Party selected consisted of Major West, Capt. TURNER, and Sergeants Holyland, Neale, Wheway, Stedmond, Wakeling, and Clarkson.

March 5th 1915
STEENWERKE FRANCE.

Left ZEMERZELE at 9 AM, and proceeded in Motor Ambulance to STEENWERKE via BAILLEUL and NIEPE. Attached to 12th Ambulance (Col. FITZGERALD). This Ambulance has charge of a casualty detention Hospital for the Division. Slight cases of exhaustion, sore feet, and other ailments requiring only a few days rest and treatment, are admitted, and, when well, sent back to the Trenches. The Hospital also runs bathing apparatus, disinfecting and vermin-killing apparatus. There is also a similar Hospital for Officers.

March 6th 1915

STEENWERKE. FRANCE.

The 12th Ambulance runs an excellent Pierrot Troupe, which gives entertainments for patients and Soldiers, and is much appreciated. For troops which are likely to be quartered in any particular town for any length of time, this is an excellent idea, preventing the men from getting stale, and giving them something to look forward to.

March 7th 1915

STEENWERKE FRANCE.

Rode with Captain TURNER to LE ROMARIN. Inspected Field Hospital established by 10th AMBULANCE. Then on to PLOEGSTEERT, where the 10th Ambulance has an advanced Dressing Station. (Col. PROFFIT). Town has been heavily shelled and badly damaged. Shrapnel burst in Dressing Station. Dressing Station well organized. Use is made of large windows on ground floor, opening into receiving room, to get stretchers through. Returned to STEENWERKE in Evening.

March 8th 1915

ZEMERZEELE FRANCE.

Returned here this afternoon by Motor Ambulance.

March 9th 1915

STRAZELLES FRANCE

Left ZEMERZELLE this morning, marching via FLÊTRE to STRAZELLES, where unit is billeted in Barns.

March 10th 1915   at STRAZELLES

March 11. 1915
SAILLY FRANCE

Left STRAZELLES at noon, marching via MERRIS, and
DOULIEU to SAILLY, where the division arrived 8.30 PM.
Billeted with 1st N. Mid. Field Amb.ce. Many men fell out on the
march, owing partly to the character of the roads, which are
paved with large rough paving stones, badly jointed, and
very slippery to nailed boots — and partly to the fact that,
the men having been recommended to have boots a size
or two too large for them, have gone to the extreme, and
obtained boots so large that their feet slip about in
them. Am told this evening that 26 men of the Lincolns
and Leicesters were left sick at STRAZELLES — the
first I have heard of it.

March 12 1915.
BAC-ST-MAUR. FRANCE.

Left for SAILLY at 5 PM, arriving here 5.45 PM.
Established Field Ambulance Hospital under Captain
DIXON, with B Section of this Unit in a Theatre,
and a Hospital for Sick Officers in a private house.
Admitted 17 slight cases, chiefly sore feet, from
Staffords, Leicesters and Sherwoods. Notified A D M S
of 26 cases left at STRAZELLES, in order that
Motor Ambulance may bring them in.

March 14. 1915
BAC-ST-MAUR.

A Section Tent-Subdivision, with ½ bearer subdivision, under Capt Turner, with Lieutenant Tatlow, established detention Hospital in SAILLY.

A number of men of 5th S. Staff., and Sherwood Foresters, who were left behind with sore-feet and exhaustion, are now ready to rejoin their Units. These have now left SAILLY. Enquired of DAA and QMG how to dispose of them.

Reply: attach SHERWOODS to 5th N. Staff., and send men of 5th S. Staffs to rejoin their Unit at FERME DE BRETAGNE, near TROU DE BAYARD. These men accordingly marched off at 3 PM, under Sergt Richardson RAMC.

Very Heavy firing tonight. Orders from Brigade at 10.40 PM: "Units must be prepared to evacuate at short notice. Men to sleep with accoutrements ready to put on"

10.50 PM: Billeting parties to report at Brigade Headquarters at 7 AM.

March 15. 1915
BAC-ST-MAUR.

12.20 AM. Orders received for Brigade to move to new billeting area.

All men unfit to march to be sent to Hospital by 9.30 AM., and nominal roll, showing ailments, to be sent to Brigade office

11.45 AM. Order to move countermanded, but will be effective tomorrow, 16th

Orders by ADMS: Hospital at BAC-ST-MAUR to be evacuated

Tomorrow. Patients unfit to rejoin Units, will be conveyed to Hospital at SAILLY by motor Ambulance. Patients able to rejoin their Units, both from BAC-ST-MAUR and SAILLY Hospitals will, if their Units have left this town, be conveyed by Motor Ambulance to MERRIS, whence they will be sent to their several Units.

The SAILLY Hospital will be administered by B Section, C Section rejoining the Unit. Hospital named: N°3 Section detention.

Lieut Tatlow (Transport Officer) reports 3 Horses B Section suffering from Influenza.

March 16. 1915
SALOMÉ-DE-LA-NOIRE FARM. - VERRIER.

8.30 AM. BAC-ST MAUR Hospital evacuated by B Section, under Capt. DIXON, who then proceeded to take over SAILLY Hospital from C Section, which rejoined Unit.

10.20 AM. Unit marched out of SAILLY to new billeting area, arriving at SALOMÉ FARM at 12.30 PM. Took over 3 Farms for billeting purposes. This district appears to be unhealthy, stinking stagnant water being everywhere. The drinking water in the Farm is greenish, and fetid in taste, and leaves a very perceptible sediment which is, in itself, acting as an irritant, sufficient to cause diarrhoea. Have forbidden any water to be used for drinking purposes unless first clarified, and then boiled in Field Cooker, which has been set aside for this purpose. The Farms in this district consist of a Manure Heap, round which the Farm buildings are erected.

There have been today several cases of Sickness and

diarrhoea today, due partly to the water, and partly to the preserved rations which the troops are not yet accustomed to. A large number of men of other Units fell out owing to sore feet, due to their boots being too large.

March 17. 1915
SALOMÉ-DE-LA-NOIRE FARM.   VERRIER
In billets all day. Several cases Sickness and diarrhoea.

March 18. 1915
AYMARD'S FARM - LE PETIT MORTIER - STEENWERK RD
12.15 P.M. Orders to move to new billeting area, 3¾ miles from here. Marched off 2.30 PM, arriving AYMARD'S FARM at 3.30 PM.
Sent in marching in Strength to MERRIS (Div. Hdqrs.).

March 19. 1915
AYMARD'S FARM.
Blizzard this morning, and off and on during day.
B Section (Capt. DIXON) rejoined from SAILLY, the No 3 Section Detention Hospital having been taken over by the Canadians.
Telegram from ADMS: "Convalescent rest Station established at MERRIS. Wire for motor Ambulance when required to remove patients there".
Opened small detention Hospital in this Farm. The building is however, quite unsuited for this

March 20th 1915
AYMARD'S FARM.
Snow and frost at first, but Fine later.
All winter clothing given up by order of A D M S: Goat
skins, Horse Rugs, and either British Warms, or great
coats. These are to be collected from Unit by Motor 'Bus.
 Orders received to indent for String and packing needles
for constructing Bivouacs. Complied with.
2 Cases removed by Motor Ambulance to MERRIS.

March 21st 1915
AYMARD'S FARM.
Fine warm day. Church Parade: read Army Act and warned
men about drinking Water.
Sent in Daily state of Sick, A F A 34. and A F A 36
Board medically examined following men for discharge as
Medically Unfit:
5" Leicesters No 2107 Pte E Taylor.   Rheumatic Fever.
         "   " 866   " J.H. Jarrom   Rheumatic Fever
         "   " 1677   " A.F Wilford   Disordered action Heart
         "   " 2066   " J. Billings   Rheumatic Fever
         "   " 3397   " W. Martin   Incontinence of Urine
2" N M F A Hame..   " Muddimer   Internal Derangement Knee (Left).
4 men from L" Lincolns transferred to MERRIS Hospital.
Inoculated remainder of Transport of this Unit, who had not
previously been done.

March 22 1915
AYMARD'S FARM.
Field day with Brigade. Dressing Station established at FERME
LE GRIN by C Section. Two accidental bayonet wounds of

Leg, 5th Leicesters, admitted to Hospital, and subsequently transferred to MERRIS.

Lt. Col. Harrison, 1/4 Leicesters, reported Laryngitis and Depression. Arranged with ADMS to have him removed tomorrow to No. 5 Clearing Casualty Station at HAZEBROUKE. Also the 6 men recommended for discharge on March 21st.

Indented for 300 c.c. anti-typhoid Lymph.

One case of mumps: isolated in empty loft with B Section.

March 23. 1915. AYMARD'S FARM.

Col. Harrison, 4th Leicesters, transferred by Motor Ambulance to HAZEBROUKE Clearing Casualty Station No. 5; also 6 men recommended for discharge as medically unfit.

Todays operation: B Section formed Dressing Station at FERME LE GRIN. In afternoon rode to MERRIS to see DADMS.

March 22nd 1915
AYMARD'S FARM, STEENWERKE.

Rode in morning to 1/5th Leicesters to see Lieut ALLEN, suffering from measles. Reported case to ADMS for removal.

2 motor-Ambulances attached to this Unit.

In afternoon took Hernia Case to MERRIS, in Motor Ambulance. Saw DADMS. ADMS called this afternoon. This Unit to send 6 Officers and 160 NCO's and men on Friday, for 5 days instruction in trenches and dressing Stations. Half to be attached to 11th Field Ambulance at ARMENTIERES, the other half to the 10th Field Ambulance at ROMARIN. The first half, consisting of B Section, with following

Officers: Major WEST.
          Capt. DIXON.
          LIEUT. YATES.
          LIEUT. and Q.M. CROSS.

The second half, consisting of C Section, with following Officers:
          Capt. TURNER.
          LIEUT. WILLS
          LIEUT. TATLOW.

with one BAGGAGE Wagon per Section.

A Section, under Capt. COWPER, and LIEUT. GRAHAM, remain at AYMARDS FARM.

67 men of 4th and 5th LINCOLNS, and 4th LEICESTERS, unfit to go to trenches, to report here, and to be under medical treatment until Units return.

Return of men of Unit not inoculated, asked for and rendered. 6 men of this Unit not inoculated.

March 25th 1915
AYMARD'S FARM. STEENWERKE.

Certificate asked for and rendered today, that all Cameras have been returned to ENGLAND.

Went, by order of A.D.M.S, to ARMENTIÈRES, in Motor Ambulance, to take Brigadier General BROMMILOW, who is ill, to HAZEBROUKE Casualty Clearing Station No 5.

March 26th 1915
ARMENTIÈRES.

Unit left, with Brigade, at 2.30 PM for ARMENTIÈRES marching via STEENWERKE, LEVEAU, and NIEPPE,

arriving at ARMENTIERES at 5 P.M. C Section
left the Column at LE RABOT, proceeding to
ROMARIN and PLOEGSTEERT, to be attached to the
10th Field Ambulance. B Section, in ARMENTIERES
and LE BIZET, attached to 11th Field Ambulance.
The advanced dressing Station is at LE BIZET, in a
Convent ½ mile behind the Trenches. The Dressing Station
is in a School at ARMENTIERES, 3 miles behind
the Trenches. From there, cases are evacuated to
BAILLEUL. The tent division was employed in the
Hospital (Dressing Station), and the bearers, with 1
Officer, proceeded in parties for 24 Hours duty, at the
advanced Dressing Station at LE BIZET.

March 27th 1915
ARMENTIERES

Inspected Dressing Station. Rode with O/c 11th Field
Ambulance to advanced Dressing Station at LE BIZET,
and to Regimental Aid post of the KINGS OWN,
situated in small cottage close to trenches. The M.O.
rarely goes into trenches, the wounded being brought to
him by regimental Stretcher bearers. After attention, they
are taken to the Advanced Dressing station by Stretcher
squads of 11th Field Ambulance.

March 28th 1915
ARMENTIERES

Hospital in morning. Walked with O/c 11th Field Ambulance
to HOUPELINES to inspect Advanced Dressing Station

established in cellar of the Brewery.

March 29. 1915
ARMENTIERES
Hospital in morning. Rode to PLOEGSTEERT, to inspect Dressing Station, and C Section. 4th Lincolns at PLOEGSTEERT report 2 cases of German measles, and 8 contacts. Reported cases to O/c Dressing Station, and directed segregation of contacts. On duty tonight at LE BIZET.

Report required by, and rendered to, ADMS, on bathing and washing accommodation for this Unit.

Reported to me that the unfit men from the Battalions left at AYMARDS FARM are unable to draw rations, as their respective Quartermasters have drawn rations for the whole of their Battalions, not allowing for the men left behind. Saw Supply Officer on the matter, and arranged for rations.

March 30th 1915
ARMENTIERES
Hospital work, and returns required.

March 31st 1915
AYMARD'S FARM, STEENWERKE.
Brigade left ARMENTIERES at 9.30, arriving at STEENWERKE at noon. 16 5th Lincoln men, and 7 4th Leicesters, unfit to march, fetched in by the 2 Motor Ambulances attached to the Unit

Corporal Parker reverts to private at his own request. In afternoon, went in Ambulance to MERRIS to see ADMS. Division to be prepared for early move to new area. All goat skins and Horse rugs to be sent in Motor Ambulances tomorrow to CAISTRE, where Ambulances will remain to be painted grey, and will be temporarily replaced by 2 others. Bell Tents to be sent tomorrow to be stored at the Hospital in the monastery on MONT DES CATS.

R. M. West.
Major RAMC.
O/C 1/2 North Mid. Field Amb^{ce}

Copy. No. 5

OPERATION ORDER No. 3.
by
BRIGADIER GENERAL W.R.CLIFFORD
COMMANDING 1/1st LINCOLN & LEICESTER BRIGADE

Ref:- 1/100,000 Sheet No. 5a.   SAILLY.
                                 14th March, 1915.

1. The Brigade will march to a new Area.

2. The Lincoln & Leicester Brigade, Headquarters, 2nd Co. Divisional Train 2nd North Midland Field Ambulance will move to the Road Junction 1½ miles North West of SAILLY CHURCH. Starting point 11.35 a.m. CROSS ROADS ½ mile N.W. of SAILLY CHURCH. Order of March 5th Leicester Regt, 5/Lincolnshire Regt, 4th Leics. Regt, 4th Lincs. Regt. Headquarters Linc. & Leic. Bde, No. 2 Company Divisional Train 2nd North Midland Field Ambulance.

3. All 1st and 2nd Line Transport will accompany Battalions.

4. Billeting parties will proceed from Brigade Headquarters under Capt. Viccars at 7 a.m. and meet Units at Road Junction ½ mile South of L in LES HAISES BSES at midday.

5. Report will be sent to point mentioned in paragraph 4.
   Issued at 11-30 p.m. to Cyclist Orderly. sd/ R.L.ADLERCRON, Major,
   Copy No. 1. 4th Lincs Bde. Maj., Linc.& Leic.Bde.
           2. 5th Lincs
           3. 4th Leics
           4. 5th Leics
           5. 2nd North Midland Field Ambulance
           6. No. 2 Coy., A.S.X.
           7. North Midland Division.
           8. War Diary.

Fall in 10.50
March off 10 oc
March off 11

To O/C. Saille Hospital 1/2 N.M.F.A.

Enclosed Brigade Orders; A and B Sections will probably pass your Hospital at Saille at 11.20. Be prepared to fall in to your position in the Unit by then, please. — Return these orders by bearer.

   [signature]
   Major
   O/C 1/2 N.M.F.A.

Bec-St. Maure
15.3.15

Recd
E.D.Jetten

Copy No. 6

OPERATION ORDER No. 4.
by
Brigadier-General W. R. CLIFFORD,
Commanding Lincoln & Leicester Infantry Brigade T.F.

1. The Brigade Billeting area has been altered.

2. The new billeting areas will be indicated to Battalion, 2nd North Midland Field Ambulance and No. 2 Company Divisional Train Billeting Officers (except the 4th Leicester Regiment which remains in its present billets) at 8-30 a.m. tomorrow at Brigade Headquarters.

3. The Move will be carried out independently by Units.

4. Starting point 1-30 p.m.

5. Reports to present Headquarters till 1 p.m. afterwards as indicated later.

Issued at
10-30 p.m.
       sd/ R.L. Adlercron, Major,
  Brigade Major, 1/1 Linc. & Leic. Bde. T.F.

by Despatch Rider.
to No. 1. War Diary
   2. 4/Lincs. Regt.
   3. 5/Lincs. Regt.
   4. 4/Leics. Regt.
   5. 5/Leics. Regt.
   6. 2nd North Midland Field Ambulance
   7. No. 2 Company A.S.C.

OPERATION ORDERS BY BRIG GEN A.J.CLIFFORD
Commanding Lincs - Leic Bde T.F.

MOULIN MESSEAN
20/3/15.

Reference 1/100000 HAZEBROUCK.

INTENTION/.
1. The Brigade supported by Artillery will attack the Farm which is 300 yards N.E. of the M. in LE KIRLEM.

2.(a) The 5th Leicestershire Regt. will carry out the assault on the enemy's trenches on a frontage extending 200 yards N. and 200 yards S. of the above-mentioned farm at 10-20 a.m. supported by the fire of No   Battery R.F.A. which will open fire at 10-0 a.m. on this section of the trenches in co-operation with 4/Lec & 5/Lincs Regt and all Machine Guns on either flank till 10-20 a.m. when all fire will be concentrated on the farm and the infantry assault by the 5/Leicester Regt will commence.

(b) The front line of trenches now occupied will be held firmly throughout the attack.
The place of the 5/Leicester Regt will be filled by 4/Leicester Regt Regt (in Reserve)

DRESSING STATION.
3. Dressing Station at Farmhouse 800 yards South of Headquarters, Windmill.

S.A.A. RESERVE.
4. The Brigade Ammunition Reserve and Tool Carts will be situated at Brigade Headquarters.

REPORTS.
5. Reports to Windmill 500 yards North East of Point 35.

sd/ R.L.ADLERCRON Maj.,
Bde Maj. L.L.L.Bde T.F.

Issued by Cyclist Orderly at 5 a.m.
to :-
Copy No 1 War Diary
2. 4/Lincs Regt.
3. 5/Lincs Regt.
4. 4/Leics Regt.
5. 5/Leics Regt.
6. O.C., R.F.A.,
7. O.C., 2nd N.M.F.A.

Copy. No.

OPERATION ORDER NO. 5
by
BRIGADIER GENERAL W.R. CLIFFORD
COMMANDING 1/1st Lincs. & Leics. Infty. Bde. T.F.

Reference Map. Belguim & France (B Series) Sheet No. 36 Scale 1/40,000.

1.
STEENWERCK
25/3/15.

1. The Lincoln & Leicester Infantry Brigade (less 1/5th Bn. Leics. Regt) 1/8th Bn. Notts & Derby Regt, 60 Divl. Mounted Troops, 2nd North Midland Field Ambulance and No. 2 Coy, Divisional Train will proceed for attachment and be billeted on the 26th instant as under :-

Unit.	Attached to	Billets.
H.Q. Linc & Leic Infty. Bde.) No. 4 Sect. Signal Co.)	11th Infty. Bde.	Near 11th Bde. Hdqrs West of PLOEGSTEERT
8th Notts & Derby Regt.	10th -do-	ROMARIN
4th Lincs. Regt.	11th -do-	PLOEGSTEERT Brewery
4th Leics. Regt.	12th -do-	LA BIZET
5th Lincs. Regt.	11th -do-	OOSTHOVE Fm.
60 Yorks Hussars	H.Q. 4th Divn.	NIEPPE
2nd Field Amb'ce (horsed portion)	10th Field Amb'ce.	Near ROMARIN.
No. 2 Coy, Divisional Train	4th Div. Train.	STEENWERCK.

2. Starting point. Cross Roads 1,000 yds South South West of STEENWERCK CHURCH at 2-30 p.m. in the following order of march, Bde. Signal Section, Brigade Headquarters, 4th Lincs. Regt 5th Lincs. Regt, 4th Leics. Regt, 8th Bn. Notts & Derby Regt, 2nd North Midland Field Ambulance, No. 2 Company, Divisional Train, The Divisional Mounted Troops will proceed direct arriving at Cross Roads of T of RABOT in B 8a at 4 p.m.

3. ROUTE. STEENWERCK-LEVEAU to Cross Roads of T of RABOT. On arrival these Units will be met by guides from 4th Division. The YORKSHIRE HUSSARS and 4th LEICESTERSHIRE Regiment will, on arrival at the Cross Roads, turn South East and proceed down the NIEPPE Road.

4. TRANSPORT. All Transport Vehicles will accompany their Batalions.

5. REPORTS. Reports to Head of Column.

sd/ R.L.ADLERCRON, Major,
Brigade Major, Linc. & Leics. Bde. T.F.

Issued by Cyclist Orderly
at   to :-
Copy No. 1. 1/8th Bn. Notts & Dorby Regt.
2. 4th Bn. Lincs. Regt.
3. 5th Bn. Lincs. Regt.
4. 4th Bn. Leics. Regt.
5. 2nd North Midland Field Ambulance.
6. No. 2 Company, Divisional Train.
7. Divisional Mounted Troops.
8. North Midland Division.
9. War Diary.

1/2 N.M. Field Institution
Vol II

Confidential

War Diary

of

1st/2nd North Midland Field Ambulance
R.A.M.C.T.

Lincoln and Leicester
Brigade.

North Midland Division.

From April 1st to April 30th 1915

R. M. West
Major

2nd North Midland Field Ambulance RAMC
Summary of War diary for April 1916

The Unit left AYNARDS FARM, STEENWERKE, where it had been billeted since March 24th, on April 6th for DRANOUTRE (BELGIUM), where it remains, having taken over from the 13th Field Ambulance. Besides allowing nightly at the Brigade Aid posts and posts about 2½ miles from Headquarters, the Unit has a dressing station, a detention hospital, a bathing establishment, and a laundry, and an observation hut. Cases from the aid posts are brought by Motor Ambulance from to the dressing station, whence they are evacuated in the morning to No 2 (Officers) or No 8 (NCOs and Men) Casualty Clearing Stations at BAILLEUL. Number of cases - chiefly gun shot wounds, treated at the dressing station during the month: 111.

The detention Hospital is used for the reception and treatment of medical and surgical cases which are likely to be fit for duty after a few days. The average number per diem has been 20.

The Bathing Establishment, under the charge of Lieut YATES, is capable of dealing with 250 men daily. These men leave their underclothes to be washed at the Laundry, which in exchange issues a clean set. By this means, pediculi have been much reduced. Two complaints only were received during the month of clean clothes being lousy, and in one case, the lice were probably inhabited afresh from dirty billets. The staff necessary to work each department consists of 1 NCO and 5 men, who have well mastered all the details. Arrangements are in progress to double both the bathing and Laundry accommodation.

The Observation Hut is used for the segregation and observation of suspected infectious cases.

The Unit also supplies 4 Stretcher bearers to the 5th Lincolns, as their bearers provide the Brigade Band; and 1 First aid man for duty in the trenches with each Battalion. This man carries Shell dressings, bandages, etc., and a Hypodermic Syringe for morphia administration, in the use of which he has been specially instructed.

The Tent Division on duty at the dressing station have worked well, and are in no way upset at the sight of Blood.

I must also praise the work of the Motor Ambulance Drivers, who are always ready and willing to work, day or night.

During the month, some officers have been detailed for duty with Units other than Medical Units: Lieut WILLS going to the 5th Lincolns, vice Major DUNCAN, RAMC, sick; and Lieut TATLOW to the 4th Lincolns, vice Major POOLE-BERRY, sick. Lieut TATLOW has since been transferred to the 1st N.M. Bde. RFA, to assist Major NICHOLSON RAMC, and his place in the 4th Lincolns has been filled by a newly joined Officer of this Unit — Lieut DRYNAN. —

Lieut BEVAN-BROWN, RAMC, and Lieut GREEN, RAMC have joined this Unit.

Capt DIXON, with Lieut GRAHAM and B Section, is in charge of a Divisional Rest Station at S. Jan CAPPELLE, for officers and men.

During the month several cases of German Measles have occurred, and have been sent to Isolation Hospital at BAILLEUL. It has been found impossible to isolate the contacts, as the men have to mix freely when in the trenches, and the method adopted to cope with the disease is to have frequent regimental inspections by the R.M.O., who at once reports any case with rise of temperature or any suspicious symptoms, and the man is admitted to the Observation Hut.

Cerebro Spinal Fever occurred in 3 cases among the 5th Lincolns

Scarlatina : 1 case, 4th Lincolns.

Mumps : 1 case, N.M. Bde. R.F.A.

Enteric : 1 case 4th Lincolns

German Measles : 12 cases, distributed as follows:

    1 case Monmouth R.E.

    1 case 4th Lincolns

    1 case R.A.M.C.

    7 case 5th Lincolns

    1 case 4th Lincolns

    1 case 5th Lincolns

A small Epidemic of Diarrhoea occurred during the early part of the month, due in my opinion, to Drinking water in the trenches saturated with decaying Animal Matter from corpses of Animals and men.

The transport has worked well, and the Horses are all in good condition.

In conclusion, I would like to say that the practice of Billeting men in Farms and Barns should be discontinued now that the Hot weather is coming. All the Farms are practically enclosures for a large heap of Manure, with a considerable amount of Liquid manure. This is sure to by flies, which will contaminate food and water. Also the men carry into their sleeping places, on their boots, a large amount of manure, which also gets onto their hands and food; and it is difficult to prevent the men from drinking the water from the farm pump. They see the natives do so without apparent ill effects — forgetting that they (the natives) are salted by generations of manure-soaked ancestors. An effort is being made to have the manure carted away into the fields; but even when this is done, the area of ground previously occupied by the heap, is soaked many feet deep, and allows a rich liquid to ooze up after every shower.

The efforts of the Military Sanitary authorities are doing much to ameliorate the insanitary conditions of the country, though the fact that we are at war appears occasionally to be lost sight of, and methods are occasionally recommended which could with ease be carried out in a suburban area in England, but which are practically out of the question out here.

R. M. West
Major R.A.M.C.
O/C 2nd North Mid Field Amb'ce, and S.M.O. Lincoln and Leicester Brigade
North Mid. Division

May 1, 1915
DRANOUTRE
FLANDERS

WAR DIARY – 2nd N.M.D. Field Ambulance

April 1 1915

AYMARDS FARM. STEENWERK.

N° 2222 Pte. Radley, 5th Lincolns, evacuated from his billet to HAZEBROUKE, suffering from Spinal meningitis: diagnosis of Epidemic Cerebro-Spinal Meningitis confirmed bacteriologically. All contacts isolated in barn. (13 contacts).

10 Measles contacts A.S.C. isolated, and to be visited daily, until April 2nd.

Visited R.M.O.s 2nd Lincolns, 5th Lincolns, and 5th Leicesters.

Major Cooke-Berry, R.A.M.C., M.O. 2nd Lincolns is ill. Detailed Captain Turner, of this Unit, to do duty for him.

Sent in War diaries for February and March.

April 2 1915

AYMARDS FARM. STEENWERK.

Detailed Lieut Graham, of this Unit, for duty with 2nd Lincolns, instead of Major Cooke-Berry, ill.

By order of A.D.M.S., sent 12 Bell Tents to the Hospital at the Monastery of MONT-DES-CATS, to be stored.

Board (medical) held, and undermentioned N.C.Os and men of 5th Leicesters recommended for discharge as Medically unfit for Active Service, and sent to HAZEBROUKE for discharge to be carried out:

252	Mercer	W.	Corpl.
2362	Richardson	A.	Pte.
1200	Evans	J.H.	"
2094	Stevens	J.E.	"
2114	Southam	W.	Corpl
2544	Catlow	J.	Pte
2263	Driver	W.W.	"
1765	Forman	W.	"

Visited R.M.O's of 4th Lincolns, 5th Lincolns, and Major Coode Berry, who is still ill.

In view of early move to new Area, detailed Capt. Turner and Lieut Graham with 8 men, to proceed tomorrow to DRANOUTRE, to take over Billets from 13th Field Ambulance.

Note that all men sent to Clearing Casualty Stations for discharge, to be entered in A and D book.

Rode into MERRIS to see A.D.M.S.

April 3rd 1915
AYMARDS FARM. STEENWERK.

Major M. Duncan. R.A.M.C., R.M.O. 5th Lincolns ill. Visited him, and ordered his removal to HAZEBROUKE Casualty Clearing Station No. 8. Detailed Lieut Wills, of this Unit, to take duty for him.

Pte Bloomfield, 5th Lincolns, a contact with Pte Radley, developed Cerebro-Spinal-Meningitis. Removed to Isolation Hospital, ST OMER. Notified ADMS.

Motored with Capt. Dixon, of this Unit, to DRANOUTRE, our new area. Inspected Hospital, Dressing Station, Headquarters, Laundry and Bathing establishment, at present occupied by 13th Field Ambulance.

The Laundry is staffed by 20 Women, who are paid 3 francs daily; and by 1 Corporal and 4 privates.

The Baths are staffed by 1 Corporal and 4 privates.

Bathing parties who are detailed by Brigade Staff Captain, provide their own Soap and Towels. Whilst they are bathing, their underclothes are taken from them to be washed at the Laundry, being replaced by clean clothes from the Laundry. Their

Khaki is issued, and used, previous to being again put on.
2⁄Lieut Wilding, R., 1st Lincolns, suffering from Scarlatina.
Removed to Isolation Hospital. Contacts isolated. Notified
ADMS.
Gunner Speck. 1st N.M. Bde R.F.A. Ammn Column = Mumps
Wired for Ambulance to remove him, and notified ADMS.

April 4th 1915
AYMARDS FARM. STEENWERK.
Rode to MERRIS to see ADMS.

April 5th 1915
Bivouac AYMARDS FARM. STEENWERK.
By order of ADMS, sent Advance party, of 12 Men and 1 NCO,
to DRANOUTRE, to take possession of billets occupied by
13th Field Ambulance.
5th Lincolns move today to BAILLEUL, on their way to
DRANOUTRE. Took over from them 10 men unfit to
march.
Detailed 1 Ambulance (Horse) Wagon to march in rear of Column,
to pick up stragglers.

April 6th 1915
DRANOUTRE.
2339 Pte Smith. J.F, 4th Lincolns, at present at BAILLEUL, reported
to me as having developed German Measles. Directed RMO to
communicate with Field Ambulance stationed there.
Received orders at 10 AM. in reply to telegram, directing this Unit
to report at DRANOUTRE at 3 PM, to replace the

13th Field Ambulance, which is moving from there today.
A and C Sections arrived 3.15 P.M., and took over the Hospital, Dressing Station, and Headquarters. N.C.O's and men in Huts. B Section in reserve in Farm 3 miles from here.

Before leaving STEENWERK, evacuated sick of Lincoln Battalions to their new Area at DRANOUTRE.

Capt Cowper's Horse badly injured in Off Hind Quarter, whilst halting outside BAILLIEUL, by Motor car driven by Capt Carey, R.E. Car skidded on wet stones, but was going too fast. Horse removed to AVD Hospital.

Rained heavily all day.

Arrangements for sick:
    Serious Cases evacuated to N°8 Casualty Clearing Station,
        BAILLIEUL.
    Slight Cases evacuated to Convalescent Depot BAILLIEUL
    Cases of Scabies to Convalescent Depot BAILLIEUL.

For working the Laundry and Baths, Corpl Kidger and Corpl. Butler, with 4 men each. Lieut Yates, of this Unit, detailed as O/i/c Baths and Laundry.

Arranged for each Section to be on duty as follows: one week at Dressing Station and for evacuating from Regimental Aid Posts; one week at Detention Hospital, and for Orderly Officers Duties; and one week in Reserve.

At 9 P.M. with Capt Turner and 2 Motor Ambulances, visited Regimental Aid posts of 4th and 5th Leicesters, 4 miles from here. Brought in one Casualty, and a case of Pneumonia from the Trenches.

One Horse left behind at STEENWERK with M. Cappon,

on account of Strangles.

Our Casualties up to date:

  1 Pneumonia   (Died)
  1 Pollus Hock   (Shot)
  1 Abscess Neck   (A.V.D. Hospital)
  1 Strangles   (M.Cappon, STEENWERK)
  1 Injured by Motor Car. (A.V.D. Hospital)

A.D.M.S., D.A.D.M.S., and Sanitary Officer called.

 Casualties:

1 1st Leicesters. 7029. Pte. Smith, Joseph.   G.S.W. Scalp.

April 7. 1915
DRANOUTRE

Lieut. Green RAMC, formerly attached to Staffords, reported today for duty with this Unit.

Last night the Motor Ambulance convoy from Regimental Aid posts (2 motors) stuck in mud at roadside 3½ miles from here. Another Ambulance was sent to bring in the patients, and this morning the two Ambulances were dragged out of the mud, and reported here at 8.30 A.M.

At present, the number of casualties at the Regimental Aid posts is wired to Brigade Office at 6 PM, and forwarded to this Unit. I would recommend that this information be sent later – say, 9 PM, as it often happens that cases turn up after the 6 o'clock return has been sent in; and in some cases possibly there would not be accommodation for them in the Ambulances, necessitating sending down other Ambulances late at night. It is not dark until after 7 PM, and men wounded are unable to venture out of the trenches to the Aid Posts until dusk sets in.

Casualties:

2	2" Leicesters.	2652.	Pte Sangster.	G.S.W. Head
3	2" Leicesters.		Lieut. Whittingham	G.S.W. Foot. R.
4	5" Leicesters.	1336.	Pte. Freear. L.	G.S.W. Buttock L.
5	2" Leicesters.	2971	Pte. Wilson J.E.	G.S.W Shoulder. R.

April 8th 1915
DRANOUTRE

B Section (Capt Dixon), with transport and 1 Motor Ambulance to report today at Convent at S' JAN CAPPEL, for duty at Dressing station to be evacuated today by a Section of the 12.F Field Ambulance.

Sent parcel of broken Teeth Plates to ADMS, to be forwarded for repairs.

2 Cases of Measles in the Detention Hospital today:
    5930 Sapper Chapman M. Monmouth R.E.
    2127 Pte Wigston. H. 2" NMFA. R.A.M.C.

23 Contacts from Detention Hospital, 16 men from the Hut occupied by Wigston, and 4 Nursing orderlies. sent, in charge of Sergt. Perry, to M. HUYPHEN'S Farm, 2 miles from here.

Notified ADMS, and had the 2 Cases removed to Isolation Hospital, BAILLIEUL.

On duty to night with convoy for Regimental aid posts.

Casualties:

6	5" Leicesters	1634	Pte. Holt B.J.	G.S.W. Face, and Groin, R.
7	108" Batt? RGA	20564	Gun' Flux. C.E.	Crushed hand, R.
8	2" Leicesters	2367	Pte. Horne. L.W	G.S.W. Arm. R.- Amputated
9	2" Leicesters	2109	Pte Rowbottom E.	G.S.W. Hand. R. L
10	2" Leicesters		Lieut. Pappsill. H.	G.S.W Thigh. L.

April 9th 1915
DRANOUTRE

Sent back to their various Units, men who have been working at the Laundry and Baths, as this Unit is now stopping the Laundry, etc.

Had Detention Hospital scrubbed out after Measles.

Casualties:

11   2" Leicesters   3417   L.Cpl. Garnes, H.   G.S.W Hand L. Self inflicted
12   5 Leicesters   7861   Pte Hutt J.J   G.S.W Hand L.   "
13   5 Leicesters   1792   Pte Sharman, G.   G.S.W Face L.

April 10th 1915
DRANOUTRE.

In morning, took Lieut Neve R.B, 52" Batt.? R.F.A, suffering from chronic Appendicitis to No 2 Casualty Clearing Station, BAILLEUL. for admission.

Went to ST-JAN-CAPPEL to see A.D.M.S., who tells me Major Poole-Berry, RAMC, M.O. 2° LINCS, wishes to resign on account of ill health, and directed me to appoint one of my officers to replace him. —— ADMS also directs that Lieut. Brogden, RAMC, M.O. 2° LEICESTERS, be transferred to the A.S.C. for duty, as his health will not stand trench work, and that Major McAllister Hewlings RAMC be transferred to the 2° LEICESTERS from the A.S.C.

Suggested to ADMS that Company Commanders of Battalions when in the Trenches, should be supplied with a length (3 feet) of stout rubber tubing for use as a tourniquet (SAMWAYS) in cases of severe Hæmorrhage from the Extremities, when the ordinary tourniquet was not effective. Approved of.

Went to Advance Medical Store Depot. Railway siding at
BAILLEUL Station, and indented and drew Medical Stores.
In afternoon rode to HUYPHEN'S FARM to see Measles
contacts: all doing well. Inspected Laundry and Baths.
By direction of DADMS. N. Mid. Division, released the
13 men of 5th LINCS. who were contacts with Ptes RADLEY
and BLOOMFIELD, on April 1st and 3rd. (Epidemic Cerebro-
Spinal Meningitis).
    Casualties:

14.   4th Leicesters. 2277 Pte Langton, Jas. G.S.W Foot, L. Self Infl.

April 11. 1915. Sunday.
DRANOUTRE
Service in morning: Rev Ashby.
ADMS, N. Mid. Div. called, and inspected dressing. Reported to
ADMS that some stretchers are of a narrow pattern and will
therefore not fit in the grooves made for their reception in the
Motor Ambulances; also that in others, the "runners" become
splayed out by the weight of the patient, and are therefore
too wide to fit the grooves. Directed by ADMS to return
all such defective stretchers to Ordnance Stores, and
have them replaced.
Lieut TATLOW, RAMC, from this Unit, proceeds to
4th LINCOLNS, for duty, vice Major Poole Berry, invalided.
Lieut TATLOW reported tonight at Regimental Aid post of
his Battalion.
Rode over to inspect Measles Contacts at HUYPHEN'S FARM.
ADMS directs that minor Cases be sent to Detention
Hospital of 1st NMFA. at LOCRES, instead of being

sent to Convalescent Depot at BAILLEUL.
O/c 1 NMFA states he has not much sick.
A D M S, asked by O/c 4ᵗʰ LEICESTERS, wishes to know:
1. Whether each R M O has Antitetanic Serum and Syringe?
   Answer: most Battalions have serum, and all have Hypodermic Syringe. It is however thought that it is better to leave the administration to the F.A. Dressing Station, on account of difficulty of ensuring Asepsis.
2. Whether each R M O has phials of Iodine?
   Answer: all R M O's have Tincture of Iodine; and I have recently indented for Iodine Ampoules, which will be issued to the R M O's.
3. Whether R M O's are in possession of Shell Dressings?
   Answer: No. Shell dressings were issued to the F.A. only. Should these, or some of them, be issued to R M O's?

On duty tonight for Evacuating Regimental Aid-posts. The wounds are chiefly Gun shot Wounds: those in the head accounting for the deaths. The entrance and exit wounds are in most cases small, and I have not yet seen any exit wound which would suggest that any but the ordinary bullet had been used. The entrance wound is sometimes so small, that unless looked for, may escape notice. The amount of shock in wounds of the extremities is remarkably small, and the pain not very acute. The difficulty is to get the cases, especially the lying down cases, to the Regimental Aid posts.

This is due to several causes: the impossibility of moving cases except in the dark; the necessity of moving them without any light from a lantern, etc., being used; the fact that the bearers, and in some cases, the guides, are not well acquainted with the route to be taken to the Aid Posts; The heavy nature of the soil — in places liquid mud knee deep, in others a slippery wet yellow clay. Many cases from the more distant Trenches take from 5 to 7 hours to bring in. One case, the bearers of which started off with on the night the man was hit, only did half the distance on that night; had to leave the patient in a dug-out during the day; and resume their retreat on the Aid Post on the next night, arriving about 2 AM on the night after the man had been wounded.

Casualties:

15	N.M.D. Field Co. R.E.	545	2/Lt. Roberts, W.G.	GSW. Upper Arm. L.
16	"	453	Sapr. Collett, W.	GSW. Neck
17	5th Lincolns	3155	Pte. Norriss, R.	GSW. Thorax. L.

April 12 1915

DRANOUTRE

Major Poole-Berry, RAMC, returned from Trenches last night, having been relieved by Lieut TATLOW RAMC. The former proceeded this afternoon to Rest Station at ST JAN CAPPEL, by order of ADMS.

In morning, demonstrated use of Elastic Tube Tourniquet to Officers of 5th LEICESTERS.

Major McAllister-Hewlings, RAMC, reported for duty with 4th LEICESTERS, vice Lieut Brogden RAMC, to report

for duty with A.S.C., vice Major McAlister-Hewlings.
Lieut Brogden, whose Unit, the 4. Leicesters, goes tonight to the Trenches, reports 21 men unfit for duty, and wished to send them to my Detention Hospital. I admitted 6 of them who were ill, and sent the remainder back to their Billets, as there is no room in the Hospital for Tired men.

Casualties:

18	4. Lincolns.	2699	Pte Street P.C.	G.S.W. (Grenade) Eye R.
19	5. Leicesters	2297	Pte Ball, A.	G.S.W. Knee R. Self Inf.
20	NMD N°1 Fd. Coy R.E.	570	Spr. Worrall E.	G.S.W. Back and Thigh R.
21	5. Lincolns.	2368	Pte Pearse C	G.S.W. Hand L.
22	NMD N°1 Fd. Coy R.E.	351	Spr. Correll, A.	G.S.W. Neck.
23	4. Lincolns	2426	Pte Baker C.	Contused Wound Face
24	4. Lincolns.	2461	Pte Watson J.E.	G.S.W. Thigh R. and Penis.
25	5. Lincolns	1870	Pte Eyre H.	G.S.W. Back.

April 13th 1915
DRANOUTRE

Last night at 11.30, a Zeppelin flew over DRANOUTRE towards BAILLEUL, estimated height 3000 feet, showed no lights. When over BAILLEUL, dropped 14 Bombs, which exploded with loud noise. The Zeppelin then retraced its course towards the N.E., being ineffectively shelled as it passed over the British Trenches. Damage reported: 3 Civilians and 4 Horses killed, 1 Sentry wounded. Inspected Billets and visited Measles Contacts at HUYPHEN'S FARM. Rode into BAILLEUL to advanced Medical Store Depot.

Orders from ADMS to distribute one Haversack of Shell-dressings to each R.M.O: sent accordingly, to 4th and 5th Leicesters, and 1 N.M.D.BFA, and 5th Lincolns.

Issued Samway rubber Tourniquets to 4th Leicesters.

Scarlatina Contacts with 2119 Pte Wilding, 4th Lincolns, who was taken ill on April 4th, to be released from quarantine, by order of DADMS.

The Convalescent Depot at BAILLEUL will be closed until 15th April.

Lieut Geoffrey Stanniland, 4th Lincolns, reported killed today by Shell.

1415 Pte Neale, 5th ~~Lincolns~~ Leicesters (contact with Lieut Allan, 5th Leicesters) removed to Isolation Hospital suffering from Measles. Contacts segregated in Barn, but to be allowed to do duty in trenches, apart from others.

2090 Pte Askey R., 5th Lincolns, sent into Detention Hospital here with Diagnosis of Urticaria, by Lieut Wills, RAMC, MO. 5th Lincolns, was found to be suffering from Measles. Removed to Isolation Hospital; all contacts in the Detention Hospital will be sent tomorrow to HUYPHEN'S FARM, and the Ward disinfected. The Contacts in his Battalion are, as far as possible billeted together, and will be allowed to go to trenches, but will be inspected daily by Lieut Wills.

Many cases of Sickness and Diarrhoea among men returning from trenches: I find that these men were unable to obtain Water, and drank Water from the trenches, probably contaminated with decaying corpses.

Casualties:

26   4th Lincolns   1747   Pte Holland W.   GSW Shoulder L.
27   5th Lincolns   2081   Pte Whitworth R.   GSW Leg R.

April 14. 1915
DRANOUTRE.

Rained nearly all day.

Removed measles contacts to M. HUYPHEN'S FARM. There are now there 40 Contacts.

Lieut George Harvey, 4th LEICESTERS, gunshot wound left Temporo-parietal region. Brain lacerated and exuding. Came in 12.15 A.M. Sent at once to No 2 Casualty Clearing Station, BAILLEUL. Wrote to his Father.

Weekly return of Wounded required by Brigade, to commence next Saturday.

Casualties:

#	Regiment	No.	Name	Wound
28	4th LEICESTERS		Lieut Harvey. G.	GSW Skull
29	"	2502	Pte Wood. A.	GSW Finger, 3rd R.
30	"	2245	Pte Brailsford F.	Incised Wound, Head.
31	4th LINCOLNS	2268	Q.M.Sgt Botham J.	GSW Thorax, perforating
32	"	999	Pte Danbury W.	GSW Shoulder R., Back, Forearm
33	"	2568	Pte Barnett S	GSW Head
34	"	1003	C.Sergt Maj Peasgood. A.	GSW (Shrapnel) Forearm L
35	"	2042	Pte Hatliff. A.	GSW Forearm L
36	"	1639	Pte Beale E	GSW (Shrapnel) Head
37	5 LEICESTERS	1876	Pte Smith. G.	GSW Neck and Arm R.

April 15. 1915
DRANOUTRE

Visited Measles Contacts at HUYPHENS FARM. All

Well. Went to BAILLEUL to N°2 Casualty Clearing Station to enquire after Lieut. HARVEY: Trephined last night, and conscious today. Wrote to his Father.

A.D.M.S. Called today.

A Committee to regulate the sanitation of the Village, is composed of:

    Major R.M. WEST. R.A.M.C. — President
    Capt P. ASHBY. Chaplain — Officer detailed by Brigade.
    Lieut PARBERRY. R.A.M.C — Div¹ Sanitary Officer
    M. J H LOUF, Mayor. — Local representative.

1204, P/e Turner, 5th LINCOLNS. who was sent to Hospital at ST JAN CAPPEL from here on April 13th, with symptoms of Influenza, has developed Epidemic Cerebro Spinal Meningitis. Directed Lieut Wells R.A.M.C, R.M.O 5th LINCOLNS, to isolate Contacts, and watch men of Company to which TURNER belongs.

Major SLEIGHT, 5th LINCOLNS, sent to N°2 Casualty Clearing Station, suffering from effects of recent attack of Influenza.

Sent to R.M.O. 4th LINCOLNS 17 sets of Underclothing to be used in cases of Scabies.

4 cases of measles removed to Isolation from 4th LINCOLNS:
    2087 Pte Leake, C.E   D Coy.
    2431 Pte Chester   A Coy.
    2047 Pte Christmas   B Coy.
    1176 Pte Woodham   A Coy.

These mens Companies will be isolated for Billeting purposes, and will be inspected daily, by R.M.O., but will be sent to Trenches with remainder of Battalion.

Casualties:

38	5th LEICESTERS	8001	Comp Sgt Maj.	Kermick J	GSW Upper Arm R. Bullet Extracted
39	"	2214	Pte	Heath J	GSW Finger 3rd L Self Inf'd
40	"	2916	Pte	Braybrooke W.	Incised Wound Face
41	1st NM Fd Coy. R.E.	554	Sapper	Dowell W	GSW Thorax, perforating
42	4th LINCOLNS.	2644	L.Cpl	Howson A	GSW. Foot R. Self Inflict'd
	"	1944	Pte	Oveston E	GSW Finger L. R. Slight

April 16th 1915

RANOUTRE

Order from A.D.M.S: detail 4 men from your Unit for duty for first aid in the Trenches, with 5th Lincolns: following detailed:

    Pte Smith H.J.
    Pte Hurst A.
    Pte Pratt G.H.
    Pte Ball A.

Excessive number of sick sent up from trenches, especially by 4th LEICESTERS. In consequence, board of Enquiry, held on 1968 Pte Sylvester, 4th LEICESTERS, who reported sick, suffering from slight corn on foot.

Sent report to A.D.M.S in the matter of the Epidemic of Trench Diarrhoea, which in my opinion, is due to drinking water contaminated with decaying animal matter, and holding much sand in suspension; and not, as has been suggested, to the Maconochie's Ration.

Lieut Harvey, ti deciatus, not so well today. Temperature 102°, and semi liquid brain matter discharging from opening in skull.

Lieut Shaw, A.V.C. sent to N°2 Casualty Clearing Station, suffering from penetrating wound Knee-joint, L, caused by his horse colliding with Motor Lorry yesterday, whilst he was riding it.

Major L Wykes, 4° LEICESTERS, suffering from Trench neurasthenia, sent to Rest Station at ST JAN CAPPEL.

2552 Pte Lawson 5ᵗʰ LINCOLNS, and 1881 Pte Holderness. G.W., 5ᵗʰ LINCOLNS, removed to isolation, suffering from Measles.

Went into BAILLEUL this morning to enquire after Lieut. HARVEY, and to obtain stores from Advance Medical Store Depot. ADMS called today. Wishes 9 gall. casks, sawn in two, to be placed in Trenches for Drinking Water: the tops to be covered with Muslin, and a Tap inserted near bottom.

Casualties:

44	522 Pte Underhill. E. 1 NMF Coy. R.E.	G.S.W. Back
45	5ᵗʰ Leicesters 2208 Pte Evans, W.	G.S.W. Groin
46	5ᵗʰ Leicesters 2275 Pte Reed, A.	G.S.W. Leg, R.
47	4° Leicesters 1765 Pte Wesson A.	Foreign body in Eye
48	5ᵗʰ Leicesters 1584 Pte Perceval A.	G.S.W. Forearm L.

April 17. 1915.

DRANOUTRE

Message from D.D.M.S. 2ⁿᵈ Corps: "In case of a forward move, all medical units should arrange for safe storage of all extra equipment with Field Ambulance or Rest Station, accumulated during the Winter".

2323 Pte Hands, Harry, 5ᵗʰ LINCOLNS, removed to Hospital suffering from Measles.

Order from A.D.M.S.: Shell dressings to be issued as follows:
- 8 per Battalion
- 3 per Brigade of Artillery
- 18 per Field Ambulance
- 1 for each other Unit

Examined and reported to Div'l Sanitary Officer, and Supply Officer on piece of Tuberculous Beef sent in by O/C 1st LINCOLNS.

Sanitary Committee, consisting of Major WEST, Capt PASHBY, Lieut PARBERRY, and M. LOUF, Burgomaster of DRANOUTRE, met this afternoon, and directed that the following measures be taken by the Mayor within the next 10 days:

1. All manure heaps to be cleared away, and deposited in fields away from buildings, and covered with earth.
2. All inhabitants to keep their houses clean.
3. All Privies to be furnished with tight fitting lids, and all openings by which flies could gain access, closed.

The Commune is unable to bear any of the expenses involved.

Lieut Harvey slightly better.

A.D.M.S. called.

Complaint from 1st Lincolns that one Company has been infested by Lice from clean clothes supplied by Brigade Laundry. Capt Turner and Lieut YATES went to inspect clothing, but this had been burnt. Men probably infested the straw in the Huts, after being in Trenches, and subsequently got their clean clothes infested from the dirty straw. Reported to Brigade.

Heavy Artillery firing from 7 PM to 8 PM this evening.

Ordered by Brigade to vacate Huts occupied by Unit, and to move into VITTORIA FARM, and ST LUCIA FARM. Engineers to occupy Huts.

Casualties:

49	4ᵗʰ Leicesters	3005	Pte Cook. W.	G.S.W. Side. R.
50	4ᵗʰ Leicesters	3526	Pte Jones G.H	G.S.W. Shoulder L
51	4ᵗʰ Leicesters	1187	Pte Ball, T.	G.S.W. Back
52	5ᵗʰ Lincolns	1768	Pte Robinson C.	G.S.W. Legs B.L
53	5ᵗʰ Lincolns	3224	Pte Stanley, W.F.	G.S.W. Back.

April 18ᵗʰ 1915
DRANOUTRE.

Orders from Brigade Headquarters to move our billets from the Huts we now occupy, to VITTORIA FARM, and Sᵗ LUCIA FARM, on the LOCRE ROAD, and to shift our transport lines to Sᵗ LUCIA FARM. The latter is unfit for habitation, being infected with Scabies, and having a foul-smelling manure heap.

Inspected billets, Hospital and Dressing Station, and rode out to visit contacts at M. HUYPHENS Farm. All well so far.

Church parade by Rev. Ashby, at 3 P.M.

Casualties:

54	5ᵗʰ Leicesters	1333	Pte Webster T	G.S.W. Arm L.
55	5ᵗʰ Leicesters	494	Capt Colver W.	G.S.W. Back.
56	5ᵗʰ Lincolns	2373	Pte Cox J	G.S.W. Head R.

April 19ᵗʰ 1915
DRANOUTRE.

Inspected Billets and sanitary arrangements.
In afternoon, rode to Sᵗ JAN CAPPELLE to see ADMS.
Inspected REST HOSPITAL (Capt. DIXON).

Sapper Jones, A.S., died on his way up from the Regimental Aid
Post this morning. Wired his C.O.

Casualties

57	5th Lincolns	1903	Pte	Roberts Jos	G.S.W. Arm L
58	5th Lincolns	963	Pte	Gooderham V	G.S.W. Arm L
59	5th Lincolns	1409	Cpl	Walls W	G.S.W. Neck
60	5th Lincolns	2251	Pte	Darrell F	G.S.W. Back
61	5th Lincolns	1640	Pte	Clapham T	Dislocated Shoulder
62	5th Lincolns	2190	Pte	Crisp W	G.S.W. Abdomen
63	5th Lincolns	2213	L/Cpl	Eastwood T	G.S.W. Thigh L
64	No 1 Siege Co. Mon. R.E.	6305	Sapper	Williams G	G.S.W. Thigh R
65	1st NMFd Co R.E.	790	Pte	Jones A.S.	G.S.W. Head [DIED]
66	5th Lincolns	2110	Pte	Heathcote A.	G.S.W. Head

Of the above, I wished Pte Jones A.S. who has been at the
Aid post since the night of 17th–18th, suffering from G.S.W.
Abdomen, to remain another 24 hours, but Lieut. TATLOW,
R.M.O. 5th Lincolns insisted on sending him up to the
Dressing station, against the wish of the O/i/c Motor Ambulance
Convoy. Have reported the matter to ADMS

April 20th 1915
DRANOUTRE
Lieut Erskine Dugnan, RAMC, reported today for 7
day's training with this Unit.
Inspection of Transport this afternoon by ADVS, and
O.C. A.S.C. – Satisfactory.
Wrote asking ADMS whether cases sent to Casualty
Clearing stations could be followed up, as regards their
subsequent movements? – Reply: No.

2325 Private Reed, L., B Coy. 5th Lincolns, removed to Isolation Hospital, suffering from measles.

Casualties:

67	5th Lincolns	3328	Pte	Smith H.	G.S.W. Fore-Arm R.
68	5th Lincolns	2372	Pte	Green T.	G.S.W. (graze) Shoulder R.
69	5th Lincolns	3158	Pte	Allcock H.	G.S.W. Back, and Shoulder
70	5th Lincolns	1727	Pte	Stow W.	G.S.W. Thorax, and Fract. Humerus
71	5th Lincolns	1436	Pte	Oxtoby J.	G.S.W. Calf, R.
72	4th Lincolns	220	Sgt.	Walker F.	G.S.W. Foot. R.
7	N.M.Div.RE	556	2/Lt	Higginbotham G.	G.S.W. Chest.

April 21. 1915
DRANOUTRE

On duty last night at aid posts.

Went to BAILLEUL this morning to convey Capt. Hadfield, 5th Lincs., to No 2 Casualty Clearing Station (wounded). Purchased 5 Barrels of 700 litres capacity each, to be used as Bathing tubs in Brigade baths: price 50 francs each. Also 10 smaller Barrels, for use for Drinking Water in trenches.

ADMS called this afternoon.

Lieut BEVAN-BROWN RAMC, reported here this afternoon for a week's training with Unit.

Memo received from ADMS: All Measles Contacts to be examined daily for 16 days by the R.M.O's, and their Evening Temperature and pulse rate recorded on a Nominal Roll. Any rise of temperature or pulse rate to be at once reported to me, and steps taken to isolate and watch the suspect.

Communicated above to all RMO's of Battalions in Brigade.

Directed by ADMS to supply 1 good first aid man for

duty with each Battalion in the Trenches.

Lieut YATES, O/i/c Brigade Bathing arrangements, reports to me that sufficient men are not bathed daily, — 60 Today, instead of 200, and he complains of the inefficiency of the Water cart fatigue supplied by the Battalions: this morning they had to be fetched, as they had not turned up at 10.30 AM, although they are due at 7 AM. They get their cart embogged at the stream, they gallop it up the hill, so that the Barrel falls off and is broken: this happened yesterday, and again today, leaving only one barrel in use. Our pump being in the hands of the R E for repairs, the Belgians at the Brewery, lent us theirs: this also has been broken by the Water Fatigue. They omitted to bring up enough water to the Brewery, where the baths are, yesterday; in consequence both Tank and Boiler ran dry. Lieut YATES suggests that arrangements be made to hire the services of the Belgians employed at the Brewery. On the occasions when they have lent a hand, things have worked smoothly, and, as they do not begin brewing until Evening, they could well do the work of supplying water during the day.

- note by A D M S : no false dentures can be supplied to troops.
- Called at N° 2 Casualty Clearing Station to ask after Lieut Harvey, : slightly better.

- Casualties:

74	5th Lincoln Regt		Captain Hadfield, J.H.	G S W Buttock L
75	5th Lincoln Regt	2420	Pte Crowercroft. W	G S W Buttocks B - L
76	4th Lincoln Regt	1822	Cpl. Cannon T	G S W Thigh R, Comp Fract Femur
77	4th Lincoln Regt	2620	Pte Archer B	G S W Forearm L

April 22. 1915
DRANOUTRE

Sent report to Brigade in the matter of the Brigade Baths.

DADMS called this afternoon. Went over to S'JAN CAPPELL with him to see ADMS. Latter wishes a good man sent to trenches with each Battalion, equipped with Dressings and Hypodermic Syringe for Morphia, to render first aid.

Manure heap in Village are being cleared away.

Lieut Hurst, 5" LINCOLNS, shot through head last night, died in 2° Casualty Clearing Station, Bailleul.

Lieut HARVEY, 4" LEICESTERS not so well.

Casualties:

78	Derby, RFA.	545	Pte Ruston A.	Crushed Foot ? Fracture Metacarpus	L
79	4" Lincolns	—	Lieut Hurst. W.B.	G.S.W. Head.	
80	4" Leicesters	2842	Pte Blackwell L.	G.S.W Hand L.	Reg R.

April 23. 1915
DRANOUTRE

Inspected contacts at HUYPHENS FARM, and detailed 22 men of this unit to report at Headquarters for duty. Rode to BAILLEUL. Lieut TATLOW RAMC, RMO 4" LINCOLNS, reports that he will not be able to take Temperature and Pulse of the measles contacts of his Battalion; instructed him to do his best.

Brigade Staff Captain asked for accommodation for 10 officers and as many men as possible tonight, as 3 Battalions are halting for the night in the Village on their way through. Arranged as far as possible.

Casualties:
Nil.

Directed by ADMS to detail 2 efficient men to proceed to the trenches, to be attached to the 2 Battalions in [?], for the purpose of rendering first aid, giving hypodermic of Morphia etc. Men detailed:

    Private: Freeman
    Private: Ashlin.

April 24, 1915.

DRANOUTRE

7 Officers of Dublin Fusiliers billeted here last night. This morning, the Dublin Fusiliers, Royal Irish Fusiliers, Seaforth Highlanders and 6° Batt. Sherwood Foresters passed through here on their way North. In afternoon, walked to MONT ROUGE, overlooking the plain of YPRES. The latter being heavily shelled by the Enemy, and on fire in several places. A Village to the North of YPRES in flames. — ADMS called this Evening.

Casualties:

81	2196	Pte Lucas A.	4° Leicesters	G.S.W. Forearm L
82	2927	Pte Wykes A.E.	4° Leicesters	G.S.W. Buttock R
83	3263	Pte Chapman W.	4° Leicesters	G.S.W. Chest L
84	1310	Pte Vallance W	5° Leicesters	G.S.W. Foot R

Detailed 4 men to proceed tonight to the trenches to act as stretcher bearers to 5° LINCOLNS, as the latters bearers, being in the Divisional Band, do not do duty in Trenches.

Names of Details:

    Pte Smith W.G.
    Pte Ball A.
    Pte Smith W.H.
    Pte Hitchcock W.

Strong reflection in sky over YPRES at 11 PM, and heavy shelling.

April 25. 1915
DRANOUTRE.

Church parade by Brigade Chaplain this morning. Visited Measles contacts, and released all the men who were isolated 17 days ago.
Case of suspected Cerebro-spinal meningitis sent to BAILLEUL:
    1108. Dr BOWNER, B. Amm. Column. 2nd NMBde RFA
Warned R.M.O. – Capt RICHMOND, RAMC.

    Wire from ADMS this Evening, directing that 2 Motor Ambulances be sent to 1st N.M.F.A at LOCRE, to help evacuate Wounded from battle at YPRES.

    2nd Lieut MOUNTAIN, 5th LINCOLNS, admitted to Hospital with Temperature.

    Casualties:

85	2705	4th Leicesters	Pte	Gask W.	GSW. Arm L
86	2286	4th Leicesters	Cpl	Russell. G.	GSW. Scalp.
87	7153	5th Leicesters	Pte	Gamble T.	Bayonet W. Forearm L. Self Inflicted
88	1434	5th Leicesters	Pte	Hewitt A.	GSW Flank L

April 26. 1915
DRANOUTRE

Inspected billets, baths and laundry – 2 Ambces returned this Morning.
1505 Pte Plumb Thos. 4th Leicesters, removed to Isolation – Scarlatina
ADMS Called this afternoon. Directed that 2 Motor Ambulances be sent to LOCRE tonight for duty with Surgeon general PORTER, for evacuating wounded from Battle of YPRES.

By Telephone message from ADMS, Lieut TATLOW RAMC, transfers tonight from 4th Lincolns to 1st NMBde RFA, for duty with Batteries, vice Major NICHOLSON, RAMC, who takes on the Brigade Ammunition Column. Lieut DRYNAN RAMC, reports tonight for duty

with 4th Lincolns, vice Lieut TATLOW, RAMC, transferred to Artillery.
Very heavy firing all afternoon in direction of YPRES.
6 Electric torches purchased today for use of Bearers.
12 Small corks, fitted with Taps and moveable lids sent to Trenches to hold Drinking Water.

89	2130	5th Lincolns	Cpl.	Woods J	G.S.W. Face
90	2153	5th Lincolns	Pte	Johnson W	G.S.W. Scalp and Hand L.
91	1955	5th Leicesters	Pte	Hurst E.	G.S.W. Foot L
92	1418	5th Leicesters	Pte	Devons G.	G.S.W. (Shrapnel) Leg R.
	2219	5th Leicesters	Pte	Smith W.E.	G.S.W. Buttock R.

April 27. 1915.

DRANOUTRE.

Heavy cannonade North of YPRES all afternoon. Thick sea-fog at 5 P.M, until 8 P.M, when firing ceased, to be subsequently resumed.
Inspected billets and baths and laundry.
Pte Plumb, 4th Leicesters, who was sent to Isolation yesterday, with diagnosis of Scarlatina, is reported to be a case of German measles.
Casualties:

94	3247	4th Leicesters	Pte	Daley C.	G.S.W. Thigh R. Fracture Femur
95	1373	1st Mons.	Rfn.	Green W.	G.S.W. Leg R
	2316	5th Leicesters	Pte	Rossell J.	G.S.W. Leg L
97	1979	5th Lincolns	L/Cpl	Heath O	G.S.W. Head.
98	578	1st N.M. Coy R.E.	Spr.	Griffith A	G.S.W. Head.
99	2426	4th Leicesters	Pte	Freeman J	G.S.W. Leg L.

Order by 2nd Corps: Men liable to be exposed to asphyxiating gases during engagement to wear cloths tied over mouth, previously wrung out in water.
Order from ~~DDMS~~ DADMS: All infectious, or suspected infectious cases,

To be specially and immediately reported to A.D.M.S.

April 28. 1915
DRANOUTRE

2440 Pte Goodacre A, A Coy., and 1365, Pte Barber C. A Coy, 2nd Lincolns, contacts with measles, sent up from the Trenches with Temperature and Headache, admitted to Observation Hut. Reported cases to A.D.M.S. Inspected Billets and Measles contacts at Huyghens Farm; latter released from quarantine today. Inspected Baths and Laundry. At latter, muslin is being dyed khaki, with Dot. Rermeny., to make face masks for men to wear as protection against Enemy's asphyxiating gases. — Private Thorpe, R.A.M.C. detailed for first aid duty in trenches with 4th Leinsters, until May 3rd.
Battle round YPRES continues.

Casualties:

100	5th Lincolns	2108	Pte. Quantrill G.	G.S.W. Shoulder L.
101	5th Lincolns	2179 2/Lt. Nash E.		G.S.W. Hand L. Self Inflicted.
102	2nd Lincolns	1593. Pte. Van Elk B.		G.S.W. Shoulder L.

April 29. 1915
DRANOUTRE

Capt. Salaman 5th Lincolns, sent to St JAN CAPPELLE rest station, suffering from Trench Neurasthenia.

1414 Pte BAKER.W. C Coy. 5th Lincolns, removed to isolation, suffering from Measles: was sent up during the night from the Trenches.

1524 Pte BROWN G. A Coy. 5th Lincolns, sent to Isolation, with symptoms of Cerebro Spinal Meningitis.

Sapper Salt 1 Field Coy. R.E, admitted 8 P.M. with G.S.W. back of Neck L, exit wound through maxillary border R upper jaw. Said to have been shot at

whilst strolling in a Wood between DRANOUTRE and LOCRE; probably sniped.
Afternoon rode to St JAN CAPPELL to see ADMS. Inspected Rest Station.
YPRES burning this afternoon, but little shelling.
   Casualties:
       Nil.

April 30th 1915
   DRANOUTRE
2200 Pte Smith E.E. A Coy 4th Leicesters — Enteric Fever — removed to
isolation.
1530 Pte Davison. F. B Coy. 5th Lincolns. — Measles — removed to
isolation.
Inspected the Farm "ROLICA", where some men of 5th Lincolns
are billeted. A bad billet, very offensive smell from sewage pump.
Reported Billet as unfit for Habitation, both to Brigade HdQrs.
and to ADMS. Pte Smith. E.E. (above), with Enteric, came from
this billet. Also 2/Lieut STANDEN, with suspected Enteric.
Major SLIGHT, Capt INGLEBY, Lieuts MOODY and MOUNTAIN,
5th Lincolns — all from this billet, have been lately suffering
from symptoms suggesting Influenza — but possibly mild Enteric.
— Return asked for, and sent, of proportion of Wounds to Hand,
compared with wounds of other parts of the body.
   DADMS called this afternoon.
   Sent in report to ADMS re Watercarts, which are not
strong enough to stand the wear and tear of the local
roads.
   A 6th Motor-Ambulance has reported for duty, — a Ford.

Casualties:

103	4" Leicesters	564	Pte Cumming B.	G.S.W. Thigh L.
104	4" Leicesters	2405	2Lpl. Ball J.G.	B.W. Hand L. (Accidental)
105	4" Leicesters	3241	Pte Southall L	G.S.W. Arm. Upper R.
106	4" Leicesters	2447	Pte Hewson C.	G.S.W. Hand R.
107	4" Leicesters	1717	Pte Asher W.	G.S.W. Cheek
108	4" Lincolns	1613	Pte Sellett C.	G.S.W. Leg R.
109	4" Lincolns	988	Pte Selby J.W.	G.S.W. Thigh R.
110	1" F. Coy R.E.	392	Spr Underhill T	G.S.W. Hand R.
111	1 F. Coy R.E.	476	Spr Salt F.	G.S.W. Neck L. and Upper Jaw R. ? Sniper

Pte Scott detailed for trench duty with 5" Leicesters.

121/56/

131/56/

46th Division.

1/2nd N.M. Field Ambulance

Vol III

121/56/

May, 1915.

Summary of War Diary of the
2nd North Midland Field Ambulance, R.A.M.C.T.
138th Brigade
46th Division.
May 1st — to — May 31st 1915.

———

This unit has been at DRANOUTRE all this month. One Section (B Section) under Major Dixon is on detached duty at St JAN CAPPELLE, where a Divisional Rest Station has been established.

The health of the Unit is good. One Officer, Capt. COWPER, was sent to the Base, on account of appendicitis. One man was killed, and another wounded whilst working as stretcher bearers in the trenches.

Lieut CHALLENOR, from the Divisional Ammn Column, is attached to B Section for instruction, and 7 reinforcements to replace men gone sick, have arrived from Base.

The general character of the work done by the Unit is much the same as last month. I have, however, moved one of the regimental aid posts into dug outs nearer the trenches, as the former location of this aid post was too far in rear of the firing line. The bearers of the Unit now evacuate direct from the dug out, by way of a communication trench, onto the KEMMEL – LINDENHOEK Road, where the ambulances meet the wounded.

During the month, 207 wounded were passed through my dressing station, and the average daily number of sick in my detention hospital is 20.

Practically every Officer, N.C.O. and man in the Units is detailed for some special work. Besides the ordinary work of evacuation from the trenches to the Dressing Station, the unit provides a Detention Hospital, Observation Hut, Tents for treatment of mild infectious cases, a Laundry, Baths capable of bathing 900 men a day, Baths for cases of Itch, and a Disinfector. In addition, a course of instruction for ambulances of the New Army is being held.

Sickness:

In the Brigade, about a dozen cases of Paratyphoid have occurred, and 2 to 3 cases of Enteric Fever. An investigation for the discovery of possible "carriers" is being undertaken, and so far one suspicious case has been found and segregated. A mild form of German measles continues, causing the men attacked to be ineffective for a week or 10 days. No cases of Gassing have occurred in this Brigade. All N.C.O. and men are supplied with respirators, and are being instructed daily in their use.

Promotions:

During the month, Major R. M. West O/C Unit, was promoted to Lieut. Colonel (Temporary), and Capt. F. Dixon to Major (Temporary).

R. M. West
Lieut. Colonel R.A.M.C.

June 1. 1915

O/C 2nd N. Mid. Field Amb^{ce}
138th Bde.
46th Divⁿ

~~Casualties:~~

May 1. 1915. DRANOUTRE

Report received that DUNKIRK has been bombarded by the enemy from the Sea. — Brigadier Genl CLIFFORD ill — Lumbago.

Casualties:

112	4o Lincolns	2034	Pte Burrows T	GSW Thigh R
113	4o Lincolns	1977	Pte Mullinger J	GSW Shoulder R
114	5th Leicesters	3205	Pte Towers S	GSW foot L
115	5o Lincolns	721	Corpl Scales C	GSW Thigh R
116	4o Leicesters	2648	Pte Taylor F.	GSW Abdomen R.
117	4o Leicesters	2629	Pte Sabni C	GSW Neck R.
118	4o Leicesters	1739	Pte Shipley E	GSW Foot L
119	4o Leicesters	1769	Pte Toon A	GSW Leg L
120	4o Leicesters	2708	Pte Hopkinson L	GSW Shoulder R
121	4o Leicesters	1656	Pte Gent E	GSW Floor of Mouth

May 2. 1915.

DRANOUTRE

2713 Pte Pollard, T, A Coy, 4th Leicesters sent to BAILLEUL with ? Enteric.

Arrested a man, civilian, for behaving in suspicious manner in Woods where Pte Salt was shot on April 30th. Remanded.

At 4.30 PM, Heavy cannonnade from direction of YPRES, followed at 5.30 by strong smell of Chlorine in Village.

Service 3 PM by Rev. Ashby.

Major Martin, 5th Leicesters, sent to Divisional Rest Station, St JAN CAPELLE, having had neck grazed by ricochet of Bullet last night.

Lieut Dalgleish, 4o Leicesters, sent to No 2 Casualty

Clearing Station, BAILLEUL, with G.S.W. Brachial Artery, L.
By order of N/K Midland Division, sent 2 Motor Amb^ces
to Headquarters Stafford Brigade, at NEUVE EGLISE, this
afternoon.

Casualties:

122 4ᵗʰ December 3677 Pte Lewin J.   G.S.W. Arm and Shoulder R.
123 5ᵗʰ December 2519 Pte Hadland W. G.S.W. Neck R.
124 5ᵗʰ December 3399 Pte Fuller J.   G.S.W. Thigh R.
125 2ᵗʰ December 2738 Pte Spong A.   G.S.W. Head
126 5 December   —   Major Martin B?   G.S.W. Head, Neck, Arm (Slight)
127 4 December   —   2 Lieut Dalglish K. G.S.W. Leg L, Arm L.

May 3. 1915.

DRANOUTRE.

Inspected and reported on Farms occupied by troops: all are
soaking in sewage and manure; and the barns are dusty and
rat-infested. Advised that troops, during coming hot season, be
either placed in huts or bivouacked. — Sent application for
bath shed to be erected for treatment of Scabies. — In
morning DADMS called. In afternoon ADMS called. Went
with him to inspect sanitary arrangements for disposal of
Sewage by cremation. Water well — no odour.
Many cases of asphyxiation by Chlorine Gas used by Germans
in Hospitals in BAILLEUL. Intense œdema of Bronchi, with
profuse exudation into tubes, causing death by "drowning".
Treatment recommended: Emetics, Oxygen, pilocarpine.
Troops to be instructed in use of face masks — two layers of
muslin, between which are tea leaves, which must be wetted before
use, with anything, even Urine.

Casualties:

128	4ᵗʰ December	2662	Pte	Pettifor H	GSW Wrist L. Fracture forearm
129	4 December	2674	Pte	Barnes W.	GSW Foot L
130	5 December	1601	Pte	Dawthrop J	GSW Arm L
131	4 Lincolns	1380	Pte	Croft G.	GSW Leg R-L
132	4 Lincolns	2153	Pte	Mylands W	GSW Shoulder L
133	5 Lincolns	1907	Pte	Heseltine T	GSW Arm L. Fracture

Message received this evening from DDMS NMD: Gentle inhalations of Chloroform or Amyl Nitrite strongly recommended for Chlorine Gas poisoning. Tell Field Ambulances of Brigade to supply each Regimental Medical Officer with extra Chloroform.

May 4ᵗʰ 1915
DRANOUTRE

Casualties:

134	5ᶜ Lincolns	1683	Pte	Harrison G.H.	GSW Knee R.
135	5ᶜ Lincolns	599	2/Lt	Wilsea	GSW Head.
136	5ᶜ Lincolns	586	Cpl	Fowler W.E	GSW Thigh R.
137	5ᶜ Lincolns	1394	Pte	Goulden P.	GSW Leg L
138	5ᶜ Lincolns	1787	Pte	Kirk E.	GSW Face L
139	5ᶜ Lincolns	2290	Pte	Anderson J.E	GSW Scalp.
140	5ᶜ Lincolns	3201	Pte	Hope S.	GSW Chest R (Shrapnel).
141	5ᶜ Lincolns	2798	Pte	Maran R.H.	GSW Knee R.
142	4ᶜ Lincolns	3365	Pte	Gaiton S.C	GSW Head.
143	5ᶜ Lincolns	1419	Pte	Elliott C	GSW Forearm L
144	5ᶜ Lincolns	2322	Pte	Gregory J	GSW Buttock L
145	5ᶜ Lincolns	2534	Pte	Butteriss R	GSW Chest R.

May 5th 1915
DRANOUTRE

2396 Pte Playfer H. 5th Lincolns, German Measles - Isolation.
16573 Gunner Teale G. 1 N.M.B. R.G.A. German Measles - Isolation

Reply received from Bde. Headquarters in answer to my application asking that a shed for bathing itch cases be erected, and promising that this shall be done.

A.D.M.S. called this morning.

Motored into BAILLEUL and purchased 25 Barrels for water in the trenches. — Called at No 8 Casualty Clearing Station, and examined cases of Chlorine gas poisoning: Cyanosis, great dyspnœa, extreme weakness, delerium, breathing quickened — in one case 75 per minute — Lungs waterlogged, and frothy fluid bubbling from mouth and nose. Venous bleeding useless, as blood is tarry, and will not flow. Vomiting the best remedy, with Pituitrine and oxygen, and Sylvester's method.

Casualties:

146 Mons. R.E. 6608 Sappr. Woods B. GSW Phalanges L. Comp Fract
147 5th Lincolns 3089 Pte Lamming T. GSW Phalanges L. Comp Fract
148 4th Leicesters 2499 Pte Ward E.C. GSW Ankle L.
149 5th Lincolns 1465 2.Cpl Uzzle E. GSW Head.
150 5th Lincolns 3425 Pte Marshall G.W. GSW Scalp.

May 6th 1915
DRANOUTRE

2642 Pte Smith J.C.E. 5th Leicesters, German Measles removed Isolation.

Rode to BAILLEUL, and bought 25 Barrels for Holding drinking water in Trenches.

ADMS called in afternoon, and brought 400 Gauze Masks for wearing to counteract effects of Gas used by Germans. Between the layers of Gauze, which are large enough to cover the Eyes, is a pad of Cotton Waste, soaked in 10% Sodium Hyposulphate, Sodium Bicarbonate, and kept moist by addition of 1% Glycerine.

Casualties:

151 2ᵈ Lincolns 2150 Pte Woodcock W.   GSW. Head
152 4ᵗʰ Lincolns 2358 Pte Chesher F.W. GSW. Abdominal Wall.
153 1 NMBdRE.   543 Spr. Daniels J.   GSW. Thorax.

May 7. 1915
DRANOUTRE.

Capt. Nicholson, 5ᵗʰ Lincolns, and 2/Lieut Smyth, 5ᵗʰ Lincolns, sent to Isolation — German Measles.

Applied to ADMS for permission to erect 3 Bell Tents for treatment of German Measles.

Went to LINDENHOEK at 1PM to bring in GSW. Head, with symptoms of Cerebral pressure.

DADMS Called. A Thresh's disinfector has arrived for use of Division.

Casualties:

154 5ᵗʰ Lincolns 1796 Pte West.C   GSW. Forearm L
155 5ᵗʰ Lincolns 1886 Pte Salmon E.V   GSW Scalp
156 5ᵗʰ Lincolns 1821 2/Lt Dee A.   GSW. Knee L
157 5ᵗʰ Lincolns 1164 Sergt. Willmott G.W. GSW. Head.

{ Note: These Casualties should have been entered on May 5,
{ Those of May 5 on May 6ᵗʰ, and those of May 6ᵗʰ
{ on May 7ᵗʰ —

May 8 1915
DRANOUTRE.

Very heavy gun fire since early morning, lasting till evening, in direction of YPRES – HILL 60.

Casualties:

158	2° Lincolns	7543	2/Lt Pike A.	GSW Tonsil L. Side
159	2° Lincolns	3601	Pte Richards T.	GSW Phalanx R.
160	2° Lincolns	7196	Pte Lewis L.	GSW Head
161	2° Lincolns	2509	Pte Wicklwright T.	GSW Shoulder R.
162	2° Lincolns	1863	Cpl Cayless C.	GSW Knee L.
163	2° Lincolns	992	Pte Oster B.	GSW Forearm R.
164	5° Lincolns	2476	Pte Fox G.H.	GSW Leg R.
165	2° Lincolns	1697	Pte Hirst A.	GSW Eye R.

May 9th 1915
DRANOUTRE.

Enemy pierced our line E of YPRES last Evening, but hear today that a counter attack on our side was successful in pushing him back. German Aeroplane brought down near KEMMEL this Evening. German Trench blown up near LINDENHOEK this Evening. 2° Lieut A. CLARKE killed by Shrapnel in Trenches this Evening. (2° Leicesters). Lieut. MOUNTAIN, A Co. 5° Lincolns admitted to Isolation Hut this Evening suffering from Measles. — Church Parade 12 noon by Rev. P. ASHBY.

Casualties.

166	2° Lincolns	1782	Cpl. Tyne R.	GSW. Scalp.
167	2° Lincolns	1661	Pte Leech J.	GSW. Scalp
168	2° Lincolns	2265	Pte Astill L.	GSW. Back L.

Sent War Diary for April to A.G. Base.

May 10. 1915
DRANOUTRE

2612 Pte Pollard, W^m, A Coy. 4th Leicesters, Enteric : removed Isolation : Inoculated in October twice.

451 Spr McCabe. E. 1st F.Coy R.E. German Measles : Admitted

1402 Pte Rollinson P. C Coy. 5th Lincolns. German Measles : admitted.

1680 Pte Wright H. C. Coy. 5th Lincolns   ,,   ,,

2613 Pte Lowthorpe W. C. Coy. 5th Lincolns   ,,   ,,

Have pitched two Bell Tents for treatment of cases of German Measles.

A D M S called today, and reports that the Officer Commanding 5th Lincolns has complained to Divisional Headquarters that the Medical Officers of this Unit, when they go to the Aid posts at night, do not wait long enough for cases to come in, but leave about 12 midnight. This is absolutely incorrect, as my Officers rarely leave the aid-posts until dawn is breaking. On the other hand, my Officers state that the O/C the 5th Lincolns interferes with their work at the aid posts, by himself advising as to the disposal of casualties from the Battalion under his Command.

1450 gauze and cotton waste respirators for use against gas fumes arrived tonight from ST OMER.

Inspected several farms, and find the manure heaps, which were ordered to be cleared away last month, have in many cases not been touched - in others, although cleared, the manure pit is being refilled.

Casualties

168	4° Leicesters	3376	Pte	Scrivens P.A.	GSW Knee R. Shrapnel.
169	4° Leicesters	1765	Pte	Wesson	GSW Head
170	4° Leicesters	2896	Pte	Budworth W	GSW Head
171	4° Leicesters	1513	Pte	Hill H.	GSW Knee L. Phalanges R. Shrapnel.
172	4° Leicesters	2473	Pte	Roe S.	GSW Knee R. Calf L. Shrapnel.
173	4° Leicesters	2422	Pte	Dongh L.	GSW Face and Head. Shrapnel
174	4° Leicesters	2131	Pte	Charity H.	GSW Leg R. Shrapnel
175	4° Leicesters	2889	Pte	Storer J.	GSW Thigh L
176	4° Leicesters	1925	Pte	Collett F.	GSW Shoulder R. Shrapnel
177	5° Leicesters	1203	Pte	Sturges T.W	GSW. Face
178	5° Leicesters	153	Corpl.	Monk S.	GSW Arm R
179	5° Leicesters	2194	L.Cpl.	Richardson E.	GSW Thigh R.
180	5° Leicesters	1479	Pte	Hunt J.T.	GSW Wrist R. Shrapnel
181	4° Leicesters	3114	Pte	Johnson W.	GSW Scalp
182	4° Leicesters	1886	Pte	Looms F.	GSW. Face.
183	4° Leicesters	1273	L.Cpl	Dodge S.	GSW. Back L. Concussion. Deafness
184	4° Leicesters	1357	Pte	Kilbourne E.	GSW Arm R, Back, Shoulder Shrapnel.
185	1° NM.Fd.Co, R.E.	234	Sergt.	Baker J.W	GSW. Face L

May 11. 1915

DRANOUTRE

1 AM This morning message recieved that a trench occupied by some of 4° Leicesters had been taken by the Enemy, and retaken by the Leicesters with loss of 50 wounded. Prepared Hospital, and took down 4 Ambulance Motors. Report exaggerated. One trench had been grenaded, and Capt. HAYLOCK, and 1 Sergeant, 4° Leicesters, killed. Several wounded. Returned 4:30 AM. at 7.40 AM, telegram to bring in 5 lying and 2 sitting cases

●●● 5th Lincolns. Took Cars to LINDENHOEK, and went
u●● bearers to Aid post of 5 Lincolns at ONE TREE FARM.
The route from LINDENHOEK is exposed, and could be
made safer by a sunk road. Reported on this to Brigadier.
A number of cases of continued fever without other symptoms beyond
Headache and furred tongue, probably Para-Typhoid cases — Typhoid
modified by inoculation.
YPRES has been burning since yesterday morning.

Casualties:

No.	Unit	No.	Rank	Name	Wound
186	4 Lincolns	1679	Pte	Bramfield H.	G.S.W. Hand L (Self Infl.)
187	5 Leicesters	1297	Pte	Bowley H.	G.S.W. Foot L
188	5 Leicesters	1427	Pte	Holland H.	G.S.W. Abdomen
189	4 Leicesters	3281	Pte	Hufton W.	G.S.W. Face L
190	4 Leicesters	1036	Pte	Franklin J.	Grenade W. Thumb-Hand L
191	4 Leicesters	1329	Pte	Cope A.	Grenade W. Face
192	5 Lincolns	1023	2/Lt	Shore H.	G.S.W. Knee R
193	5 Leicesters	3291	Pte	Smith S.	G.S.W. Arm L
194	5 Leicesters	2295	Pte	Stevenson J.	Grenade W. Buttock-Thigh
195	4 Leicesters		2nd Lieut	Russell G.E.	Bayonet wound Neck (Accident)
196	4 Leicesters	1380	Pte	Hawkesworth W.	G.S.W. Abdomen
197	4 Leicesters	2431	2/Lt	Goadby A.	Grenade W. Leg L, Head, Arm
198	4 Leicesters	412	Pte	Gill F.	Grenade W. Foot R - Leg L
199	4 Leicesters	2429	Capt	Reading	Grenade W. Arm (Fracture) and Leg
200	4 Leicesters	2683	Pte	Taylor C.	G.S.W. Thigh R
201	4 Leicesters	3170	Pte	Campbell A.	G.S.W. Arm L

May 12. 1915
ANOUTRE.

5857 Sapper McConkey Wm. No 1 Siege Coy. A Mons Engineers, removed to Isolation — Cerebro-Spinal Meningitis.

Pte Brown J. 8th NMFA RAMC: On the Night of May 10th, when E1 Trench was grenaded by the Germans, and evacuated by the men holding it, Pte Brown remained in the Trench and attended to the Wounded. ~~Have notified ADMS~~.

This Unit to undertake the mixing and supplying of the Solution for dipping the Gas-Respirators: Lieut Bevan Brown to be the Officer responsible for this. The solution is as follows.

Hyposulphate of Soda	10 lb
Sodium Carbonate	2 lb
Glycerine	½ pint
Water	1 gallon

Squeeze the Respirators nearly dry in above solution. When a respirator has been used against Gas, it should be treated with solution half the above strength.

Instructions from ADMS to send more RAMC Personnel to keep in trenches: consulted with Brigadier General, and arranged that 2 RAMC men for 1st aid work, be sent to each Battalion instead of 1, as formerly.

Two Vacuum flask bottles sent from ADMS for collecting gas fumes in trenches: in charge of 1st aid RAMC men in trenches.

190 Respirators received from ADMS. Retained 100 for use of this Unit, and sent 90 to Brigade Headquarters.

Casualties
202 5ᵗ Lincolns 3584 Pte Bluitte —   GSW Thigh L
203 5ᵗ Lincolns 1314 Sgt Gray T.   GSW Thorax
204 5ᵗ Lincolns 2816 Pte Jackson F   GSW Wrist L Thigh R
205 5ᵗ Lincolns 1685 Pte Miller C   GSW Arm L and R
206 5ᵗ Lincolns 135 Sept Lansing P. GSW Neck
207 4ᵗ Lincolns 1243 Dr Flear B   GSW Hand L
208 5ᵗ Lincolns 2501 Pte Robinson J GSW Forearm L
209 5ᵗ Lincolns 1751 Pte Bale T   GSW Knee R

May 13. 1915.
DRANOUTRE.

Heavy Rain all day.
DMS 2ⁿᵈ Army called and Inspected Dressing Station and Hospital.
ADMS called.
DADMS called.
Mixed 18 gallons of Solution for dipping Respirators.
No shelling direction of YPRES. Continuous shelling direction ARMENTIERS.
Sent in report on classification of cases for last 14 days.
Lieut McKNEE RAMC took blood for Vidal test from one of the cases of suspected Paratyphoid.

Casualties:
210 5ᵗ Lincolns. 2385 2Cpl Stafford L. GSW Leg R. Fracture
211 4ᵗ Lincolns 2442 Pte Hayward H.   GSW Trigger Finger. Accidental
212 5ᵗ Lincolns 1441 2Cpl Smalley J.J GSW Arm L
213 5ᵗ Lincolns 1884 Pt Cram W.H.   GSW Face
214 5ᵗ Lincolns 1482 Pt Cave J   GSW Knee R
215 5ᵗ Lincolns   Lieut Sheel H.   GSW Leg L
216 4ᵗ Lincolns 2775 Pte Parrot —   GSW Thighs R and L

May 14th 1915
DRANOUTRE

332 Pte Hunt H. A Coy 4 Leicesters, Enteric (inoculated sick(ful)) to Isolation.
Heavy rain all morning, clearing in afternoon.

Pte Green, C Section 2nd N.M.F.A. R.A.M.C., shot in neck 7.30 AM
and killed. Buried tonight at ONE TREE FARM.

Casualties:

217	4th Lincolns	2074	Pte Hurst L.	G S W Face
218	4th Lincolns	1741	Pte Hanges J	G S W Finger
219	4th Lincolns	282	Sergt. Herrick W.	G S W Fore Arm R.
220	4th Lincolns	2515	Pte Cooke P.	Trench Mortar W. Thigh R.
221	4th Lincolns	2129	Pte Stewart F.	G S W Hip R.
222	4th Lincolns	2493	Pte Robinson R.	G S W Head.
223	4th Lincolns	2382	Pte Sandall F.	G S W Thigh L.
224	4th Lincolns	2512	Pte Clark J.	G S W Thigh R.
225	1 N M F Coy R.E	534	Sapp Brittain J	G S W. Head.
226	5 Leicesters	1751	Pte Dale T.	G S W Knee R.
227	5th Lincolns	2816	Pte Jackson F.	G S W. Thigh R. Wrist L.
~~228~~	~~5th Lincolns~~	~~1884~~	~~Pte~~	

May 15. 1915
DRANOUTRE

Fine cold day. Very little firing to be heard.
Rode to St JAN CAPPELLE and inspected Divisional Rest Station.
Permission obtained from Brigadier to start Brigade Cricket Club.

Brigade and division re-numbered:
    138th Brigade
    46th Division.

Casualties:

228 4"Lincolns 1173 Cpl. Cripit J. GSW Back (Shrapnel).
229 172"Coy RE 1771 Cpl. Farr W. GSW Abdomen
230 4"Lincolns 2665 Pte Wardle W GSW Head.
231 5" Lincolns 1543 Pte Wilson W. GSW Arm L
232 4" Lincolns 2 Lieut. Marris G. Shock: Trench Mortar

May 16. 1915
DRANOUTRE.
Fine Hot day. — Church Parade, Bishop of Pretoria.
ADMS called: reports men of Suffolks suffering from Neuritis, and analysis of Water from stream, which they drink, and which flows from German trenches near WYTESCHAETE, reveals presence of Arsenic. Has directed me to procure specimens from stream running from LINDENHOEK past KEMMEL for analysis.
Capt. COOPER, 4" Lincolns, shot last night in trenches.
Number of men admitted Hospital last night suffering from shock and deafness, from explosion of bomb from trench mortar.

Casualties:

233 4"Lincolns 1009. Cpl. Woods J.L. GSW Hand L
234. 5"Lincolns 2258. Pte. Jenkinson W. GSW Shoulder R.

May 17" 1915
DRANOUTRE
Heavy rain all day. Roads very bad. Rode this morning to KEMMEL to procure samples of Water from stream to East of Village, but was informed samples had already been taken this morning and despatched to ADMS.

Casualties:
235 4 December 2108 Pte Charlesworth J   GSW Hand L. S.I.
236 4 December 3403 Pte Miller WJ   GSW Nose.
237 4 December 1557 Pte Toseland F   GSW Forehead
238 4 December 7561 Pte Corrigan E   Periscope splinters face
239 5 December 2ⁿᵈ Lieut Selwyn C   GSW Thigh R L. both Femora Fractured
240 5 December 1776 2Cpl Minchley J   Shell Wound Buttock
241 4 December 1576 ACpl Cepper G   Shock

May 18ᵗʰ 1915
DRANOUTRE
Heavy Rain nearly all day. New baths and laundry opened today.
Two baths set aside for Scabies – to be under direct Advice of RAMC.
Stream at WYTSCHAETE poisoned by Germans, contained
1 gram of Arsenic to the pint.
Lieut Oakbury, Div¹ Sanitary officer called. A THRESH apparatus
to be attached to Baths for disinfection.
Casualties:
242 4 December 3054 Pte Price AE   Bayonet W. Scalp. accidental
243 5 December 1494 Pte Lord S.   GSW Thumb. R.

May 19ᵗʰ 1915
DRANOUTRE
Wet day. Started new Baths this morning: in addition to officers
Baths, and Scabies baths, 700 men can be bathed daily, but
owing to lack of accommodation in Laundry, only 450 can be
supplied with clean underclothes.
Capt Cooper RAMC, of this Unit, became ill at 11.30 AM with
abdominal pain and vomiting. Diagnosis: Biliary Colic

In evening, removed to No 3 Casualty clearing Station, BAILLEUL.
List of all NCOs and men who have suffered from Enteric Fever at any time, asked for and promised: some cases of Enteric having occurred, a search to be made for Contacts. Several cases of Paratyphoid in the Brigade.
A D M S examined men said to be unfit for trench work with a view to employing them on Lines of communication.
   Casualties: Nil

May 20th 1915
DRANOUTRE.
Fine day. Capt Cooper, R.A.M.C, of this Unit evacuated from No 3 Casualty clearing Station, BAILLEUL, to BOULOGNE.
This afternoon the Enemy blew up one of our trenches, near LINDENHOEK. Several casualties reported.
   Casualties: Nil

May 21st 1915
DRANOUTRE.
Submitted new scheme to Brigadier and A D M S, for better care of Wounded in trenches: The R.M.O. to remain in the advanced Dug-outs, whence he could quickly and without much risk reach the trenches if wanted. He would collect his wounded in his Dug out. Pack-Horse Farm will be taken over by me as an advanced dressing station, one of the Officers of this unit going there with the stretcher bearers, and remaining all night. At the main dressing station, an officer of the Unit will be on duty, to receive the cases sent up from the advanced dressing station. Scheme approved of.
The blowing up of our trench by the Germans resulted in

9 men being killed, chiefly by being buried in the debris, and one Officer of R.E. killed whilst attending to repair of damage. One Officer, Lieut DYSON, 5ᵉ Lincolns, was still buried this morning, but was subsequently dug out none the worse after 14 hours.

Casualties:

244. 1NMFCoRE. 495 Sapp. Baker C.F.   GSW. Hand L
245. 5ᵉ Lincolns 1170 L/Cpl Barnes E.   GSW Thigh R.
246. 5ᵉ Lincolns 3264 Pte Bee S.   GSW Back - Shoulder
247. 5ᵉ Lincolns 2138 Pte Turner C.J.   Bruised back
248. 5ᵉ Lincolns 2314 Pte Tomlinson F.   Bruised back
249. 5ᵉ Lincolns 2647 Pte Wells C.A.   GSW Thigh L
250. 5ᵉ Lincolns 1132 L/Cpl Smith A.   GSW Hand R
251. 5ᵉ Lincolns 1683 Pte Hearn J.   Fract Fibula R. - Humerus L
252. 5ᵉ Lincolns 1324 Pte Crouch T.   Bruised back
253. 5ᵉ Lincolns 2736 Pte Adams R.A.   Cut forehead
254. 5ᵉ Lincolns 2173 Pte Dakin E.   GSW Hand L
255. 5ᵉ Lincolns 1516 Pte Reed A.   GSW Cheek
256. 5ᵉ Lincolns 1618 Pte Bloomfield F.   Fract Clavicle L
257. 5ᵉ Lincolns 1662 Pte Holmes A.   Bruised Legs
258. 5ᵉ Lincolns 1236 Pte Graham A.   Bruised Pelvis
259. 1NMFCoRE 623 Spr. Johnson J.   Lacerated Ear L
260. 5ᵉ Lincolns 1181 Pte Bradley H.   GSW Thumb L
261. 5ᵉ Lincolns 3165 L/Cpl Bond R.   Shock
262. 5ᵉ Lincolns 1788 Pte Charlesworth H.   Shock
263. 5ᵉ Lincolns 2275 Pte Smith R.   Bruised Arm R. - Shock
264. 5ᵉ Lincolns 2273 Pte Middleton J.   GSW Hand L
265. 5ᵉ Lincolns 580 Pte Tomby J.   Shock
266. 5ᵉ Lincolns 3160 Pte Brown M.   Shock

Most of above were due to **mine explosion**.

May 22. 1915
DRANOUTRE

Fine warm day. In morning ADMS called. Went with him to inspect 4th Leicesters, who have gone into bivouac. Orders from ADMS that if Measles increase, must take a Barn to segregate them in. Major GRESSON, commanding 4th Leicesters, suffering from over work; to go to St JAN CAPELLE Rest Station tomorrow. Major MARTIN takes command of 4th Leicesters.

Casualties

No.	Unit	Regt. No.	Rank/Name	Injury
267	5th Lincolns	991	L/Cpl Taylor W.	Bruised Hand - Shock
268	5th Lincolns	2473	Sgt. Turvey R.	Bayonet W. Thigh L
269	5th Lincolns	2440	L/Cpl Laurence C	GSW Wrist L
270	5th Lincolns	2428	Pte Gabbitas W.	GSW Leg R. Foot L
271	5th Lincolns	2777	Pte Hodkinson J.	Crushed Legs - Shock
272	5th Lincolns	2786	Gibson H. Pte	Crushed Legs - and Chest
273	5th Lincolns	1864	L/Cpl Stubb G.	GSW Scalp
274	5th Lincolns		Lieut. Dyson E.	Bruised back

May 23. 1915
DRANOUTRE

Fine warm day. Heavy gun fire near Hill 60. Lieut CHALLENOR, RAMC., M.O. Div' Amm. Column, is attached to B. Section, at Rest station, St JAN CAPPELLE, for instruction from 15th Inst.

Casualties:

No.	Unit	Regt. No.	Rank/Name	Injury
275	4th Lincolns	812	Sgt. Crick A.	Periscope Wound face
276	5th Lincolns	3197	Pte. Gilfoy N.	GSW. Shoulder R.
277	4th Lincolns	2507	Pte. Brocklesby T.	Foreign body in Eye

May 24, 1915
DRANOUTRE

Fine, Warm. Inspection at LOCRE by Commander 2nd Army (General PLUMER). In afternoon went to S'JAN CAPPELLE to see Major Dixon, on account of complaint made by NCO i/c Motor Ambulances, that Motor Ambulances are overladen, and that men having no business there, are found riding in them. Saw DADMS. In view of cases of paratyphoid, am having nominal rolls of all men who have had typhoid prepared, and certain selected cases are bacteriologically examined. Lce Cpl DAWSON, 4º Lincolns, found to be a Carrier, and removed to BAILLEUL. Very heavy firing last night, both gun and rifle. Gas used last night by Germans against our troops at YPRES: over 1000 cases said to have been brought into BAILLEUL today. Germans are also accused of using overhead bombs, which, on bursting, discharge liquid formalin.

Casualties:
278 4º Lincolns   2358 Lce Cpl Gurnley G.   GSW Skull
279 4º Lincolns   2528 Pte   Greaves G.   GSW Hand L. Accidental
280 4º Lincolns   2844 Pte   Woodford C. Injury Eye R
281 4º Lincolns   2335 Pte   Walter H.   Shell Wound Scalp
282 4º Leicesters 1280 Pte   Shipman W.   GSW Scalp

May 25th 1915
DRANOUTRE

Fine, Warm. Sent 220 Respirators to 5º Lincolns. Visited Casualty Clearing Station at BAILLEUL, and examined some gassed cases. As a result, I reported to ADMS:
1 Many men have not been shown how to wear respirators
2 Cotton Waste in respirators is often in lumps, with spaces allowing passage of air in between.

3. Owing to absence of Waterproof bags, the pads get dry.
4. Respirators do not always fit tight round the Nose
ADMS called this afternoon. — Several fresh German Measles, all mild cases, this last week.

Casualties.
283 4 Lincolns   1868 Pte Wyldes R.   GSW Knee L.
284 4 Leicesters 2116 Pte Beaver J.   GSW Thigh R. Femur F.act.
285 4 Lincolns   1281 Pte Aukland W.   GSW Neck.
286 4 Leicesters 2593 LeCpl. Jones G.J. GSW Face.

May 26 1915
DRANOUTRE
Fine. Warm. Last night 10 PM Zeppelin flew over Village.
ADMS called. Went with him to inspect Farms to be occupied by Cambridge Battalion, passing through on way to ARMENTIERES.
  Orders that in future, Units requiring respirators, will indent on Ordnance.
  This Evening, a time fuse which some men of 5th Leicesters were examining, exploded, injuring 6 of them.
  Sent Circular Memo by Surg. General Porter, subject: Asphyxiating gases and use of respirators, to M.O-s of Battalion
  Casualties:
  Nil.

May 27 1915
DRANOUTRE.
Went to St JAN CAPPELLE to see ADMS with reference to some men recommended for Lines of Communication. Drew from Ordnance

respirators and bags for this Unit. N.C.O. and men to be instructed
and drilled in their use.— Rev. UFFIN, Congregational Chaplain, arrived.
Casualties:

287 5⁵ᵗʰ Lincolns 1616 Pte Reed A.   G.S.W. Face.
288 5ᵗʰ Lincolns 1252 Cpl Kirk F.   G.S.W. Head, Arm R, Thumb R. ⎫
289 5ᵗʰ Lincolns 2457 Pte Topham W.   G.S.W. Thigh R, Leg R.   ⎬ Accidental
290 5ᵗʰ Lincolns   769 Cpl Nelson R.   G.S.W. Arm and Chest   ⎪ explosion of
291 5ᵗʰ Lincolns 1065 2ⁿᵈ Lt Jackson W. G.S.W. Hip R.   ⎪ portion of
292 5ᵗʰ Lincolns 2468 Pte. Fell C.   G.S.W. Arm R.   ⎪ Shell.
293 5ᵗʰ Lincolns 2646 Pte Tomlinson T. G.S.W. Face, Hand L.   ⎭
294 5ᵗʰ Leicesters 1672 Pte Pepper B.   Injury to Eye L.

May 28. 1915
DRANOUTRE
Cool, cloudy. Capt. Turner instructed unit in use of respirators.
Col. A.D.M.S. called this afternoon. The Field Ambulance, of Kitcheners
Army, is attached to the 1ˢᵗ and 2ⁿᵈ Field Ambulances for 8 days'
instruction, being billeted at LOCRE with 1ˢᵗ F. Amb ᶜʸ. Instruction
starts tomorrow. Royal Scots, from Ypres, and Argylls, billeted in
DRANOUTRE, coming from YPRES. Went in Ambulance to
POPERINGHE to return two R.E. men from Hospital to their billets
at VLAMERTINGHE.
Casualties
295. 5ᵗʰ Leicesters 1319 Pte Saddington. G.S.W. Head.
296. 4ᵗʰ Lincolns 2812 Pte Richardson G. Incised Wound Scalp.

May 29. 1915
DRANOUTRE

Fine. Warm. Men of 2/1st Field Ambulance, New Army, attached to this unit for instruction.

Casualties:

297. R.F.A. Dr. Newton H. Comp. Fract. Skull (Kick).
298. 2ⁿᵈ Lincolns 2399 Dvr. Drake H. Grenade W. Thighs and Legs
299. 5ᵗʰ Lincolns 2475 Cpl. Coles J. G.S.W. Face
300. 2ⁿᵈ Lincolns 2712 Pte Kirk R. Grenade W. Leg R.
301. 5ᵗʰ Lincolns 1251 Cpl Copping C. G.S.W. Head.
302. 5ᵗʰ Lincolns 2696 Pte Bradbury E. G.S.W. Head.
303. 4ᵗʰ Lincolns 2306 Pte Snaider H. Grenade Knee, Hand L.
304. 4ᵗʰ Lincolns 1831 Pte Pearse H. G.S.W. Head.
305. 4ᵗʰ Lincolns 2661 2Cpl Tipler C. Grenade W. Thigh L.

May 30. 1915
DRANOUTRE.

Fine, Cold. N Wind. Church Parade this Evening.
Little firing.

Casualties:

306. 4ᵗʰ Lincolns 2523 Pte Flemming J. G.S.W. Hand L.
307. 4ᵗʰ Lincolns 2496 Pte Scott S. G.S.W. Thigh R.

May 31. 1915
DRANOUTRE

Fine warm day. NE Wind. In afternoon rode to LINDENHOEK, and walked to Regent Street Dug Outs, where Regimental Aid post of 4ᵗʰ Leicesters and 5ᵗʰ Lincolns have been established. Appear to be very suitable for the purpose, being near Trenches and in dead ground.

The idea is that this Field Ambulance shall bring the Motor Ambulances to LINDENHOEK Aid post (4: Lincolns and 5: Leicesters), and send bearers up by way of the communication Trench (Regent Street) to the Regent Street Dug Outs to bring down the wounded. This procedure will be adopted tonight.

A Zeppelin at 8.30 PM N.W of DRANOUTRE. Steering W.

Casualties:

308	4: Leicesters		Lieut. Abell. J.G.	GSW Neck
309	5: Lincolns	2606	Pte Langton D.	GSW Thigh L } Grenade
310	5: Lincolns	2335	Pte Feller H.	GSW Arm R
311	5: Lincolns		Lieut. Dixon O.	GSW Arm R
312	4: Leicesters		Captain. Faire R.	Grenade Wound Neck
313	7: R.Bde	306	Pte Wardle J.	Grenade W. Legs, Chest, Arm R.
314	5: Lincolns	1345	Pte Norcock A.	Grenade W. Thigh L
315	7: R.Bde	295	Pte Coleman J.	Grenade W. Forehead.
316	7: R.Bde	245	Pte Reeves J.	Grenade Thigh R.
317	4: Lincolns	2423	Pte Ward S.	GSW Scalp
318	4: Lincolns	2403	Pte Fletcher J.	GSW Scalp
319	7: R.Bde	2431	Pte Prosser W.	GSW Hand R.

June 1st 1915

DRANOUTRE.

Fine Warm Day, N.W wind.

Casualties

320	4: Lincolns	2655	Pte Scholes J.	GSW Scalp.
321	110: H.Batty, R.F.A	8781	Dr. Wheeler W.J.	Lacerated W. Scalp- Accidental.
322	4: Leicesters	2621	Pte Raven E.	GSW Thigh and Arm L.

121/6390

46th Division
121/6390

H₂ N.M. Field Ambulance

Vol III

June 15

June 2. 1915
DRANOUTRE.

Fine warm. NW Wind. ADMS called this morning. Went with him to
LINDENHOEK to inspect Dug outs, via Regents Street.
This afternoon rode to BAILLEUL to visit 3rd NMFA. This evening
7 men, base details, reported here for duty.

Casualties:

323	6'Lincolns	1999	Pte	Rudkin G.	GSW Neck
324	6'Lincolns	1976	Pte	Lawrence H.	GSW Wrist R.
325	6'Lincolns	2551	Pte	Sharpe H.	Bayonet W Hand. R
326	6'Lincolns	2374	Pte	Vann H.	Bayonet W. Thigh L
327	6'Lincolns	2584	Pte	Evans H.	GSW Thigh R.
328	2nd NMFA	2306	Pte	Martin J.	GSW Ear L.
	RAMC				

June 3. 1915
DRANOUTRE

Cloudy Day. Wind N.W. - Drill Squads with respirators. Rode to
LOCRE to 1st Field Ambulance, to arrange with them, according to
ADMS instructions, for them to evacuate any wounded of this
Brigade from KEMMEL sector of trenches, now occupied by 5th
Lincolns

Casualties

329	7th A Bde	7320	Pte	Pinterford H.G.	GSW Neck
330	5 Lincolns	2397	Pte	Hill E.	GSW. Hand R.
331	5 Lincolns	1203	Pte	Smith H.	GSW Scalp

June 4. 1915
DRANOUTRE

Foggy Morn, fine afternoon. Wind SE-SW. Sent MO to Ambulance

to KEMMEL, with Capt TURNER, RAMC, to evacuate
Col JONES, O/c 5ᵗʰ Leicesters, wounded by High Explosive Shell.
Later went myself to bring in body of Col JESSOP, O/c 5ᵗʰ Lincolns,
killed by same shell, which also killed 2 men and a horse,
exploding opposite 5ᵗʰ Leicesters' Headquarters in KEMMEL.
ADMS called. All N.C.O.'s and men of Unit to have smoke
helmets.

Casualties
332 5ᵗʰ Lincolns 7027 Pte. Cragg. A. GSW Thorax
333 5ᵗʰ Lincolns 8912. Pte. Hodson A. GSW Head.

June 5ᵗʰ 1915
DRANOUTRE
Fine Day. Fog in Morning. Wind NW-SW. 44ᵗʰ Field
Ambulance, attached for training, left today. In afternoon
visited dug-outs, and prospected for water. One good well
found in ruined cottage, but also found Human and Cow's
bodies in its vicinity. Smoke Helmets issued to men.
Lieut Col. Jessop buried in DRANOUTRE Churchyard
this afternoon.

Casualties.
334 5ᵗʰ Leicesters 1766 Pte Walkinson C   GSW Face. Comp Frect
335 5ᵗʰ Lincolns 1527 Pte. Price F   Bayonet wd Lower Jaw
                                           Finger L

June 6ᵗʰ 1915
DRANOUTRE
Fine Day. Fog in Morning. Wind NW-SW. M.O. 5ᵗʰ Bucks and
Oxford L.I. reported for training. Church parade 12 o'c. by
Rev Ashby. Two cases Enteric among civil population, a

man and his wife, reported by Civil Doctor. Cases removed to
the Cliers Hospital, and house disinfected and put out of
bounds. Inspected Bivouacs of 5ᵗʰ Leicesters.

Casualties:

336 5ᵗʰ Leicesters 1647 Pte Woodcock M. GSW Knee R
337 5ᵗʰ Leicesters 1250 2ⁿᵈ Lt. Smith W. GSW Face
338 5ᵗʰ Leicesters 1750 Pte Eyre F.G. GSW Leg
339 5ᵗʰ Leicesters 726 2ⁿᵈ Lt. Gilbert N. GSW Hand R.

June 7. 1915
DRANOUTRE

Visited Bivouacs of 5ᵗʰ Leicesters. Civilian Case of Enteric Fever
on Kemmel Hill reported by civil doctor, and removed to
isolation.

Casualties

340 5ᵗʰ Leicesters 1766 Pte Crite F. B. wound Hand L. (3.6.15)
341 5ᵗʰ Ox. and Bucks L.I.- 10891 Pte Smith G. GSW. Shoulder L.
342 5ᵗʰ Leicesters 1569 Pte Whitworth J. GSW. Elbow R.
343 5ᵗʰ Leicesters - L/Cpl Jones C.H. GSW Back and Hand L
344 5ᵗʰ Lincolns 1203 Pte Smith H. GSW Scalp

June 8ᵗʰ 1915
DRANOUTRE

Fine, warm. 98° in shade. Rode to Rest Station at Mont
des CATS. Called to see ADMS at S. JAN CAPPEL. Inspected
rest station there: appears to be working well. Also
Baths for troops.

Casualties.
3●● L⁴ Leicesters 2256 Pte Freeman A. GSW Head
326 L⁴ Leicesters 3536 Pte Leeson G. GSW Neck
~~327~~

June 9. 1915
DRANOUTRE.
Fine morning. Warm. Thunderstorm in afternoon. Rode to
LINDENHOEK, and went to Regent Street dug outs. Prospected
for Water, which is getting scarce.
Casualties.
347 L⁴ Lincolns 580 Pte Cook A. Appendicitis
328 5 Leicesters 1646 Pte Bassett H. G S W Head
329 L⁴ Leicesters Capt. and Adjt. Dyer-Bennett. GSW Leg R. B.W. Chest.

June 10. 1915
DRANOUTRE.
Heavy Thunderstorm in early morning. Close day, with thick
mist. Experiments tried with Smoke Helmets prove them very
efficacious, without the Respirator.
Casualties
    Nil.

June 11. 1915
A D M S Called. Dull day. Wind N.W.
  Casualties.
350 5 Leicesters 2324. Pte Yates A. G.S.W. Shoulder R. (7.6.15)

June 12. 1915
DRANOUTRE

Hot close day. Wind S.E. Rode to Kemmeel to inspect dressing station (aid post), and try and find a more suitable one. As KEMMEL is being shelled daily with high explosive shells. Nothing suitable in KEMMEL.

351 1st Leicester Lieutenant Bruce H. Grenade Wd Eyes and Skull.
352 1st Leicester 1656 Cpl Sidney Pte G.S.W. Thigh R.
353 1st Lincolns 2653 Pte Rees T.S. Grenade Wd Chest, Arms, Hand, Neck
354 1st Leicester 2315 Pte Thompson Jos. G.S.W. Hip R.
355 1st Leicester 1301 Pte Salm F G.S.W. Scalp.
356 1st Lincolns 2211 Pte Hopper C. G.S.W. Neck
357 1st Lincolns 2567 Pte Carter A. G.S.W. Neck
358 1st Lincolns 2916 Pte Martin J. G.S.W. Scalp
359 1st Lincolns 2564 Pte Ashling G. G.S.W. Buttock
360 5th Ox. and Bucks 10852 Pte Blundy A. G.S.W. Arm L
361 1st Lincolns 2160 Pte Hutchinson T. G.S.W. Nose (Periscope)
362 5th Ox. and Bucks 10776 Pte Donald R. G.S.W. Forehead
363 1st Lincolns Lieutenant Newton R.W. Grenade Wd Head

June 13. 1915
DRANOUTRE.

Hot close day. Wind W. Rode to trenches to ascertain whether firing trenches are wide enough to permit stretcher being carried through; too narrow and too tortuous. Shortly after leaving Trench F4, high explosive shell burst on parapet, injuring 12 men. In evening went to St JAN CAPPELLE to see A.D.M.S. It is proposed to make dug outs for the left Trench Sector, similar to those in Regent St (Right Trench Sector) for use as medical aid posts, and to evacuate from there instead of from Kemmell

Casualties:
364 4th Lincolns 3378 Pte Smith H.   GSW Ear and Neck
365 4th Lincolns 2379 Pte Robinson W. GSW Arm L
366 5th Lincolns 2225 Pte Crowstone J. GSW Foot R.
367 4th Lincolns   75 Sergt Brown H.   GSW Face.
368 4th Lincolns 2677 Pte Gilliatt H. GSW Shoulder R
369 5th Lincolns 2406 Pte Chambers E. GSW Foot L
370 5th Lincolns 2706 Pte Dann J.E.   GSW Back R.
371 5th Lincolns 2299 Pte Stainton J. GSW Skull (slight).

June 14. 1915
DRANOUTRE
A.D.M.S. Called this morning. Fine day. Cloudy. Wind N.E.
In afternoon went to St JAN CAPPELLE to conference with A.D.M.S.
and O/C's 1st and 3rd Field Ambulances with reference to a
Battle Practice tomorrow.
3 Reinforcements arrived today.

Casualties:
372. 4th Lincolns 1868 Pte Wydles R.B.   Old G.S.W. Knee L
373. 5th Lincolns 2327 Pte Robinson F.   GSW Neck.
374. 5th Lincolns 1863 Pte Stevenson J. GSW Knee R.
375. 5th Lincolns   825 Corpl McKenzie J.W. GSW Head, Arm L, Back.
376. 5th Lincolns 1541 L/Cpl Blanks C.F. GSW Forearm L, Face
                                           Shoulder L, Hand R.

June 15. 1915
DRANOUTRE
Fine day, Wind N.E,
Battle practice: communications.
Heavy firing S. this afternoon and Evening.

KEMMEL Village being constantly under shell fire, is unsafe
for an Aid-post, so a dug out on the KEMMEL - VIERSTRAAT
road, is to be made.

Casualties.
(McKenzie, Robinson and Wyolles should be on today lists)

June 16·1915
DRANOUTRE.

Fine Hot day, Wind N·E - N·W. Went to Dug-outs to meet ADMS, and
DDMS 2nd Army, who inspected arrangements. Whilst up there,
Shrapnel burst in trench, injuring 9 men. Several High Explosives burst in
front of dugouts.

Casualties
377 1° Leinsters   9653 Pte. Harding S.C.   GSW Scalp
378 10° Durh.L.I. 19402 Pte Armbruster. G.   GSW phalanges L.
379 5° Leicesters   1379 Sgt Bell H.W.   GSW Shoulder L
380 6° K.O.Y.L.I. 13183 L/Cpl. Bowser A.J.   Fractured ribs L. (mine Explosion)
381 2° NMFA.Name. 2460 Pte. Potter E.S.   GSW Leg R. (slight)

June 17 1915
DRANOUTRE

Fine warm day. Wind N. Lieut Manfield RAMC, from 5° Leinsters, reported for
duty with this Unit.
4.30 PM Telegram from ADMS: "All leave cancelled. Be prepared to move
whole Field Ambulance at short notice" - Acknowledged receipt.

Casualties
382 5° Leicesters 2145 Pte Manning T.S   GSW Forearm R. Comp·Fract.
383 5° Leicesters 1433 Pte Foister G.   GSW Scalp
384 4° Leicesters 1796 Cpl. Pratt H.   GSW Leg, Arm, Neck

385 4'Leicesters 1295 Pte Tebbett W. GSW Leg R., Arm, and Neck
386 4'Leicesters 3446 Pte Widdowson J. GSW Leg R.
387 5'Leicesters 501 Sgt. Harris J.E. GSW Thigh L. Front
388 10 Durh LI. 12599 Cpl. Stevens J. GSW Shoulder L. Legs L-R.
389 4'Leicesters 3574 Pte Francis D. GSW Leg L, Arm L, Hand L.
390 4'Leicesters 2962 Pte Johnson B. GSW Thigh R.
391 4'Leicesters 2160 Pte Spiers W. GSW Leg L
392 4'Leicesters 3096 Pte Rowe T.H. GSW Leg L, Arm L, Scalp, Thorax
393 4'Leicesters 1977 Pte Chandler P. GSW Shoulder L
394 5'Leicesters 2493 Pte Newbold W. GSW Neck and Arm L
395 10 Durh LI. 12640 Cpl. McHugh H. GSW Chest L

June 18. 1915
DRANOUTRE.

Fine Day. Fresh N E Wind.

In afternoon Went to KEMMEL to select site for dug-out for Aid post, and arrange for its construction. Site in railway cutting.

Casualties.

396 4'Leicesters 1625 Pte Beaumont A. GSW Periscope, neck
397 10 Durh LI. 17023 2Lt Heaviside A. Bayonet W. Thigh R. Accid.
398 10 Durh LI. 12573 Pte Foster J.W. GSW Neck
399 5'Lincolns Lieut Riggle H.B.: Contused Wound Ankle R.
          caused by Grenade dropping on it.

June 19th 1915
DRANOUTRE
Fine Warm. Wind N.E.
Went to St JAN CAPPELL to see ADMS. This division has orders to move to new area, commencing Tomorrow. This Unit to move on Tuesday night, 22nd June.
Casualties:
400 4 Lincolns 773   La Cpl Turpin, A.   GSW Shoulder R.
401 4 Lincolns 1186 Pte Lomas. W   GSW Wrist L

June 20. 1915
DRANOUTRE
Section of 2/2nd Northumbrian Field Ambulance, under Lieut CROWLEY, arrived to take over. Lt. Col West, O/c Unit proceeds on leave.
Casualties:
402 5 Lincolns 2816   Pte Jackson F.   GSW Thighs
403 5 Lincolns 2001   Pte Strubb W   GSW Legs, Buttock R.
404 5 Lincolns 2081   Pte Whitworth R   GSW Shoulder L
405 5 Lincolns 2953   Pte Sherriff E.J.   GSW Phalanges L, and Abdl. Wall.
406 5 Lincolns 3235   Pte Wilson C   GSW Phalanges L
407 5 Lincolns 1591   Pte Goodwin W.   GSW. Back
408 5 Lincolns   Lieut. Disney S.C.W. GSW Arm L. Thigh R.
409 10 Durh L.I. Lieut. Fairburn   GSW Head and Arm R.
410 5 Lincolns 2331   Pte Neville H.   GSW Arm R.
411 10 Durh LI 20800 Pte Whittingham A   GSW Scalp.
412 10 Durh LI 9398   Pte Walker J.   GSW Leg L. Foot L.
413 10 Durh LI 8684   Pte Woods E   GSW Legs
414 10 Durh LI 13012 Pte Scutter T.H   GSW Neck, Side and Shoulder L
415 10 Durh LI 12475 Pte Spooner N   GSW Hand L. and Face.
416 4 Lincolns 2929   Pte Gee. E.   GSW Hand L

June 21. 1915
Casualties.
217 4th Lincolns. 2526 Pte Good E.   GSW Arm L
418 4 Lincolns. 3191 Pte Franklin E. GSW Forearm R.

June 22. 1915
WIPPENHOEK FARM. ~~VLAMERTINGHE~~. POPERINGHE.
138th Brigade and this Unit moved from DRANOUTRE for new billets S.W. of VLAMERTINGHE, at 9 P.M., arriving 12.30 A.M. Lieut WILLS. RAMC. M.O. 5 Lincolns proceeds on leave. Lieut GREEN, RAMC, of this Unit takes his duties during his absence. Detention Hospital taken over by 2/2nd Northumbrian Field Ambulance. Wounded collected by us.

June 23rd 1915
WIPPENHOEK FARM. ~~VLAMERTINGHE~~. POPERINGHE
Lieut DRYNAN, RAMC, MO. 4 Lincolns, proceeded on leave.

June 24th 1915
WIPPENHOEK FARM. ~~VLAMERTINGHE~~. POPERINGHE.
Rest camp established at FARM. — 4 Hospital Marquees, and 2 Operating Tents. Wounded evacuated from HOOGE by 3rd N.M.F.A, assisted by an Officer, Motor Ambulances, and Bearers, from 1st and 2nd NMFA.

June 25 1915
WIPPENHOEK FARM.- ~~VLAMERTINGHE~~ POPERINGHE.
A.D.M.S. called.

June 26 1915
WIPPENHOEK FARM. ~~FLAMERTINGHE~~ POPERINGHE

Lt Col West, o/c Unit, reports for duty on return from leave. A.D.M.S called. Heavy thunderstorm this evening.

June 27. 1915
WIPPENHOEK FARM. ~~FLAMERTINGHE~~ POPERINGHE
Fine. Warm. Wind S.W-S.E. ADMS called.
DDMS, 5th Corps (Col. NICHOLS) called, and inspected Camp.
Rain in Evening.

June 28. 1915
WIPPENHOEK FARM. - POPERINGHE
Showery. Wind SV. The unit camp now comprises 4 Hospital Marquees, and 4 Bell Tents — besides an Operating tent for dressing room and dispensary, and accommodation for 80 convalescents in a large barn.

In afternoon, Surgeon General TREHERN called and made a short inspection. Rode to RHENINGHELST to visit ADMS.

In Evening, went with Evacuation convoy to inspect Estammet 1 mile W. of YPRES, proposed as a dressing (advanced) station, but found it unsuitable. — 9 Shells into POPERINGHE this Evening.

June 29. 1915
WHIPPENHOEK FARM. POPERINGHE.
Showery day, with very heavy rain tonight. Wind SW-W.
Most of patients admitted here are suffering from deformed feet.
A few cases of Influenza. About 130 patients altogether.

June 30th 1915
CHIPPENHOEK FARM - POPERINGHE.

Fine day - cloudy. Wind S.W.

Motored to Divl Headquarters to see A.D.M.S. A.D.M.S. called in afternoon, and disposed of some chronic cases, chiefly bad feet, by detailing them for duties with the Sanitary Section, etc.

At 9 P.M., caught a man dressed as a French Soldier in the long corn at back of officers tents. Sent him to the Farm he states he came from to be identified. All found correct.

This Evening, at Sun-set, two "Sun-dogs" appeared, one on either side of the Sun, and lasted 20 minutes.

D/
6439

46th Division

121/6439

2nd North Midland Field Ambulance

War

from 1st to 31st July 1915

July 15

Abstract from War Diary of 2nd North Midland Field Ambulance
R.A.M.C.

138th Brigade — 46th Division

In the Field.

for the month of July 1915

This Ambulance has charge of the 46th Divisional Rest Station near POPERINGHE, which I established here on June 22nd.

The number of patients to be accommodated is limited to 200.
The average number in the Rest Station is 160.
The largest number, during a rush, was 240.
Of the above, 50% are returned to duty,

    25% sent to Mt DES CATS Casualty Clearing Station for a further 7 days rest. The majority of these are returned to duty,

    25% evacuated to C.C.S.

The prevailing type of illness has been Enteritis, characterised in a large number of cases by Mucous Stools with Haemorrhage, griping, and great debility.

"Influenza", or Trench Fever accounts for a large number of sick.

Neurasthenia furnished a number of cases: some obviously genuine, with loss of speech, stammering and Tremors. In other cases, although difficult to prove, the reality of the disease was doubtful.

Several cases of exhaustion were admitted, chiefly young soldiers, who complained of the weight of their equipment

The distance from the Bivouacs to the trenches is considerable, 8 miles; and I believe it would be an increase in the effectiveness of Battalions if packs could be carried in the transport, even though the latter had to be increased for the purpose.

For the amusement and occupation of patients, entertainments by the Divisional Pierrot troupe have been organized; and convalescent patients, besides having short route marches and physical drill, are put on light fatigues about the camp.

A number of patients admitted, were from the re-inforcement drafts which came out in June, and their quality, as a whole, leaves much to be desired: Hammer Toe, flat foot, chronic asthma and Bronchitis; and, in one case, contracture of the right arm and hand due to scarring after old burn, were noted.

The Works undertaken by the Unit during the month, were:
1. Establishment of Baths at POPERINGHE.
2. Taking over, cleaning, and white washing a steam mill at VLAMERTINGHE, to be used as a dressing station.
3. Construction of Medical Dug-outs at KRUISSTRAAT, to serve as advanced dressing station.
4. Construction of Shelter trenches for reception of Sick and personnel, at rest-station, for in case of shelling.
5. Sanitary measures at rest station; construction of shelters and Huts at rest station.

During the month 2 Officers from the Base reported for duty with the Unit; and one Officer was sent to replace a Regimental Medical Officer (sick) with his Battalion.

The Officer Commanding the Unit was sent to the C.C.S. suffering from Enteritis, but has since rejoined.

On July 30-31 the Unit provided 3 Officers and 100 men for duty as stretcher bearers behind the firing line during the attack on HOOGE.

R M West
Lieut Colonel R.A.M.C.
O/C 2nd N. Mid. Field Ambulance
O/C 46 Div' Rest Station.

1.8.15

War Diary for
July, 1915
of the
2nd North Midland Field Ambulance
R.A.M.C.
138th Brigade
46th Division

July 1. 1915
WIPPENHOEK FARM. - POPERINGHE.

Dull cold day. - Misty. Wind W.

Lee Cpl. FRAMPTON, E., 4th Leicesters, removed to isolation, suffering from Scarlatina.

Major F. Dixon and Lt. B. BROWN, RAMC, proceed to England on 5 days leave, due to return July 7th.

The physical quality of the re-inforcements sent to the Division this week leaves much to be desired: some of the men sent out having previously been rejected for Active Service abroad. Sent a report on the matter to the ADMS.

July 2nd 1915
WINDENHOEK FARM. POPERINGHE.

Dull warm morning. Wind S.W. - Fine warm afternoon.

Surg. General Porter called in afternoon, and inspected the Camp. States that this is a Divisional rest station, and that the accommodation is limited to 200 patients; that they are not to be kept in for more than 7 days; if longer, are to be sent to MONT-DES-CATS.

Lieut Foster, S.B., from 2/2 Field Ambulance, LUTON, reports for duty.

DADMS and Divl Sanitary Officer called.

July 3rd 1915
WIPPENHOEK FARM - POPERINGHE.

Fine day - Very Warm. Faint S W Wind. Took 36 men to KRUISSTRAAT, 1 mile West of YPRES, to dig 3 dug outs for medical aid-posts. Called on Brigadier-General Cliffall. In afternoon, General Allenby,

G.O.C. 5th Corps, with Colonel NICHOLS, DDMS, and Col BEEVOR, ADMS 46th Division, inspected the camp. — M. _____, a French interpreter, attached to the Unit today.

July 4th 1915
WIPPENHOEK - POPERINGHE.

Fine day. Very Warm. Wind S.W. Thunder threatening.
Church Service by Rev Ashby in Morning.
In afternoon rode to MT DES CATS.
Surg. Genl. TREHERNE visited camp this afternoon.

July 5th 1915
WIPPENHOEK, POPERINGHE.

Fine day, but cloudy. Wind NW.
Visited Dug-outs at KRUISTRAAT, ½ mile W. of Ypres.
In afternoon visited ADMS. Baths to be started at POPERINGHE in Convent, to be staffed eventually by non-efficients. Detailed Cpl. BUTLER, who had charge of baths at DRANOUTRE, with 4 RAMC men, and 6 invalids, to start work — the RAMC men to be gradually replaced by invalids.
Complimentary order from G.O.C. Vth Corps on state of Field Amb'ces.
Lieuts Cross and MANFIELD proceed on leave, returning on July 11th.

July 6th 1915
WIPPENHOEK - POPERINGHE.

Fine warm morning. Many Showers in Evening. Wind S.W. — Drew 2 more Hospital Marquees from MONT DES CATS, making 6 in all. 170 patients at present in Rest camp. In morning called at Div'l Head quarters to see ADMS. Detailed 1 Corporal and 10 men to get baths, being established in Convent at POPERINGHE, in working order. Visited baths with ADMS.

July 7 1915
WIPPENHOEK - POPERINGHE.
Cloudy Day - Warm. Strong S.W Wind. Clouds of dust. By order of ADMS, detailed 15 men from Unit, and 10 convalescents from various regiments, for fatigue work at the Baths. Called on ADMS in morning, and also on M.O 5th Leicesters, Lieut BARTON R.A.M.C. in connection with outbreak of Enteritis which has occurred in a company, occupying a particular Trench. Probably due to Drinking Water.
Lieut GRAHAM proceeds on leave.
Major DIXON and Lieut BROWN, returned from leave, and report for duty.
1 H.D. Horse died last night : Colic.
All afternoon, heavy showers of rain from S.W.
Pte Ball of this Unit sent to N°10 C.C.S. with Appendicitis.

July 9th 1915
WIPPENHOEK. - POPERINGHE
Raining off and on all day. Wind N.W - S.W. Cold.
Called on ADMS in morning, and accompanied him to inspect baths.
In afternoon DADMS called.
Pitched 2 extra Hospital Marquees, making 6 in all.
All tents to be stained with Cutch.

July 10th 1915
WIPPENHOEK - POPERINGHE.
Fine day: Cloudy. Wind S.W - S.E.

In morning called on A.D.M.S. The Division to take over new line of Trenches, tonight, from S. of YPRES to Hill 60.

100 Stretcher bearers, under M.O. from 3rd Field Ambulance, to be stationed at Dug Outs, at point to be settled later. This Unit to provide 60 bearers towards the total.

In afternoon. Unit Sports.

July 11. 1915
WIPPENHOEK - POPERINGHE.
Dull day. Cold. Wind S.W.

Church Service in Morning by C.O.
Rev. B. Fleming, R.C. to transfer to 1st E. Amb'ce tomorrow.
B Section, on duty at Hospital Tents, to be relieved tomorrow by C Section. The officers of the Section which relieves, taking duty for a fortnight.
Lieut Cross, and Lieut MANSFIELD, report for duty, after leave of absence.
YPRES and POPERINGHE both out of bounds, unless on duty.
All men inoculated once, to be re-inoculated.

July 12. 1915.
WIPPENHOEK - POPERINGHE.
Showery morning. Fine cool day. Wind N.W.
Received from Ordnance 126 stretchers. — Large influx of patients

owing probably, to the fact that Division is taking over new line of Trenches tonight.

Rev B. Fleming, R.C. Chaplain, left unit for attachment to Sherwood Foresters. Lieut GRAHAM R.A.M.C. reports for duty.

July 13. 1915
WIPPENHOEK. – POPERINGHE.

Lieut GREEN, R.A.M.C., of this Unit, gone on leave.
Showery day. Cold. Wind N.W. – S.W. Some shells dropped on POPERINGHE. Called on 1st N.M.F.A.

July 14. 1915
WIPPENHOEK. – POPERINGHE.

Fine morning. Heavy showers of evening and night.
Large influx of sick men – 220 in Hospital. I have no doubt that many of these men are shamming, in order to get out of Trench Duty, but it is difficult to prove. Evacuated a number to M.I. DES CATS, and C.C.S. at HAZEBROUCK.
Col. Sir A. BOWLBY. A.M.S., called.
A fresh well is being sunk; soil Clay, then sand and clay. No water yet (6 feet).
Orders received to to dig shelter trenches and Dug-outs, in case of shelling.
Case of shock after Shelling, with symptoms of Chorea and aphasia.
Collection of sick from Battalions much delayed, owing to slackness of R.M.O's, in not having their Cases ready, necessitating 2 or 3 unnecessary journeys of Ambulances. Reported to A.D.M.S.

July 15. 1915
WIPPENHOEK — POPERINGHE.
Fine day, cloudy. Wind N.W.
Commenced digging trench and traverses. In afternoon called on ADMS. Told him to carry on with Rest Station for Corps walk.
All itch cases to be treated at VLAMERTINGHE, under Capt BUTLER, in a disused Mill. Scabies cases to be sent there tomorrow to clean up the building. POPERINGHE shelled yesterday.

July 16 1915
WIPPENHOEK — POPERINGHE
Fine to Showery.
Went to VLAMERTINGHE and took over deserted Steam Flour Mill for dressing station and Itch Hospital. Place to be cleaned and White washed. Called on ADMS.

July 17. 1915. POPERINGHE
Fine, cloudy. Wind NW.
Cleaned out Barn at WIPPENHOEK FARM for reception of patients. Visited VLAMERTINGHE MILL.

July 18 1915.
WIPPENHOEK. POPERINGHE
Fine day. Wind NW, fresh.
Visited dressing station at VLAMERTINGHE. Called on ADMS.
In afternoon Rode to MONT DES CATS and saw Surg.
Gen PORTER, DMS 5th Corps.
231 Patients in Rest Station.

July 19 1915

WIPPENHOEK - POPERINGHE

Fine day. A.D.M.S. called. Surg Genl PORTER, DMS
V° Corps, inspected Camp. Colonel Sir A BOWLBY, and
Colonel Sir W. Herringham, AMS, called.

July 20 1915

WIPPENHOEK - POPERINGHE

Fine day. Wind N.W. Cool.
VLAMERTINGHE in morning, to inspect Dressing Station.
Afternoon: Band entertainment for Patients by Stafford Brigade.
Over 60 Patients - mostly neurasthenics - from 5 Divisions. As
there are 280 patients in cur station, sent 106 to C.C.S.
at HAZEBROUKE.
Trench with 21 prisoners, captured by us at HOOGE last night,
after mine explosion.

July 21. 1915

WIPPENHOEK - POPERINGHE.

Fine day. Cloudy. Warm. Wind N.W.
A D M S called in morning.
In afternoon, went to C.C.S. at MT. DES CATS, to see Serjt Major
WATTS, who was evacuated to there on 19th, with PARA typhoid.

July 22 1915

WIPPENHOEK - POPERINGHE.

Showery day, Fine intervals.
Lieut PUDDICOMBE, RAMC, from N° 6 Hospital, ROUEN, reported today
for attachment to Unit.

July 24th 1915
WIPPENHOEK FARM. - POPERINGHE.

Fine day - Cloudy - cool. Wind S.W - N.W.
Afternoon went to M. DES CATS, to see Serjt Major WATTS.
In evening, detailed scout BEVAN BROWN, R.A.M.C, for duty
with 5th Batt North Staffordshire Regiment. Took him to BLAUW-
-POORT FARM, W. of Hill 60, which is his Aid post.
Unofficial Orders received that the Rest Station is to move to
new area. Went to see A.D.M.S. about it. (Orders confirmed).

July 25th 1915

WIPPENHOEK FARM. - POPERINGHE

Fine day, Warm Wind N.W.
A.D.M.S. called this morning and this afternoon
Orders to move cancelled: instructions to stand fast.
220 patients in Hospital.

  NOTE: a large number of men fall out from Battalions and
report sick, on account of the weight of their packs. In my
opinion, this weight is excessive, especially to a young soldier.
It would repay Battalions to allot 2 or 3 G.S Wagons for the
carriage of packs, if they have to be taken up to the trenches,
even though the transport line should thus be increased. The
wastage from men thus breaking out would be diminished by
$\frac{1}{3}$rd.

July 26th 1915
WIPPENHOEK FARM. POPERINGHE
Fine day, with Showers. - Wind N.W.

July 29th 1915
WIPPENHOEK FARM, - POPERINGHE.

Proceeded in Motor Ambulance to MT DES CATS to enquire after
Sergt. Major WATTS. Will return to duty tomorrow.
Then to Officers Hospital on MONT NOIRE, to pick up Capt.
NICHOLSON R.F.A., who returns to duty.
Lt. Col. WEST, O.C. Unit, suffering from Enteritis.
Major DIXON, of this Unit, suffering from dislocation Acromial End
Left Clavicle.

July 30. 1915
WIPPENHOEK FARM, POPERINGHE.

75 men under Capt. TURNER, with Lieuts. GREEN and FOSTER
proceeded to dug-outs at KRUISSTRAAT, under orders from ADMS.
to assist 1st NMFA in collecting wounded.
Lt. Col. WEST proceeded to MT DES CATS, sick.

July 31. 1915
WIPPENHOEK FARM. POPERINGHE.

ADMS orders 3 officers and another 100 men to proceed to KRUISSTRAAT
to relieve the party who went yesterday. Detailed Lieuts YATES,
MANFIELD, and PUDDICOMB with 35 men - no more being
available. Capt TURNER, with Lieuts GREEN and FOSTER, returned,
with 1 Horse Ambulance Wagon. The men remained to assist bearers
of 1st F. Ambulance.
Shell dropped in No 3 C.C.S, Bailleul, this morning.
Action at HOOGE last night and this morning.

21/0807

46th Division

1/2nd N.M. Field Ambulance

Vol VI

August/15

August 1915

Abstract from War Diary of 2nd N. Mid F.A.
R.A.M.C. T.
138th Brigade   46th Division
In the Field.
For the month of August 1915

The Unit remained in charge of the 46th Divisional Rest Station at WIPPENHOEK until August 20th, when the rest station was taken over by the 3rd NMFA, and I moved to a Field S. of POPERINGHE, on the POPERINGHE — WESTOUTRE Road, where I established my headquarters.

At the same time, I took over from the 1st NMFA, the advanced dressing stations at KRUISSTRAAT, at the ZILLEBEKE Railway Embankment, and also a new dressing station at CHATEAU ROSENTHAL. These dressing stations are all in dug-outs, that at the CHATEAU, having in addition 2 Steel Tubular Tunnels, capable of accommodating 12 lying cases in each.

On several occasions I have had to collect wounded from MAPLE COPSE, on account of part of the trench leading to the Railway dug-outs, being impassible: the wounded, in consequence, having to be brought to MAPLE COPSE. I have asked that dug-outs be constructed for me there, as there is at present no accommodation available.

I have repaired or reconstructed the Dugouts in the Railway and at the CHATEAU, as many of them had fallen in.

The casualties this month have not been numerous.

A considerable number of cases of Mucous diarrhoea with haemorrhage have occurred: the cause does not appear to be constant.

1.9.15

R. M. West
Lieut. Colonel R.A.M.C.
O/c 2nd N. Mid. Field Amb
46 Division

August 1, 1915
WIPPENHOEK FARM. - POPERINGHE

Lieuts YATES and PUDDICOMBE, with 56 men, returned today.

August 2nd 1915
WIPPENHOEK FARM - POPERINGHE

Anniversary of declaration of War.

August 3. 1915
WIPPENHOEK FARM - POPERINGHE

4 Sick officers arrived. ADMS instructions that they be kept here, as MT DES CATS is full.

August 4. 1915
WIPPENHOEK FARM - POPERINGHE.

Anniversary of Mobilization of Territorial Army for War.
Operating tent pitched for sick Officers.

August 5. 1915
WIPPENHOEK FARM - POPERINGHE.

Instructions from ADMS: Cases of Shock not to be admitted to rest-camp without Medical Certificate that there has been actual physical Shock.

August 6. 1915
WIPPENHOEK FARM. - POPERINGHE.

Marquee pitched for Sick Officers - the Operating tent to be used for nursing.

August 9. 1915
WIPPENHOEK FARM - POPERINGHE
B Section take over duty in Hospital.
Wooden Shed erected for Orderly Room.

August 12. 1915
WIPPENHOEK FARM - POPERINGHE
Lieut GREEN, RAMC, of this Unit, detailed for regimental duty temporarily, with Sherwood Foresters. Lieut KEITH-COHEN, RAMC, from N°1 General Hospital, reports for attachment to this Unit, for training.
Inspection this afternoon by General PLUMER, C.i.C. 2nd Army, and Surg. General PORTER. DDMS.
Lieut-Col. WEST, O/c Unit, reports for duty, discharged from Hospital.

August 13. 1915
WIPPENHOEK FARM - POPERINGHE
Heavy Showers in morning, Wind S.W.
ADMS Called.

August 14. 1915
WIPPENHOEK FARM - POPERINGHE.
Fine day, with showery intervals. Wind S.W.
Red Cross have sent Mobile Coffee Stall: a superfluous luxury.

August 15 1915
WIPPENHOEK FARM. POPERINGHE
Heavy Showers early Morning, with Thunder. Wind S.W. Some shells in Poperinghe. 50 Cases Enteritis in Hospital. Sent off War Diary for July.

August 16 1915
WIPPENHOEK FARM. POPERINGHE

Rode to Headquarters to see A.D.M.S. this morning. This unit to take over collecting Wounded in YPRES salient on 20th., the 3rd Field Ambulance to take over this rest-station. Visited 1st Field Ambulance, who take over Dressing Stations at VLAMERTINGHE and BRANDHOEK. Thundery weather.

August 17 1915
WIPPENHOEK FARM. - POPERINGHE

Lieut Col West and Major Dixon R.A.M.C., proceeded to x Lieut FOSTER KRUISTRAAT Dug-outs, for 24 hours instruction, previous to taking over. Gassed in evening by shells.

August 18 1915
WIPPENHOEK FARM. POPERINGHE. x Major Dixon
Lieuts MANFIELD and FOSTER x proceeded to KRUISTRAAT Dug outs for 24 Hours instruction, previous to taking over

August 19. 1915
WIPPENHOEK FARM. POPERINGHE.

Lt Col. West and Lieut KIETH COHEN proceeded to the Dug outs in ZILLEBEEK railway embankment, where the latter remains on duty, relieving the 1st N.H.F.A. Heavy shelling with high explosives.
Major DIXON ill - Nephritis: to be sent to C.C.S tomorrow. 260 patients in rest Station.

August 20. 1915
POPERINGHE

Unit evacuated Div¹ Rest Station at WIPPENHOEK FARM, and proceeded to field S. of POPERINGHE, previously occupied by 3ʳᵈ NMFA. The 3ʳᵈ NMFA took over Div¹ Rest Station.

Lieut Col West, with Lieut GRAHAM and Lieut MANFIELD, with 30 NCOs and men, proceeded by route march to KRUISTRAAT to take over Dressing Station at Dug-out Huts, and also Dressing Station in Railway Embankment near ZILLEBEKE LAKE.

Lieut Col WEST and Lieut GRAHAM at KRUISTRAAT (N°1 Dressing Station), and Lieuts MANFIELD and R. COHEN at Embankment (N° 2 Dressing Station).

Lieut YATES, with Quartermaster, remains at POPERINGHE Camp.
Capt. TURNER proceeds on leave to England.
Sergt. Major WATTS proceeds on leave to England.

August 21. 1915
KRUISTRAAT. YPRES.

Heavy rain. ADMS came to KRUISTRAAT. Accompanied him on round of inspection to Railway Dug-outs, and to CHATEAU ROSENTHAL on the Lille road, which this unit will take over for Dressing Station N° 3. In afternoon went with ADMS to call on ADMS III⁽ᵈ⁾ 2ⁿᵈ.
In evening, Lieut FOSTER and 25 men arrived to take over N° 3 Dressing Station. Took them there to guide them. Much intermittent heavy shelling, with Crumps and shrapnel at KRUISTRAAT.

Aug 22. 1915
KRUISTRAAT - YPRES.

Inspected Dressing Station N° 2. In Evening Lieut PUDDICOMBE with 25 men arrived to complete Dressing Station No 3. Guided them there. Went to Town Major in YPRES for leave to remove bricks.

August 23. 1915.
KRUISTRAAT. - YPRES
Party to collect Bricks went into YPRES, when heavy shelling began. ASC man reported wounded. Went in with Motor Ambulance, and found Lce Cpl WELLS, and Pte COLLINGTON with the man, in spite of the shelling. Got man away, and reported the action of the above two men to ADMS
Inspected Dressing Stations Nos 2 and 3.

Aug. 24. 1915
KRUISTRAAT. - YPRES
Inspected dressing stations. Went into POPERINGHE to inspect the Camp. Called on ADMS. This morning and afternoon many Cramps about KRUISTRAAT, and VLAMERTINGHE.

Aug 25. 1915
KRUISTRAAT - YPRES
Inspected dressing stations. Shelling as usual. Hot fine Day. Wind NW

Aug. 26. 1915
KRUISTRAAT. - YPRES.
Hot, Fine day. Wind N.W. Inspected dressing stations in morning. In afternoon, CAPT. TURNER reported back for duty after leave. Took him round the dressing stations, as he will take over tomorrow

August 28. 1915
POPERINGHE

Rode to KRUISSTRAAT, and inspected Dressing Stations Nos 1, 2, 3.

August 29. 1915
POPERINGHE

Went with ADMS to KRUISSTRAAT, and inspected Dressing Stations 1. 2. 3.

August 31. 1915
POPERINGHE.

Went in Motor Ambulance to KRUISSTRAAT, and inspected Dressing Stations 1. 2. 3.

August 27. 1915
POPERINGHE.

Capt. TURNER reported at KRUISTRAAT this morning, and took over charge of dressing station. Lieut Col WEST returned to the Camp at POPERINGHE.

No 1 Dressing Station has 2 Officers and 34 men, including Transport
No 2 Dressing Station has 1 " " 33 "
No 3 Dressing Station has 2 " " 50 "
                       5   117   Total 122.

Sketch map of disposition of dressing Stations:

Sept '15

½ N.M. 2°. Comm.

Sep - Oct '15

Vol VII

War Diary
of
1/2nd N. Mid. F. Amb.
R.A.M.C.

September 1915.

Sep - Oct 15

September 1. 1915
POPERINGHE
Rode to KRUISSTRAAT, and inspected dressing Stations 1.2.3
Wet day.

September 2. 1915
POPERINGHE
Motored to KRUISSTRAAT, and inspected dressing stations 1.2.3

September 3. 1915
POPERINGHE
KRUISSTRAAT dressing Station taken over by 3rd Division F.A.
Capt. TURNER moved to N°2 dressing station, with Lieut GRAHAM.

September 4. 1915
POPERINGHE
Wet day. Motored to DICKYBUSH to inspect Farm, proposed as a dressing station, instead of KRUISSTRAAT, but found it in possession of RFA. Went to KRUISSTRAAT and to N°3 dressing Station

September 5. 1915
POPERINGHE.
Wet morning. Motored to KRUISSTRAAT, and arranged for Motor Ambulances to be parked at Mill at VLAMERTINGHE. ADMS on leave. Fine afternoon, but Cool. Lieut MANFIELD reports for duty at the Camp, from N°2 Dressing Station.

September 6. 1915
POPERINGHE.

Fine warm day. Cloudy. Motored to KRUISSTRAAT, and guided ~~Lieut. Manfield~~ a re-inforcement party to CHATEAU ROSENTHAL. Inspected this and also No 1 Dressing Station. Accompanied by Capt. TURNER, visited aid post of 3rd Division at MAPLE COPSE. As some of our wounded have to be taken there instead of to their own aid post in the Railway Cutting, it is necessary that we should have a dug-out for them in MAPLE COPSE. Reported this to ADMS.

 Lt. Col. Wraitt, 1st NMFA, is acting ADMS, during leave in England of ADMS.

September 7th 1915
POPERINGHE
Sent Lieuts MANFIELD and COHEN to No 2 Dressing Station to relieve Lieuts. FOSTER and PUDDICOMB, who return to camp for duty.

September 8th 1915
POPERINGHE.
Visited No 1 and 2 dressing Stations. Sent 2nd report to ADMS relative to dug-out in MAPLE COPSE. Fine warm day. Wind N-NE. Visited DADMS.

September 9th 1915
POPERINGHE.
Went this evening to No 2 Dressing Station (CHATEAU ROSENTHAL) to relieve Lieut. COHEN, proceeding on leave tomorrow.

September 10. 1915
POPERINGHE
At CHATEAU ROSENTHAL. Visited 2nd pass ... Canal Bank,
No 1 Dressing station, and ZILLEBEKE Station. Fine, Hot.

September 11. 1915
POPERINGHE
Returned to Camp at POPERINGHE last night. Lieut YATES
relieves me at No 2 Dressing Station. Fine Hot

September 12. 1915
POPERINGHE
Fine Hot. Church parade with 1st NMFA. Visited DADMS

September 13. 1915
POPERINGHE
Fine. Hot. Visited ADMS, who returned from leave last night.
DDMS 5th Corps (Col Nichols) inspected camp this afternoon.
Lieut FOSTER relieves Capt TURNER at Dug-outs tonight

September 14. 1915
POPERINGHE
Lieut Col WEST proceeds on leave. Capt TURNER in Command.
Order from ADMS postponing change-over until Monday 20th

September 17. 1915
POPERINGHE
Verbal order from ADMS not to change-over until Wednesday 22nd
at earliest. New scheme for evacuation of wounded from

ARMAGH WOOD by means of new dug-outs at I 24. C. 6. 8 (Ref. Sp 28/70000). Until these dug-outs are ready, the Brigade Battle Headquarters are to be used as temporary advance dressing stations. This will do away with collecting from MAPLE COPSE, which is outside our divisional area. Q.M.S. WHEWAY and 8 men sent up to occupy them. Lieut PUDDICOMB proceeds on 14 days' leave.

September 19. 1915
POPERINGHE.

Orders received from ADMS to change-over tomorrow, 20th. — 1000 sand-bags sent up by Motor Ambulance for new dug-outs in ARMAGH WOOD. Requested C.R.E. to have road leading to new Dug-outs levelled. Q.M.S. WHEWAY and his party, relieved by Sergt. BRANSTONE and 8 men. — 17 N.C.Os and men sent to the WHITE MILL, VLAMERTINGHE, under Lieut. FOSTER, to take over dressing station from 1st NMFA. Lieut GRAHAM returned from Railway dug-outs to POPERINGHE. 1 Officer and 24 men from 3rd NMFA, arrived at railway dug-outs, and a similar party at CHATEAU ROSENTHAL, to take over collecting from this Unit; an equal number of my men returning to POPERINGHE.

September 20th 1915
RHENINGHELST

Handed over to 3rd NMFA, the Collecting posts at ARMAGH WOOD, Railway dug-outs, and CHATEAU ROSENTHAL. Lieut GRAHAM, with 30 NCOs and men, and C Section equipment, proceeded to VLAMERTINGHE, and took over the dressing station at the WHITE MILL, from the 1st NMFA. — The Headquarters of this Unit moved from the POPERINGHE-WESTOUTRE Road, to

to a site on the POPERINGHE - RENINGHELST Road, near the
Lo Town. - Lieut YATES and MANFIELD, with remainder of
men from dug-out, proceeded to VLAMERTINGHE. Lieut FOSTER
proceeds on leave. Troop train shelled at VLAMERTINGHE. 25 wounded.

September 22ⁿᵈ 1915
RENINGHELST
Orders to prepare upper floors of WHITE MILL for wounded.

September 23. 1915
RENINGHELST
Lieut Col WEST returns from leave. Lieut COHEN ill in England.
Inspected dressing station at VLAMERTINGHE. — Raining.

Sept 24. 1915
RENINGHELST
Wet morning. Practised loading Wagons. In afternoon, inspected
Gas-helmets, and issued Iron-rations. Inspection of Wagons by ADMS.
Orders received to be prepared to move at short notice, as an assault
on the Enemy lines is to take place tomorrow.

Sept 25. 1915
RENINGHELST
Wet cold day. Inspected WHITE MILL Dressing Station in morning; 40
wounded last night. Motored to advanced Medical Store at GODERSVELT for
drugs, etc. required.
Capt. C.R. FLAXMAN RAMC from ETAPLES, reported for duty with
Unit.

September 26, 1915
RENINGHELST.

Fine day. Wind N.W. Inspected Dressing Station at WHITE MILL. Lieut YATES proceeds on leave to ENGLAND, being replaced at WHITE MILL by Capt. FLAXMAN. Attack commenced yesterday morning continuing: 3rd Division, supported by 11th Division, assaulted German trenches near HOOGE. Took 3 or 4 lines of trenches, but had to abandon them. 200 prisoners and 2 Officers (Germans) taken at HOOGE. Wire received that the French have taken, in CHAMPAGNE, 70 guns and 16,000 prisoners.
Afternoon, rode to WIPPENHOEK to 1st NMFA. Church Parade 2 o'c. by Canon HUNT.

September 27, 1915
RENINGHELST.

Following promotions in Gazette: Lieuts. to be Captains:
   R.B.M. YATES, M.B.   April 1.
   B.S. WILLS, FRCS Eng.   April 22.
   T. GRAHAM M.B.   April 26
   S.R. FOSTER M.B.   May 27
   G.H.H. MANFIELD   April 1.
Inspected the WHITE MILL at VLAMERTINGHE.
Orders received this evening that 46th Division is to join the 1st Army near ARRAS. Rode to KRUISTRAAT to the Brigade Headquarters.

September 28, 1915
RENINGHELST.

Inspected WHITE MILL, VLAMERTINGHE.
Bulletin reports that the French and the British have taken 21,000 prisoners at LENS and ARRAS.

Army Form W.3091.

Cover for Documents.

Nature of Enclosures.

War Diary

1/2nd North Midland. F.A.

October 1915

Notes, or Letters written.

War Diary
of
1/2nd. N. Mid. F. Amb.
R.A.M.C.

October 1915.

October 1, 1915

RHENINGHELST

Fine cold day. Orders to move to new area at village of LABEUVRIERE W. by S. of BETHUNE. Motored over to locate billets, travelling through LOCRE - BAILLEUL - VIEUX BERQUIN - MERVILLE - HINGES - CHOCQUES, and back through BETHUNE - ESTAIRES - LEVERRIER - BAILLEUL. Later: Billeting area altered, the Division to move to neighbourhood of GONNEHEM, N.E. of BETHUNE.

In evening 27th Field Ambulance arrived from neighbourhood of BETHUNE to take over tomorrow.

October 2nd 1915

RHENINGHELST.

Struck camp and packed equipment. Division moved out to march to new area at 7 PM. This unit marched. The 1st and 3rd Field Ambulances went by motor Bus.

Marched to VIEUX-BERQUIN, via LOCRE - BAILLEUL - OUTERSTEEN. Arriving 2.30 AM Oct. 3rd. Fine night, cold.

Capts. TURNER and YATES proceeded, with 40 men by 'Bus, to take over billets at farm CENSE-LA-VALLEE, near GONEHEM.

October 3rd 1915

VIEUX-BERQUIN

Unit, with Division, arrived here 2.30 AM. Billeted in Barn. Marched 16 miles. In evening, Unit moved, with Division to their destination GONEHEM, starting at 8 PM, and arriving 2 AM Oct. 4., marching via MERVILLE - COLONNE - ROBECK.

October 4th 1915
GONNEHEM - FRANCE

Unit arrived 2 AM at Farm CENSE-LA-VALLÉE. Very dark night, and difficult to follow column. Difficulty in finding the Farm, where unit is now Billeted. Unit marched 13½ miles.
In morning motored to BETHUNE, 5 miles, to report to ADMS 26 Divn.
In afternoon ADMS, DADMS called.

October 5th 1915
GONNEHEM - FRANCE
~~Late last night orders to move to new billeting area received~~.
Men resting all day. Tonight orders to move tomorrow to new Area received.

October 6th 1915
FOUQUIERES - France
Left GONNEHEM with division at 11.AM, arriving at FOUQUIERES at 3 PM, marching via GONNEHEM - CHOCQUES - FOUQUEREUILLES - GOSNAY. Billeted in CHATEAU, with 1st NMFA, and attached to 11th Division. Fine day. — 2 miles S.E of BETHUNE. ADMS called.

October 7th 1915
FOUQUIERES - FRANCE

Fine day - Warm. Tidied up camp, where men are under Canvas. Reported arrival to Brigade Headquarters. ADMS called. Lieut PUDDICOMBE, RAMC, will not return for Active service abroad.

October 8th 1915   FOUQUIERES.
Lieut-Col West with A.D.M.S. & Capt Turner motored to VERMELLES to

inspect dressing station. Col. West
severely wounded at entrance to
dressing station by a coal-spirit
shell which burst in road 8 yards
away. A shrapnel bullet penetrated
hand & right lung just missing
the spine. Wound dressed at
VERMELLES & Col. West removed
to SAILLY LABOURSE, & later on to
No 6. Officers Hospital, BETHUNE.
Condition serious. Chauffeur also
wounded by same shell but not
severely.

Capt. Turner assumed temporary
command of unit.

Oct. 9th. 1915 FOUQUIERES.
  Visited Col. West. Condition satisfactory. Instructions received from
A.D.M.S. to the effect that extra
stretchers are to be obtained (if needed)
from C.C.S. Extra blankets to be
obtained from D.A.D.O.S.

Oct. 10th. 1915. FOUQUIERES.

  Instructions received from ADMS
to send cases of sick to 3rd F. Amb.
Attended conference at Div. Hdqrs.
on subject of impending attack.

Col. West progressing satisfactorily.

Oct. 11th. FOUQUIERES

In morning visited dressing stations at VERMELLES, trenches & aid posts together with A.D.M.S & Capt. Yates. In evening attended conference of divisional M.O's. Twenty four empty petrol tins received from A S C! making 50 available altogether for taking water to aid posts.

Col. West going on well.
Lieut. Renwick A.C. reported for duty.

Oct. 12th. VERMELLES

In morning visited VERMELLES with Capts. Graham & Foster. Found CHATEAU occupied by party of 9th Division, & Brewery about to be handed over to party of 3rd F. Amb., Guards Div. Went in search of A.D.M.S. & with him visited D.D.M.S. XI th corps who gave orders that both places were to be handed over to us.

At 3.30 P.M. the following personnel proceeded by route march to VERMELLES

All 7 M.O's. A section complete with equipment. B & C sections bearer sub-divisions together with 12 orderlies 2 clerks & 2 cooks.

Arrived about 8 P.M. & proceeded to
unpack equipment & take over
Dressing Stations at BARTS Dugouts.
The transport returned to FOUQUIERES
with the exception of handling
cookers & one water cart at
Brewery & one water cart at Chateau.
Five stretcher squads were sent
to BARTS. These brought in some
casualties which occurred in the
46th Division as they moved in.
  The personnel remaining behind
at FOUQUIERES consisted of
2 M.P., transport section & 25 N.C.Os
& men.

Oct. 13th. VERMELLES
Personnel distributed as follows:—
  At Brewery. 6 M.O's.
                A sect. tent subdivision.
  At Chateau. 2 M.O's. 2 clerks. 2 cooks
                8 orderlies. C section equipm.
  At BARTS. 1 N.C.O. 4 orderlies.

A large stock of dressings & medical
comforts & 50 petrol tins full
of water were placed in BARTS
to replenish Regt. Aid Posts.
  The D.A.D.M.S & Major MacAlister

Hawlings took charge of Chateau.
Five wheeled stretchers (two our own
& three from 3rd F. Amb. Guards Div)
were placed by dug-out at end
of BARTS ALLEY to assist in
bringing cases to Brewery.

The Brewery was reserved for
stretcher cases, walking cases
being dealt with at the Chateau.

Twenty motor ambulances of
46th Division & five lent by
Guards Division were parked
under the command of Lieut.
Durward to remove casualties
from Brewery. Nine horse
ambulances & 14 motor lorries
were placed at disposal of
D A D M S to remove walking
cases from Chateau.

During the morning 83 cases
of gas poisoning were brought
in: 26 to Brewery & 57 to Chateau.
These were caused by our own
gas escaping from cylinders.
With one or two exceptions they
were not of a serious nature.

At 1.15 P.M. all three bearer sub-
divisions proceeded to trenches.
Three squads were left at end

of BARTS ALLEY in charge of
wheeled stretchers. The remainder
were placed in BARTS.

Capt. Foster was placed in command
of all the stretcher squads with
orders to keep in touch with R.M.O's
& superintend the removal of
casualties from the Reg. Aid Posts
by way of BARTS ALLEY which
was reserved solely for the
removal of wounded.

At 1.45 P.M. visited Aid Posts
together with Capt. Foster. Casualties
were already beginning to arrive
in considerable numbers owing to
the German bombardment of our
reserve trenches.

At 2 P.M. the Division attacked
the HOHENZOLLERN Redoubt & the
trenches immediately south of it,
the Lincolns & Leicesters on left,
Staffords Brigade on right,
Monmouths following & Notts &
Derby in support

A shell struck Brewery about
3 P.M. injuring an R.E. & corporal

At 4.20 P.M. an urgent message
arrived from aid-posts asking
for every available stretcher squad

Three squads were made up from personnel at Brewery & despatched immediately to trenches together with six squads from 46th Div. Sanitary Sect. which had arrived to assist. At the same time I visited BARTS & found BARTS ALLEY filled by hundreds of walking cases making their way back, whilst BARTS itself was crowded with men who had walked so far & then collapsed. Progress up the trench was almost impossible owing to the number of wounded pouring down it, so returned & at 5.10 P.M despatched an urgent message to A.D.M.S. asking for all available stretcher squads. In response to this 80 bearers from 3rd N.M. F. Amb. & 32 from 1st N.M. F. Amb. arrived by driblets during the night & also 12 bearers from 84th F. Amb. with 2 wheeled stretchers. All these were sent to trenches as soon as they arrived. About 9 P.M. the 3 squads in charge of wheeled stretchers were sent into the trenches & motor ambulances used bring cases down from BATTN HEAD in Trenway.

Before 6 owing to heavy fire from S.M.G.s that our Stretcher Squads were clearing from Aid Posts. This was due to the large number of cases that 2nd K.O. brought in from near BARTS, which it was necessary to clear before proceeding further up the trench. The stretcher squads took many hours to make a single journey, owing to the extreme difficulty in moving along the crowded communication trenches which were congested with wounded walking down, & bombs, water & ammunition going up. It was not till about 9 P.M. that our squads began to remove cases from Aid Posts & not until the following morning did we begin to receive casualties from the front line trenches. The numbers of stretcher cases passed through Brewery were:-

Noon. 39.   8 P.M. 138
6 P.M. 97   9.15 158   11.15. 202.
7 P.M. 121.   10.15. 180

At the Chateau to which the
walking cases were directed
very large numbers were received
The number of which a record
was obtained was 690, but
1100 tallies were used & the
D.A.D.M.S. estimates that about
400 more of the slighter cases were
sent on by horse ambulances
& motor lorries no treatment being
attempted. There was at one time
very great congestion the
available transport being insuff-
icient for the number of cases
for most of whom not even
cover could be found. Fortunately
the night was fine & warm so
that no great hardship was
entailed.

Many walking cases drifted
into the 36th F.Amb. dressing
station which they had to pass
on their way to the Chateau;
some of the slighter cases
finding that they would have
a long wait before they could
receive attention walked on to
other dressing stations.

Captains Armitage & Parbury

arrived to take over from the O.C. the
Field Ambulance. Long talk with
Capt. Thomas, K.A.M.C. and
Lt. Ind. Yorks W. relieving the
P.M.O.'s. Wired requesting either one
the P.M.O.'s did not desire to be
relieved.

Lieut. Renwick went to Chateau
about 9 P.M. to assist the two
M.O.'s already there.
Total number of cases passing
through Chateau estimated at
1500 by D.A.D.M.S.

Oct. 14th. VERMELLES.
Cases were brought into Brewery
as follows:
Oct. 13th. 11.15 P.M.   202 cases
     14th. 12.15 A.M.   220
            1.15   241
            6 A.M.   293
            8 A.M.   309
            Noon.   385
            2 P.M.   399
            4 P.M.   440
            6 P.M.   450
            8 P.M.   469

About 1 P.M. a report was received

from trenches saying that some hundreds of wounded were still lying in forward trenches & the redoubt. Forwarded this to ADMS by motor cyclist & asked for 250-300 fresh stretcher bearers as my own were becoming exhausted. Gave same message verbally to DADMS. No other application for assistance made.

His report as to numbers of wounded proved to be quite accurate, 343 cases being brought in of subsequent to noon of the 14th.

Sixty bearers of the N.M.D. Cycle Coy arrived in the morning & 50 men of the R.F.A. in the afternoon. The R.A.M.C. bearers were so exhausted by the afternoon as to be of very little use, having been on duty for 24-36 hours continuously. During the evening most of them were gradually withdrawn for a meal & a few hours sleep, their places being taken by the cyclists & R.F.A. mentioned above.

Stretcher cases were brought in

such numbers allow of it being said that the Battle of L__ Loos was the __ enabled to cope with this.
A great number were brought out on to the Chateau, which was but __ of a large number of the Dressing Station was used & the building handed over to the 3rd. F. Amb. & Brigade Div. order of the A.D.M.S., 46th Div., casualties being taken to the Chateau. The D.D.M.S. XIth Corps visited the Brewery about 7 P.M.

The same night the 46th Div was withdrawn from the trenches with the exception of the Notts. & Derby Brigade which remained till the following night. The trenches were taken over by the Guards Division.

Capts. Cooke & Brogden arrived to assist the M.O's. During the afternoon 3 N.C.O's were brought up from Fouquieres to assist, & another party of 12 bearers arrived from 84th F. Amb. to relieve those who came the previous evening.

At 10 P.M. visited trenches with
2 stretcher squads including
three sent by Guards 3rd F. Amb.
Guards Div. & searched several
miles of trenches returning at
6 A.M. Eleven wounded found
& brought in. Stretcher cases
arrived at Chateau in a steady
stream through night. Five
slightly wounded Germans treated, four
at Brewery & one at Chateau.

Oct. 15th VERMELLES.

Shortly after midnight 2 Officers
& 120 men of 59th F. Amb.
arrived & reported to Capt. Yates.
Half of them were sent into the
trenches. They found & brought
in about twenty wounded & were
of great assistance in searching
the communication & fire trenches
& the redoubt.

About 10 A.M. the stream of
patients ceased & as it was
certain that very few if any
wounded remained to be brought
in the personnel of the 59th F. Amb.
returned to their unit.

In the afternoon the D.M.S.
1st. Army visited the Chateau.

Orders received from A.D.M.S.
to hand over Chateau to Guards
Division at 6 P.M. but permission
was given for us to remain till
next morning in order to avoid
a night march. Capt. Spence &
50 of the most exhausted men
returned to FOUQUIERES in motor
& horse ambulances. Five squads
were left in tenders to bring
down any further casualties.
The number of cases treated up
to 9 P.M. was 47.
Returned to FOUQUIERES at 10 P.M.
leaving Capt. Mayfield in charge
at Chateau.

Oct. 16th. FOUQUIERES.
Fourteen casualties dealt with
at Chateau during night.
Remainder of unit & equipment
returned to FOUQUIERES in
morning in motor & horse ambulances.
In afternoon 50 N.C.O's & men
went to BRUAY in motor & horse
ambulances for baths.

Oct. 17th. FOUQUIERES.
No parades. Men resting

September 29. 1915.
RENINGHELST.
Wet cold day. Visited WHITE MILL at VLAMERTINGHE.
This division to move South during the next 3 days. Report
recieved that the French have broken through the German lines at
LENS with 3 divisions.
Lieut FOSTER, from leave, reported for duty.

September 30th 1915
RENINGHELST.
Capt YATES, recalled from leave, reported today for duty.

Oct. 18th. FOUQUIERES
   Parade for kit inspection 9 A.M.

Oct. 19th. FOUQUIERES

   Motored with A.D.M.S. & Col Dent
to ALLOUAGNE to see new billets
for unit.

Oct. 20th. LILLERS
   Unit proceeded by route march to
LA COUFFE Farm near LILLERS.
Sections billeted at separate farms.
In afternoon motored to ALLOUAGNE
to report to A.D.M.S.

Oct. 21st. LILLERS
   Paraded 7.45. Marched off at
8 A.M. to LA BEUVRIERE (6 miles)
for inspection by G.O.C.

Oct. 22nd. LILLERS
   Overhauling & repacking
equipment.

Oct. 23rd. LILLERS.
   D.A.D.M.S. called.

Oct. 24th. LILLERS.

Church Parade 2 P.M.

Oct. 25th. LILLERS.

Visited VERQUIN to inspect new billets. A.D.M.S. & Col. Dent called in afternoon. Very wet day.

Oct. 26th. LILLERS.

Advance party consisting of Lieut. Renwick & 8 other ranks proceeded to VERQUIN to take over hospital. Capts. Mayfield & Graham proceeded on leave.

Ext. from LONDON GAZETTE 25.10.15 Capt. A.C.F. TURNER to be Major temp. from August 20th 1915.

Oct. 27th. VERQUIN

Unit proceeded by route march to VERQUIN arriving about 2 P.M. Most of the tents were left behind as they were soaked. Proceeded to take over hospital in school. The 37th F. Amb. had left 30 patients behind of which 9 were

cases of scabies. They left two
orderlies for same. 30 new
Capt. Foster, 2 N.C.O's + 13 men
marched to HESDIGNEUL for
preliminary inspection by Corps Commander

Oct. 28th. VERQUIN

Very wet day. Capt. Foster, two
N.C.O's + 13 men proceeded to
HESDIGNEUL for inspection by
H.M. the KING. Capt. Yates with
2 orderlies + a motor ambulance
attended to render first aid.
Horse lines in very bad condition
so horses brought into school
yard.
138th Brigade requested that
an N.C.O. should be placed in
charge of baths at mine, daily
from 7 A.M to 11 A.M.

Oct. 29th. VERQUIN

D.A.D.M.S. called.

Oct. 30th. VERQUIN
Seven scabies cases & ten other cases
all of 12th Division returned to 37th
F. Amb. at LABOURSE by order of A.D.M.S

Oct 31st   VERQUIN

Brigade Church Parade 10.30 A.M.
Orders received from A.D.M.S.
to send scabies cases to 1st M.M. &A.
Lieut. MUNROE A.R. reported
for duty.

46th Division

1/2nd N.M. F. Amb.

%co³ / %oe VIII

131/762

Nov 1915

Oct. 31st. VERQUIN

Brigade Church Parade 10.30 A.M.
Orders received from A.D.M.S. to
send scabies cases to 1st N.M.F. Amb.
Lieut. MUNROE, A.R. reported for duty.

Nov. 1st. VERQUIN

Very wet day. Capt. Yates &
Lieut. Cross proceeded on leave.

Nov. 2nd. VERQUIN

Very wet day. Lieut-Col. Cuthbert
Wallace called. Return rendered
of all men used to certain branches
of engineering i.e. turning, tool making
etc.

Nov. 3rd. VERQUIN

Visited A.D.M.S. Fine day.

Nov. 4th. VERQUIN

Fine day.

Nov. 5th. VERQUIN

Motored to LESTREM with A.D.M.S.
to look for new billets. Capt.
MANFIELD returned from leave.

Nov. 6th. VERQUIN

The 138th Brigade marched to
new area at ROBECQ. One

motor ambulances [illegible]
with [illegible]
[illegible]
with Lieut. [illegible]
followed [illegible]
[illegible]
[illegible]

Nov. 7th. ROBECQ.
Left VERQUIN at noon & proceeded by route march to LABIETTE farm near ROBECQ, arriving about 3.30 P.M.
Thirty patients were transferred in motor ambulances to the 3rd N. Mid. F. Amb. at ZELOBES by order of A.D.M.S.

Nov. 8th. ROBECQ.
Called on A.D.M.S. in morning.
Lieut. COOPER. [illegible] reported for duty from base.
Capt. [illegible] S.R. detached for duty with 4th Leicesters.
Sergt. Major Watts detached for duty with No. 9 C.C.S. by order of A.D.M.S.
Promotions.
Q.M.S. McEwan to be acting Sergt. Major
S. Sergt. Williams to be acting Q.M. Sergt.

Nov. 9th. ROBECQ

Lieut. RENWICK H.C. detached for duty with 1st Monmouth Regt by order of A.D.M.S.
Small unoccupied farmhouse taken over as hospital.

Nov. 10th. ROBECQ

Requested by Brigade to supply N.C.O. & men for working baths at Gonnehem two days a week.

Nov. 11th. ROBECQ

Capt. FOSTER S.R. detached for temporary duty with 7th Sherwoods.
Very wet day

Nov. 12th. ROBECQ

Called on A.D.M.S.
Lieut. MUNROE A.R. detached for duty with 4th Leicester Regt., and Lieut. COOPER W.E. for duty with 5th Leicester Regt. Lieut. URIE reported for duty from VERSAILLES
Lieut. CROSS returned from leave

Nov. 13th. ST FLORIS
At 3.30 P.M. ordered to move.
Moved at 5.15 P.M. & marched to
ST FLORIS (4 miles) arriving about
7 P.M. Billets arranged & these were
occupied by Horses & Indian M.T.
About 10 P.M. other billets were
found, the sick being accommodated
in a school room.

Nov. 14th. ST FLORIS
Visited A.D.M.S. & 155th Fyfe Ridge

Nov. 15th ST FLORIS
Usual parades

Nov. 16th ST FLORIS
Cold & wet

Nov. 17th ST FLORIS
Showery : very cold
Called on D.A.D.M.S.

Nov. 18th ST FLORIS
Called on A.D.M.S. All scabies cases
to be sent to 3rd N.M. F. Amb. at ZELOBES.
All other sick to be sent to C.C.S.
10 NCO's & 20 men to be detailed

for duty at drying rooms. These are
farms or dug outs where men
relieved from the trenches can sleep
whilst their clothes are being dried.
The trenches are very wet, so the
men in them are relieved every
24 hours.
  Motored to BOIS PACAUT to look
for fresh billets & found suitable
farms, at present occupied by the
58th Field Amb.
  LIEUT. CANNON D.J. RAMC
reported for duty.

Nov. 19th   ST FLORIS
  Nineteen scabies cases sent to
3rd N.M.F. Amb. Remaining cases
in hospital sent to CCS, & School-
room vacated.

Nov. 20th.   ST FLORIS
  Order received from ADMS to return
all tents to Ordnance.

Nov. 21st. ST FLORIS
  G.S. waggon sent to No. 4 Field Amb.
to draw 7 wheeled stretchers.
  Ten NCO's & 20 men sent to Hdqrs. of
Brigades for duty at drying rooms.

...2 N.C.O's + 6 men sent to [?] ...
...[?] subsequently returned as the
drying rooms are not yet ready.

Nov. 22nd 1915.   ST. FLORIS

Lieut. COSTER W.F. returned from
5th Leicesters for duty with this unit.
Visited A.D.M.S. in morning + subsequently
motored to MESPLAUX + LE TOURET
to inspect dressing station + advanced
dressing station there.
Orders received from A.D.M.S. to attend
conference at his office every Monday
at 9.30 A.M.

Nov. 23rd 1915.   ST FLORIS

Lieut. CANNON with 1 N.C.O + 2 men
sent to advanced dressing station
at LE TOURET.

Nov. 24th. 1915.   MESPLAUX Farm
                    near LOCON
Unit left ST FLORIS at 9.45 A.M
+ proceeded by route march to
MESPLAUX Farm arriving at 1 P.M.
In afternoon CAPT. MANSFIELD
with 28 N.C.O's + men proceeded

to take over advanced dressing station at LE TOURET from 57th. Field Amb. In evening visited advanced dressing station & aid posts at GLORY HOLE and TUBE STATION. Wounded are evacuated from these aid posts by means of a trolley running on rails to a point on the RUE DE BOIS about 400 yards from advanced dressing station. Condition of trenches very bad, the depth of mud & water making walking extremely difficult. Number of casualties small.

In morning A D M S called. Capt. FOSTER R.A.M.C returned from 7th Sherwoods for duty with this unit.

Lieuts TATE & TIBBLES S.G reported from base for duty with this unit.

Nov. 25th, 1915.   MESPLAUX Farm
In morning inspected baths at LOCON which are to be worked by this unit. In afternoon visited advanced dressing station.
In evening called on A D M S at

LESTREM.   Capt. RENWICK R.A.M.C.
returned from 1st Yeomanry for
duty with this unit.

Nov. 26th. 1915.   MESPLAUX Farm.

Capt. GRAHAM V.C. M.C. returned from
leave & reported for duty.
Lieut. MUNROE R.A.M.C. returned from
4th Leicesters & reported for duty.
Lieut. TATE R.A.M.C. detached for
duty with 1st H.M.F. Amb.
Lieut. TIBBLES R.A.M.C. detached for
duty with 4th Kings Liverpool Regt.
    In afternoon called on A.D.M.S. &
G.O.C, together with Capt. RENWICK.
Baths at LOCON are to be worked
by XI th Corps & not by this unit.

Nov. 27th. 1915.   MESPLAUX Farm.

    In morning visited advanced dressing
station. In afternoon A.D.M.S called
with G.O.C. Subsequently D.D.M.S XI th
Corps called.
    Lieut. COOPER R.A.M.C. proceeded on
leave. S.Sergt. Foster proceeded
to England having obtained a
commission.

Nov. 28th. 1915.   MESPLAUX Farm.

In morning called on A.D.M.S. Capt. FOSTER RAMC detached for duty with N.M.D. T.E.

In afternoon Church Parade in barn.

Nov. 29th. 1915.   MESPLAUX Farm.

In morning called on A.D.M.S for weekly conference. Subsequently visited Lieut. TIBBLES RAMC M.O. 4th. Kings Liverpools who was in trenches. Found him suffering from bronchitis. Reported to ADMS.

Nov. 30th. 1915.   MESPLAUX Farm.

A D M S called in morning & inspected some chilled feet.

Lieut. URIE RAMC proceeded for temporary duty with 6th Sherwoods. Lieut. MONROE proceeded to 4th Kings Liverpool Regt. to replace Lieut TIBBLES who returned here.

200 old railway sleepers drawn from T.P.E. for horse standings. Work started on laying horse

Standings & erecting mud walls for
Shelter
• In afternoon visited advanced
dressing station. Capt. GRAHAM
proceeded to [illegible] advanced
dressing station to relieve Capt
CANNON who returned to MECHILI)

Dec.

Army Form C. 2118.

WAR DIARY
or
INTELLIGENCE SUMMARY.
(Erase heading not required.)

46th Div. F/207/1

1/2nd N. Mid. F. Amb.
R.A.M.C.
December 1915
Vol IX

Army Form C. 2118

WAR DIARY
or
INTELLIGENCE SUMMARY

(Erase heading not required.)

Instructions regarding War Diaries and Intelligence Summaries are contained in F. S. Regs., Part II. and the Staff Manual respectively. Title Pages will be prepared in manuscript.

Place	Date	Hour	Summary of Events and Information	Remarks and references to Appendices
MESPLAUX Farm	Dec 1st		Capt. YATES R.A.M.C. returned from leave & reported for duty. Lieut. TIBBLES R.A.M.C. evacuated to C.C.S. sick (bronchitis & rheumatism) Capt. RENWICK proceeded to Advanced Dressing Station to relieve Capt. MAYFIELD who returned to farm. B section took over hospital at MESPLAUX from C section; C section took over advanced dressing station from A section.	
"	2nd		In afternoon visited advanced dressing station & 138th Regt. drying rooms.	
"	3rd		Telegram received in morning :— "All leave stopped; recall officers on leave." Called on A.D.M.S.; this division to move shortly to an unknown destination. At 5 P.M. a party from 59R. F.Amb. arrived to take over advanced dressing station from which our men returned to MESPLAUX.	
"	4th		Lieut. COOPER R.A.M.C. recalled from leave, reported for duty. In afternoon called on A.D.M.S.	
CALONNE	5th		At 8.15 A.M. sent advance party of 12 N.C.O's & men under Capt. YATES to take over hospital at CALONNE from 59R. F.Amb. At 9 A.M. party from 59R. F.Amb. arrived to take over MESPLAUX farm. At 10.15 A.M. unit proceeded by route march to CALONNE arriving at 1.30 P.M. Hospital in school; 48 patients transferred in motor & horse ambulances. Two horses wagons left behind at MESPLAUX. At 9 P.M. order received from H.Q. 46th Division all H.D. horses to be replaced by L.D. or mules.	

Army Form C. 2118

WAR DIARY
or
INTELLIGENCE SUMMARY
(Erase heading not required.)

Place	Date	Hour	Summary of Events and Information	Remarks and references to Appendices
CALONNE	Dec. 6R.		In morning attended conference at A.D.M.S. Office. In afternoon called on Capt. ARMSTRONG, M.O. 5R. Lincolns. Orders received that all equipment above establishment is to be returned to Ordnance at once. Lieut. URIE R.A.M.C. returned from 6R. Sherwoods for duty with this unit.	
"	7R.		Lieut. URIE R.A.M.C. detailed for duty with 5R. Lincolns in place of Capt. ARMSTRONG who is sick. 21 H.D. Forces handed over to 19R. Div. Ammn. Col. in exchange for 42 mules. In afternoon visited D.A.D.M.S.	
"	8R.		Telegram received in morning :— "All leave stopped." Lieut. COOPER went to R.E. to take place of Capt. FOSTER who went on leave yesterday. Lieut. DOUGLAS H.T. R.A.M.C. reported from base for duty with this unit. Telegram received in evening :— "Leave re-started"; Capt. RENWICK proceeded on leave.	
"	9R.		Four NAPIER motor ambulances exchanged for SUNBEAM cars.	
"	10R.		In morning attended conference at Div. Adq'rs on subject of clothing & equipment of division. In afternoon A.D.M.S. called.	
"	11R.		Lieut. CANNON D.J. R.A.M.C. evacuated to C.C.S. sick (I.C.T. Reet R)	
"	12R.		Order received from A.D.M.S. to send a horse to LESTREM to fetch THRESH disinfector. Sent team of six mules which were unable to move it.	

Army Form C. 2118

WAR DIARY
or
INTELLIGENCE SUMMARY
(Erase heading not required.)

Instructions regarding War Diaries and Intelligence Summaries are contained in F. S. Regs., Part II. and the Staff Manual respectively. Title Pages will be prepared in manuscript.

Place	Date	Hour	Summary of Events and Information	Remarks and references to Appendices
CALONNE	Dec. 13th		Attended weekly conference at A.D.M.S. office	
"	14th		Fifteen men arrived from 9th. & Amb. & 20 from 57th. & Amb as reinforcements making up 9 over strength.	
"	15th		Sent Lieut. CROSS to reconnoitre LILLERS & BERGUETTE railway stations as this unit will probably be entraining shortly.	
"	16th		A.D.M.S. called together units near D.D.M.S. (Major LLOYD JONES) Capt. RENWICK returned from leave & reported for duty. Four A.S.C. drivers (mule) arrived as reinforcements from base. D.D.M.S. could	
"	17th		Orders received at 7P.M. This unit to march with 138th Regt. to new area to-morrow.	
"	18th		Unit left CALONNE at 11A.M. & marched with 138th Regt. to new area at THIENNES arriving about 2.30 P.M. No billets available so unit ordered to return to CALONNE. Great difficulty in turning round as road narrow & very bad & greatly congested. Had just finished turning at 4.30 P.M. when another order came to go on to NEUFPRÉ 1 mile E of AIRE. Turned once more with great difficulty, several waggons being ditched in the process. Unit left at 7.30 P.M. & marched to NEUFPRÉ arriving about 9.30 P.M. Men & animals very tired. Billets bad & unfit for accommodation whatever.	
NEUFPRÉ	19th			

Sick : So 20 were sent to No 1 CCS Station & 29 to CCS.

WAR DIARY
or
INTELLIGENCE SUMMARY.
(Erase heading not required.)

Army Form C. 2118.

Hour, Date, Place	Summary of Events and Information	Remarks and references to Appendices
NEUFPRÉ. Dec. 20R.	In morning called on A.D.M.S. for weekly conference. In afternoon B section under Capt. RENWICK proceeded to new billets at LA LACQUE 1½ miles away.	
Dec. 21st.	Lieut. DOUGLAS R.A.M.C. returned from 5th R. Lincolns for duty with this unit. Lieut. SHANKS W. R.A.M.C. from 19th Division reported for duty with this unit in place of Lieut. MUNROE who is struck off our strength.	
Dec. 22nd	Lieut. COOPER R.A.M.C. returned from R.E. for duty with this unit. Barn at LA LACQUE taken for sick as there is no accommodation at NEUFPRÉ. Orders received to send all cases of scabies to 3rd. F.M.t. Amb.	
Dec. 23rd.	All our motor ambulances proceeded to 46th. Div. Amb. Workshop Unit this evening as they are travelling independently via HAVRE. Two motor ambulances lent by 38th Division arrived at 7 P.M. to replace them.	
Dec. 24 R.	Orders received from A.D.M.S. that sick of 139th Bgde. are to be cleared by this unit, as 1st F.M.t. Amb. is entraining to-morrow. Capt. YATES with 5 N.C.O's & men & one motor ambulance	

WAR DIARY
or
INTELLIGENCE SUMMARY.
(Erase heading not required.)

Army Form C. 2118.

Hour, Date, Place	Summary of Events and Information	Remarks and references to Appendices
NEUFPRÉ. Dec. 24th. (continued)	despatched to BOESEGHEM to run medical collecting room for 139th Brigade.	
" Dec. 25th.	137 R. Bgde. & 1st F.M. & Amb. entrained to-day. Our unit sent 1 sergeant & 2 men to BERGUETTE station & a similar party to LILLERS station. These parties were supplied with medical comforts, tins of curact, & empty tins for sanitary purposes, & used in charge of medical arrangements for sick on trains. The horses & mules of 1st F.M. & Amb. were left behind & attached to this unit for rations.	
" Dec. 26th.	139 R. Bgde. moved from BOESEGHEM to new billets round ISBERGUES & the collection of their sick was taken over by 3rd. F.M. & Amb. Capt. YATES & his party returned to NEUFPRÉ. Lieut. CANNON D.J. rejoined this unit for duty.	
" Dec. 27th.	Lieut. SHANKS R.Q.M.C. detailed for temporary duty with 4 R. Lincoln Regt.	
" Dec. 28th.	Lieuts. CANNON & CROSS proceeded on leave	

Army Form C. 2118.

WAR DIARY
or
INTELLIGENCE SUMMARY.
(Erase heading not required.)

Instructions regarding War Diaries and Intelligence Summaries are contained in F.S. Regs., Part II. and the Staff Manual respectively. Title pages will be prepared in manuscript.

Hour, Date, Place	Summary of Events and Information	Remarks and references to Appendices
NEUFPRÉ Dec. 29R.	Capt. SINCLAIR J.J. R.A.M.C reported for duty with 1st. S.M. & Amb.	
" Dec. 30R.		
" Dec. 31st.	Lieut. DOUGLAS. R.A.M.C detailed for temporary duty with 5th Lincoln Regt.	

Army Form C. 2118

46
Div

WAR DIARY
or
INTELLIGENCE SUMMARY
(Erase heading not required.)

F/2041/2.

War Diary of 1/2nd. N. Mid. Field Ambulance
R.A.M.C.
January 1916

Vol I

Jan 1916

Army Form C. 2118

WAR DIARY
or
INTELLIGENCE SUMMARY
(Erase heading not required.)

Instructions regarding War Diaries and Intelligence Summaries are contained in F.S. Regs., Part II. and the Staff Manual respectively. Title Pages will be prepared in manuscript.

Place	Date	Hour	Summary of Events and Information	Remarks and references to Appendices
NEUFPRÉ	Jan. 1st.		Eight men of 46th Div. Cycle Coy. arrived, to be attached to this unit for rations.	
"	2nd.		Church Parade 11.45 A.M. by Rev. BALDWIN.	
"	3rd.		Visited D.A.D.M.S. This unit to entrain on Jan. 5th.	
"	4th.		Packing waggons.	
"	5th.		Unit left NEUFPRÉ at 8.40 A.M. & proceeded by route march to BERGUETTE station (4 miles) arriving at 10.30 A.M. Proceeded to entrain. Train left at 1.30 P.M. for MARSEILLES travelling via ORMOY — MONTEREAU — AVIGNON. Capt. MANFIELD R.A.M.C. left behind in charge of horses & mules. There are attached to, & billeted by 3rd. N.M. F. Amb. All waggons entrained except supply waggon & blanket waggon which were handed over to 3rd. N.M. F. Amb. Sergt. BAKER & Pte. SPENCER not yet returned from leave.	
"	6th.		Latrine accommodation along line very bad — in fact practically nil. Halts for too few; sometimes an interval of 14 hours between halts. Men rather crowded; 32 to a truck. Only 4 compartments provided, so two trucks used by officers. Train is shared by this unit & 3 companies of 5th. Lincoln Regt.	
PARC BORELY MARSEILLES.	7th.		Arrived at MARSEILLES 8.30 P.M. & proceeded to detrain. At 10 P.M. marched to PARC BORELY Camp (4 miles) arriving 11.15 P.M. Unit under canvas. Weather fine but cold, with very strong wind.	
"	8th.		Reported to Camp Adjutant in morning ; in afternoon called on A.D.M.S. of MARSEILLES. This unit to take over hospital in PARC BORELY.	
"	9th.		Camp Church Parade 11.30 A.M. B section took over hospital from no. 9 M.A.C.	

Army Form C. 2118

WAR DIARY
or
INTELLIGENCE SUMMARY
(Erase heading not required.)

Instructions regarding War Diaries and Intelligence Summaries are contained in F.S. Regs., Part II. and the Staff Manual respectively. Title Pages will be prepared in manuscript.

Place	Date	Hour	Summary of Events and Information	Remarks and references to Appendices
PARC BORELY	Jan. 10th		Fine day, very cold night. 100 men went to baths.	
"	11th		Fifty men went to baths; remainder for route march.	
"	12th		Usual parades; weather milder.	
"	13th		Called on 1st. N.M.F.Amb. at Camp VALENTINE. Two lorries 9 miles off. This unit arrived to-day & bivouacked to Camp VALENTINE. Capt. MANFIELD did not accompany them as he has been detached for special duty. Overflow ward opened in building just outside camp to present hospital full. Attended conference in afternoon with Colonel HODDER, O.C. 3rd N.M. F.Amb. & the R.M.O's of units in camp, on the prevention of scabies & venereal disease.	
"	14th		Information received that one of our new drafts. 127947 Pte. HUTCHINSON is deserter from 16th Royal Irish Rifles. Went to Camp VALENTINE to interview the man. He admits offence.	
"	15th		Hospital overcrowded, so two square tents (I.T.E.P) borrowed from Camp MUSSOT.	
"	16th		Church Parade 9.30 A.M. By Bishop of GIBRALTAR. Orders received from 46th.Div. that waggons are to be ready to embark at once. Hospital handed over to 3rd. N.M. F. Amb. & equipment packed. Capt. MANFIELD arrived from BERGUETTE.	
"	17th		Usual parades.	
"	18th		Usual parades.	
"	19th		Orders received from 46th Div. waggons to embark to-morrow & rest of unit on following day.	

Army Form C. 2118

WAR DIARY
or
INTELLIGENCE SUMMARY
(Erase heading not required.)

Instructions regarding War Diaries and Intelligence Summaries are contained in F. S. Regs., Part II. and the Staff Manual respectively. Title Pages will be prepared in manuscript.

Place	Date	Hour	Summary of Events and Information	Remarks and references to Appendices
PARC BORELY	Jan. 20th.		All transport of unit left at 7.30 A.M. for docks, where it was loaded on H.M.T. ANDANIA.	
S.S. ANDANIA	21st.		Reveille 5 A.M. Unit left camp at 7 A.M. & marched to docks (7 miles) arriving 9.15 A.M. Proceeded to embark on H.M.T. ANDANIA. Capt. MANFIELD left behind at transport officer in charge of horses & mules; 17 N.C.O's & men also left behind as no room for them on transport. Capt. RENWICK R.A.M.C. of this unit sent to 3rd. R.M.F. Camp Scala. At 9.30 P.M. orders received to disembark to-morrow morning.	
PARC BORELY	22nd.		Reveille 4.30 A.M. Unit proceeded to disembark & marched back to PARC BORELY Camp, arriving about 10.30 A.M.	
"	23rd.		Usual parades. Waggons disembarked & parked at docks	
"	24th.		Waggons returned to Camp.	
"	25th.		Instructions for entraining received.	
"	26th.			
In the train	27th.		Horses left VALENTINE Camp at 9 A.M. & proceeded to PARC BORELY arriving at 12 Noon. Unit left PARC BORELY at 2 P.M. & marched to ARENC Station arriving 4.15 P.M. Proceeded to entrain. Train left at 7.12 P.M. for an unknown destination.	
In the train	28th.			
PONT REMY	29th.		Reached PONT REMY at 7.15 P.M. & proceeded to detrain. This was completed by 9.15 P.M. & unit then marched to billets in village. Billeted in large co-operative stores.	
"	30th. 31st.		Accommodation good. Lieut. Col. R.M. WEST returned from England & resumed command of unit	

46th Div.

1/2 N.M. Field Amb.

March 1916

Army Form C. 2118.

WAR DIARY
or
INTELLIGENCE SUMMARY.
(Erase heading not required.) 2nd N. Mid. Field Ambulance. 46th Div.

Hour, Date, Place	Summary of Events and Information	Remarks and references to Appendices
BEAUVAL - FRANCE. March 1. 1916.	Lieut SHANKS, R.A.M.C., of this Unit, detailed for Regimental Duty with 1st Monmouths. — Capt. NEIL-KANE (T.F.) reported for duty with this Unit. Hospital has evacuated. Snow.	SOUCHEZ. [Sketch map showing TALUS DES ZOUAVES, BOYAU ERSATZ, BOYAU CABARET ROUGE, BETHUNE, BOYAU DES -, ARRAS, ST ELOY, CARENCEY, ACQ, with Dressing Stations, Main Dressing Station, 1st N.M.F.A., Regimental Aid Posts, Fire Trenches marked]
HOUVIN - HOUVIGNEUL. FRANCE. March 6. 1916.	Unit proceeded by route march to HOUVIN - HOUVIGNEUL (16 miles). Blizzard in morning. Fine afternoon. Hospital to accommodate 50 patients, established here on arrival.	
VILLERS - CHATEL. FRANCE. March 9. 1916.	Unit proceeded by route march to VILLERS - CHATEL (12 miles), where a Divisional Rest Station, Officers Hospital, and Scabies Hospital, were established. — 2 Officers detailed to go round Trenches. Cases for C.C.S. to be sent to No 30 C.C.S. at AUBIGNY.	
VILLERS - CHATEL. FRANCE. March 11th 1916.	Inspected Trenches, starting at CABARET-ROUGE. Accommodation for medical personnel poor, but can be improved. Evacuation of Wounded being done by 1st N.M.F.A. at ACQ and ST ELOY. Wounded are kept in A.D. post Dugouts until night, and are then sent down to Aid Post at ST ELOY by means of Trolley railway, from TALUS - DES - ZOUAVES. Urgent cases can be evacuated from Aid-post Dugouts by day to advanced Dressing Station in the ARRAS - BETHUNE road, and thence to ST ELOY by wheeled Stretcher.	[signature] LIEUT. COL. COMDG. 2nd North Mid. Fd Amb. R.A.M.C.

Forms/C. 2118/10

(9 29 6) W 4141—463   100,000   9/14   H W V

Army Form C. 2118.

WAR DIARY
~~INTELLIGENCE SUMMARY.~~
(Erase heading not required.)   2ⁿᵈ N. Mid. Field Ambulance. 49 "Div"

Instructions regarding War Diaries and Intelligence Summaries are contained in F. S. Regs., Part II. and the Staff Manual respectively. Title pages will be prepared in manuscript.

Hour, Date, Place	Summary of Events and Information	Remarks and references to Appendices
VILLERS - CHATEL FRANCE. March 13. 1916. -	Conference at Headquarters of A.D.M.S. - Took over 3 Wooden Huts at MINGOVAL. ½ mile from VILLERS-CHATEL, previously occupied by a French Ambulance. Each Hut capable of accommodating 60 patients. Capt. YATES in charge. Instructions received from A.D.M.S. to send 2 Motor Ambulances each evening to ST ELOY, to assist in evacuating wounded from rail-head. Also 6 bearers to allow to transport on their journey from wounded from rail-head. - Capt. the Rev. BURNHILL C.F., Four Regimental Aid posts to rail head by Trotters. reported for duty.	
VILLERS - CHATEL FRANCE. March 15- 1916.	G.O.C. Inspected Hospital	
VILLERS - CHATEL FRANCE March 18. 1916	D.D.M.S. 17ᵗʰ Corps Inspected Hospital	
VILLERS - CHATEL FRANCE March 19. 1916.	Capt. NEIL BAIN (T.C.) evacuated sick to N° 30 C.C.S.	
VILLERS - CHATEL FRANCE March 21. 1916.	Number of cases of Œdema of feet, occurring in men who have been standing for several days in Water in Trenches: in some cases followed by Neuritis and in others by Gangrene (moist) of toes. Probably due to impeded circulation from tight puttees and boots.	

Army Form C. 2118.

WAR DIARY
or
INTELLIGENCE SUMMARY.

(Erase heading not required.) 2nd W. MIN. Field Ambulance. 46th Div."

Instructions regarding War Diaries and Intelligence Summaries are contained in F.S. Regs., Part II. and the Staff Manual respectively. Title pages will be prepared in manuscript.

Hour, Date, Place	Summary of Events and Information	Remarks and references to Appendices
VILLERS-CHATEL FRANCE March 26. 1916.	Message from A.D.M.S. 12.30 A.M. Send all Motorambulances at once to report to O.C. 1st N.M.F.A. at MONT ST ELOY. Prepare to receive wounded. Instructions complied with, but no wounded. Mine exploded in Staffed lines and craters held by us.	
VILLERS-CHATEL FRANCE March 28. 1916.	Lieut CANNON. R.A.M.C. of this Unit, detailed for temporary duty with 5th Lincolns, vice Lieut URIE. R.A.M.C., admitted to Hospital. Lieut COOPER. R.A.M.C.(T.C.) of this Unit, detailed for temporary duty with 6th N Staffords., vice Capt. DALE. R.A.M.C., admitted to Hospital. Sergt POWELL, R.A.M.C., of this Unit, detailed to proceed Divisional School at AGNIERES, for instruction in Anti-Gas precautions.	

Vincent
2nd Nth Md Fld Amb Col R.A.M.C.

1/2 CP M.F. Amb.

April 1916

COMMITTEE FOR THE
MEDICAL HISTORY OF THE WAR
Date 26 JUN 1916

46

1/2 N M 7a Amb

Vol 14

Army Form C. 2118

WAR DIARY
or
INTELLIGENCE SUMMARY
(Erase heading not required.)

2ⁿᵈ NORTH MIDLAND FIELD AMBULANCE
NANCY
46 Division

Instructions regarding War Diaries and Intelligence Summaries are contained in F. S. Regs., Part II. and the Staff Manual respectively. Title Pages will be prepared in manuscript.

Place	Date	Hour	Summary of Events and Information	Remarks and references to Appendices
VILLERS (CHATEL)	April 1st 1916		10 Reinforcements arrived from base, one of whom, Pte ADCOCK, NANCY, found to be suffering from Acute Phthisis. Remainder (nineteen) found to be in good condition. All got fit for trench work in eight fifteen days.	
"	April 3		Inspection of Transport by D.D.M.S.	
"	April 4		Inspection by D.D.M.S. 17th Corps.	
A.C.Q.	April 7		Moved to take field of ACR, taking over dressing station from 1/1 N.M.F.A. who were to first station at VILLERS CHATEL. Inspection of Huts: 2 stations at main dressing station at ACQ - 1 station at advanced dressing station at ST. ELOY. 1 dugout and 6 men in dugouts behind of BOYAU CENTRALE on BETHUNE RD - 1 station at first field aid & one aid post was LA TARGETTE. These assignments are for evacuation of wounded from trenches via communication trench PAREMI-NEUVILLE ST VAAST. No room in communication trench for wounded being carried out direct. Dugouts on either of trenches PAREMY-NEUVILLE ST VAAST, numerous & in only few communication trenches - the TENTAILLE and the DE. POSTIN. Although not in the course of our actions. It is used for surplus equipment of covering of enemy first aid Drk at night from the Pyramid dispatched to St. Eloi station at NT. ST. ELOI from to communicate Drk of the following up with station and station with wounded. Evacuations taken up by motors taken along the communication trench to the Dug-out by stretcher bearers of wounded. At ST. ELOI, taking the Ordinary D.R., 2 motor shelters from the station motor ACR by motor Ambulance : one from ACR of A.D.S.A. to A.D.S.	
"	April 13		Inspection of men paced during morning driving fine show on matter of cleanliness of blanket & pocket etc. etc. The Gen. Sirprelly C.O. Reviews in the general in "parks" ; whence it is thought men might forcibly get inspiration by the great men in certain cases intermit. It sorted efficient & for our immediate.	

Army Form C. 2118

2ⁿᵈ NORTH MIDLAND FIELD AMBULANCE
R.A.M.C.T.
46 Division

WAR DIARY
or
INTELLIGENCE SUMMARY

(Erase heading not required.)

Place	Date	Hour	Summary of Events and Information	Remarks and references to Appendices
ACQ	April 14 1916		Major A.E. TURNER, R.A.M.C.T., of this Unit, proceeds to 3ʳᵈ ARMY SCHOOL of INSTRUCTION at ST POL, for a 7 days course of instruction in effects of GAS.	
MAISNIL-ST-POL	April 21ˢᵗ 1916		D.M.S. 3ʳᵈ ARMY, inspected dressing station. A.S.C.M.T. drivers attached to Unit, come under R.A.M.C. for purpose of pay and discipline.	
"	April 23ʳᵈ 1916		Unit moved to new area at MAISNIL-ST-POL, taking over from 77ᵗʰ Field Ambulance, 25ᵗʰ Division, who move to an area vacated by 46ᵗʰ Division. Established Hospital at MAISNIL-ST-POL. F.G.C.M officer for to try 2ᵉ HUTCHINSON, W. A.S.C. attached, in charge of 1ˢᵗ threatening violence to his Superior officer. 2ⁿᵈ threatening act of General bad whilst he had been confined.	
"	April 24 1916		Inspection by A.D.M.S. 46 Division.	
"	April 26 1916		30 Officers, N.C.O's and men. inoculated with (new?) Typhoid Vaccine.	

R. M. West
Lieut Colonel R.A.M.C.T.
O/C. 2ⁿᵈ N.M.F.A.

WAR DIARY or INTELLIGENCE SUMMARY

Army Form C. 2118

2nd N Midland Field Ambulance
PART 7.

Place	Date	Hour	Summary of Events and Information	Remarks and references to Appendices
			Trench Feet: This has often been used as a catch-all phrase, and is often applied to any case of affection of the foot. The real Trench foot occurs in men who have had to stand sometimes for 36 hours or so in water and cold without relief. Losing the efficiency of circulation and changing the foot gear. The symptoms are — a flaccid cold appearance of the skin which may terminate — and sometimes very rapidly — in actual painful death and gangrene. Affections of the feet, redness, tenderness, pain from roots, patches of numbness, pins and needles, shooting cramp-like pains, and slow pains or atrophies, to harsh actual chronic flat feet — these being a long-standing sequel of the foot. The recovery is very slow, turning out almost useless. Cases requiring for months or often in men who have worn unsuitable boots, or in those who work in heavy mud.

Trench Fever: A considerable number of cases of pyrexia of unknown onset, lasting from 2 days to about a week, and as indicated by a relapse lasting 4 or 5 days, has been met. In fact there were from 10 to 15 of the admissions to Hospital. The other symptoms observed are headache, pains in the head and body, and also acid resistant pains in the shins, apparently on the Tibia. The constant appearance of influenza and recovery relative to charge of those lower frequently noticed the absence of pains in the skin in epidemic fever, and continues for a considerable period after the fading of the temperature. | |

B. M. West
ADMS
o/c 2 N M F A
May 1916

Confidential

WAR DIARY

of

2nd North Midland Field
Ambulance.
R.A.M.C.
46° Division

from April 1st to April 30th
1916

J. McField

May 1916.

2nd P. M. F. Amb.

WAR DIARY of 2nd NORTH MIDLAND FIELD AMBULANCE
NAME T.F.
Army Form C. 2118

for May 1916

WAR DIARY
or
INTELLIGENCE SUMMARY
(Erase heading not required.)

Place	Date	Hour	Summary of Events and Information	Remarks and references to Appendices
MAISNIL-ST-POL FRANCE	May 1st 1916	—	Lieut B. GRAVES. R.A.M.C. T.C. reports for duty from No 2 Stationary Hospital ABBEVILLE.	
"	May 4	—	Field General Court Martial on Pte HUTCHINSON, W., A.S.C. attached to this Unit, charged with 1st Having threatening and insulting language to his Superior officer. 2nd Breaking out of guard tent in which he was confined. Composition of Court :- President- Major WROTTESLEY, Lt D.A.C. - Members: Capt. FOWLER, A.S.C., Lieut. FAIRBAIRN, Yorks Hussars	
"	May 5		Major TURNER, with C. section, moved to BAILLEUL-AUX-CORNEILLES, to take over billets evacuated by 3rd W.M.F.A. who have moved to new area.	
			Lieuts. COETZEE and FRASER, R.A.M.C. T.C. report for duty with this Unit.	
			Capt. GRAHAM, of this Unit, evacuated sick to No 43 C.C.S. FREVENT.	
"	May 6		Moved with of 139 Brigade and Monmouths to new billeting area.	
			Capt CHALLENOR, R.A.M.C.T., reports for duty with this Unit	
"	May 8		Major TURNER, with C section, rejoins for duty with Unit, from BAILLEUL-AUX-CORNEILLES, by orders of ADMS.	
LE SOUICH. FRANCE	May 9		Raining all day. Unit left MAISNIL-ST-POL 9.30 am and proceeded by route march to new billets at LE SOUICH. Scheduled Hospital, with accommodation for 80 patients established here.	
"	May 10		LIEUT. COETZEE. R.A.M.C. T.C., detailed for duty with 5th Sherwood Foresters, vice Capt GREEN, to report to this Unit.	
			Capt. PERRY. R.A.M.C. T.C., reports for duty with this Unit	
			Lieut. J.F.G.C.M. held on Pte HUTCHINSON, W. A.S.C. attached : 12 Months Hard Labour, and loss of 1 Months pay.	
"	May 11		Capt. GREEN. R.A.M.C. T.F., reports for duty with this Unit.	
			S.S. Major KEEY, A.S.C. reports for duty with Transport Section of this Unit.	

WAR DIARY 1/2" NTH MIDLAND FIELD AMB/S
ANNEXURE
for MAY 1916
Army Form C. 2118

WAR DIARY
or
INTELLIGENCE SUMMARY
(Erase heading not required.)

Instructions regarding War Diaries and Intelligence Summaries are contained in F. S. Regs., Part II. and the Staff Manual respectively. Title Pages will be prepared in manuscript.

Place	Date	Hour	Summary of Events and Information	Remarks and references to Appendices
LE SOUICH FRANCE	May 12 1916	—	Inspection by ADMS 46th Division	
"	May 13	—	Lieut GRAVES, RAMC T.C., detailed for duty with 5th N Staffords. Lieut FRASER, RAMC T.C., detailed for duty with 2nd Bde. RFA 46 Div? Capt. PERRY, RAMC T.C., detailed for duty with 1st Lincoln Battalion. Capt. BANNAN, RAMC T.F., from 23rd CCS, reports for duty, inexperienced	
"	May 14	—	Gas Helmet inspection Lieut Col. WEST proceeds on leave.	
"	May 16	—	Lecture to transport section on "Gas attack".	
"	May 17	—	Sentence of 12 months Hard Labour, awarded Pte HUTCHINSON, W., ASC attached, by F G C M on May 2nd, reduced by Army Commander to 2 months No 1 Field Punishment	
"	May 18	—	Capt. FLAXMAN, RAMC T.C., reports for duty from leave Gas Helmet tests for transport. M. COHEN reports for duty as interpreter	
"	May 19	—	Capt L.T. CHALLENOR detailed for duty with 42nd C.C.S. Lieut HALICHMAN, RAMC T.C., reports for duty with this Unit, from No 47 CCS.	
"	May 21	—	Gas Helmet inspection	
"	May 22	—	Capt YATES, RAMC T.F., of this Unit with 2 NCO's and 50 men, proceeded to CANDICAPZE to upst C.O.C. 3rd NMFA RAMC T.F., for Trench digging.	
"	May 23	—	Lieut Col WEST, reports for duty from leave Officers Lecture on gas-shells by Major TURNER.	

WAR DIARY
or
INTELLIGENCE SUMMARY

(Erase heading not required.)

Army Form C. 2118

WAR DIARY OF 2nd NORTH MIDLAND FIELD AMBULANCE, 9 AMC T.F.
For MAY 1916
R. McLeod Lieut-M. Comm. B.S

Instructions regarding War Diaries and Intelligence Summaries are contained in F. S. Regs., Part II. and the Staff Manual respectively. Title Pages will be prepared in manuscript.

Place	Date	Hour	Summary of Events and Information	Remarks and references to Appendices
LE SOUICH. FRANCE	May 25	—	Proceeded to FONQUEVILLERS, to inspect medical arrangement of advanced dressing station of 13th NMFA. Capt. FLAXMAN detailed for permanent duty with Corps Cavalry.	
"	May 28	—	Gas Helmet inspection. ADMS called. Capt. GRAHAM, RAMC T.F. joined of chest trouble. Capt. FRASER, RAMC T.C. from 2nd Oxh. M.A. 26th Divn. posted for duty.	
"	May 31	—	During the month, probably on account of the improvement in the weather and the fact the Battalions are leaving the entrances amongst the troops too much diminished. The chief causes of illness are the so-called "Trench Fever", and a certain number of cases of Pithecoides Tonsillitis. There have been a few cases of Paratyphoid, Diphtheria, and 1 case of Scabies Fever. A certain number of men have been inoculated against Paratyphoid, but the effects, I think the inoculation should be compulsory. The reaction though were worse than that caused by Anti-typhoid inoculation, as short - 24 hours, with headache, nausea, and languideness. The Gas Helmets issued by the Ordnance Service, are in many cases defective, the chief defect being that the eye pieces got out covered in vapour, - as easy they it seemed of an instrument able to remove were used to examine and screw them up, but appears to be able the fingers. Out of 80 new helmets recently examined, 15 were found defective from this cause.	

Holt Cemetery

112- N. Miro and Vine Orleans

June 1996

COMMITTEE ON
LOCAL HISTORY
Date 31 AUG 1996

WAR DIARY
or
INTELLIGENCE SUMMARY.
(Erase heading not required.)

Army Form C. 2118.

Hour, Date, Place	Summary of Events and Information	Remarks and references to Appendices
June 1st. 1916. LE SOUICH		
" 2nd " "	Capt. J.L. GREEN RAMC rejoined this unit from temporary duty with 46th Div. A.S.C. He is detailed for duty with 5th Sherwood Foresters.	
" 3rd " "	Lieut. Col. R.M. WEST, O.C. unit, evacuated to no.19 CCS sick. Major TURNER assumes temporary command of unit. Order received from ADMS :- Lieut. KALICHMAN RAMC to be sent to DDMS, ROUEN. Six wheeled stretchers drawn from Ordnance.	
" 4th " "	Lieut. KALICHMAN RAMC proceeded to ROUEN. No. 1993 Pte. J. WILLBOND detailed for motor duty with 1st Monmouth Regt. Rode to DOULLENS in afternoon to see Colonel WEST. Capt. J.E. DIXON RAMC reported for duty with this unit from 3rd H.M. F. Amb.	
" 5th " "	Motored to PAS, to call on ADMS; then to 3rd H.M. F. Amb. at GAUDIEMPRE to see rabbit wire incinerator. Then to Adv. Dressing Station at FONQUEVILLIERS to visit Capt. YATES & inspect dug-outs & trenches. Lieut. Col. R.M. WEST evacuated to base to-day	

Army Form C. 2118.

WAR DIARY
or
INTELLIGENCE SUMMARY.
(Erase heading not required.)

Instructions regarding War Diaries and Intelligence Summaries are contained in F.S. Regs., Part II. and the Staff Manual respectively. Title pages will be prepared in manuscript.

Hour, Date, Place	Summary of Events and Information	Remarks and references to Appendices
June 6th 1916. LE SOUICH	Vapour baths arranged in two bell tents at back of present bath-house. Lieut. FRASER RAMC detailed for duty with 3rd. F.M. Bgde. R¾A.	
7H. " "	Vapour baths completed. Capt. T. GRAHAM RAMC taken ill whilst on leave in England.	
8H. " "	Inspection by D.M.S. Third Army.	
9H " "	Visited 1st F. M. & Amb. at LUCHEUX	
10H " "	Very wet day. Corrugated iron incinerators erected for Burning Manure.	
11H " "	Gas helmet inspection in morning. Two carpenters sent to R.E. dump at PAS to assist in making latrine seats. DADMS called. Lieut. & 2MR CROSS proceed on leave. The Revd. Capt. UTHWATT arrives to replace Capt. GURNHILL.	
12H " "	Visited DADMS in morning. One NCO & ten men sent to 3rd. F.M. & Amb. for Travel making. One bell tent sent to 3rd F.M. & Amb.	
13H " "	Rain all day.	
14H " "	Lime advanced one room in evening	

Army Form C. 2118.

WAR DIARY
or
INTELLIGENCE SUMMARY.
(Erase heading not required.)

Instructions regarding War Diaries and Intelligence Summaries are contained in F. S. Regs., Part II. and the Staff Manual respectively. Title pages will be prepared in manuscript.

Hour, Date, Place	Summary of Events and Information	Remarks and references to Appendices
June 15th. 1916. LE SOUICH		
" 16th "	Called on A.D.M.S. for conference & subsequently visited 2nd Battle Headquarters with him	
" 17th "	Visited FONQUEVILLERS with Col. WRAITH & inspected dug-outs & trenches. Lieut. J.H. RUTTER RAMC reported for duty from 3rd H.M. F.A. Lieut FRASER RAMC reported for duty from 3rd H.M. Fld. R.F.A.	
" 18th "	For Helmet inspection in morning.	
" 19th "	Visited A.D.M.S. for conference in morning. Subsequently A.D.M.S called & inspected hospital.	
" 20th "		
" 21st "	Visited A.D.M.S for conference in afternoon. A.D.M.S VIII Corps called & inspected Hospital.	
" 22nd "	Lieut. & 2Mr CROSS reported for duty from Leave	
" 23rd "	Empty six stretcher sent to 1st H. M. & Amb.	
" 24th "	Visited A.D.M.S; then went on to 1st & 3rd H.M. & Amb.	
" 25th "	Hospital closed, all cases except three being sent to C.C.S., & waggons packed. Lieut. RUTTER RAMC sent to 1st H.M. & Amb.	

Army Form C. 2118.

WAR DIARY
or
INTELLIGENCE SUMMARY.
(Erase heading not required.)

Instructions regarding War Diaries and Intelligence Summaries are contained in F.S. Regs., Part II. and the Staff Manual respectively. Title pages will be prepared in manuscript.

Hour, Date, Place	Summary of Events and Information	Remarks and references to Appendices
June 26th 1916 GAUDIEMPRÉ.	Very wet day. In morning visited ADMS. At 2 PM unit marched to GAUDIEMPRÉ (11 miles) arriving 6 P.M. Huts assigned to unit very bad, quite unfit for occupation, so men ~~billeted~~ billeted in Barns in village.	
June 27th "	3 NCO's + 24 men sent to no. 19 CCS for duty; also 8 men to Major Brennan, + 8 men to 3rd N.M.F.Amb. ADMS called. All available stretcher bearers (70) marched to Battle Headquarters at SOUASTRE at 2.30 P.M. arriving at 3.30 P.M. Orders were then received to return to GAUDIEMPRÉ.	
June 28th "	Two NCO's sent to advanced dressing station to await Capt. YATES	
June 29th "	Tents stale returns wanted to men. Capt. DIXON RAMC, Lieut. FRASER RAMC, & Lieut. + 2 NR CROSS moved to advanced dressing station. At 5.30 P.M. all available stretcher bearers (70) moved to ADMS Battle Headquarters at SOUASTRE & are billeted in dug-outs	
June 30th "		

Forms/C. 2118/10

46th Division

1/2 N.M. Field Ambulance

July 1916

COMMITTEE FOR THE
MEDICAL HISTORY OF THE WAR
Date 13 SEP 1915

WAR DIARY or INTELLIGENCE SUMMARY

Army Form C. 2118.

(Erase heading not required.)

MEDICAL 46
1/2 NM 2nd Civil

Instructions regarding War Diaries and Intelligence Summaries are contained in F.S. Regs., Part II. and the Staff Manual respectively. Title pages will be prepared in manuscript.

Hour, Date, Place	Summary of Events and Information	Remarks and references to Appendices
July 1st 1916. SOUASTRE	At 7.30 A.M. Division attacked GOMMECOURT, Staffords on right, Notts & Derby on left, Lincolns & Leicesters in support. Casualties were dealt with at two advanced dressing stations in FONCQUEVILLERS, one staffed by 1st F.M. & Amb. & one by 2nd F.M. & Amb. Lying cases were then placed in motor ambulances while car ran night into FONCQUEVILLIERS. Walking cases went back to the dir. in the FONCQUEVILLIERS - SOUASTRE road & were there loaded onto Ford ambulance & G.S. waggons. Twenty motor ambulances, nine Ford ambulances waggons, & eighteen G.S. waggons were parked on the SOUASTRE - BIENVILLERS road in readiness. Evacuation of casualties proceeded smoothly & rapidly. By 11 P.M. 1390 wounded had been evacuated to the 3rd F.M. & Amb. at the main dressing station at GAUDIEMPRÉ. The G.S. waggons moved that night in clearing large numbers of slightly wounded. The German bombardment of our trenches was very severe & caused the following	

WAR DIARY
or
INTELLIGENCE SUMMARY.
(Erase heading not required.)

Army Form C. 2118.

Hour, Date, Place	Summary of Events and Information	Remarks and references to Appendices
	Casualties amongst men of this unit:—	
	KILLED. 1898 Pte. WARD. J.E. 42415 Pte. COPE. W.H 42606 Pte. ROSE. G.W.	
	WOUNDED 2314 Pte. HUBBARD N. 2699 Pte. WARREN W.E. 2231 L.Cpl. STORER S. ⎫ slightly wounded; 1154 Pte. PARKER A. ⎬ remained at duty. 2283 Pte. BAXTER R.E. ⎭	
	The Germans fired a great number of Lachrymatory shells, the effects of which were felt at the advanced dressing station. The R.A.M.C evacuation trench was quite useless being nearly waist deep in water. It was also heavily shelled with both H.E. & Lachrymatory. Fortunately it was not required as motor ambulances had no difficulty in going up to FONCQUEVILLIERS	
July 2nd 1916. GAUDIEMPRÉ.	Visited FONCQUEVILLIERS in morning; all quiet. At noon received order from A.D.M.S:— All personnel & transport to return to GAUDIEMPRÉ at once! fifty stretcher bearers returned from FONCQUEVILLIERS in evening. Captain PERRY R.A.M.C reported for duty from 3rd N. M. & Amb.	

WAR DIARY or INTELLIGENCE SUMMARY.

(Erase heading not required.)

Army Form C. 2118.

Instructions regarding War Diaries and Intelligence Summaries are contained in F.S. Regs., Part II. and the Staff Manual respectively. Title pages will be prepared in manuscript.

Hour, Date, Place	Summary of Events and Information	Remarks and references to Appendices
July 3rd. 1916. GAUDIEMPRÉ.	In morning rode to PAS to see O.D.M.S. who went to taken over Adv Dressing Station at BIENVILLIERS & man dressing station at LARBRET to-morrow. In afternoon rode to LARBRET to inspect dressing station there. Capt. DIXON R.A.M.C. with 1 N.C.O. & ten men proceeded to A.D.S. at BIENVILLIERS. Remaining personnel returned from FONCQUEVILLIERS.	
July 4th. 1916. LARBRET.	Captain YATES R.A.M.C. with 40 of the most exhausted men proceeded to LARBRET in motor ambulances at 9 A.M. Capt. MANFIELD with 4 N.C.O's & 20 men proceeded to BIENVILLIERS at 10.30 A.M. At 11 A.M. remainder of unit with all transport proceeded to LARBRET arriving at 12.30 P.M. Dressing station in huts capable of accommodating 1,000 patients, & a skilled [daily]. In afternoon returned to BIENVILLIERS & inspected A.D.S., dug-outs, & regimental aid posts.	
July 5th. 1916. LARBRET	Men resting & mending & cleaning clothes & kit. No. 2383 Pte. C. DEPLEDGE, 6th Stranders. killed by a shell near main dressing station this morning. Body brought into dressing station & C.O. injured ?. Capt. YATES R.A.M.C. moved to A.D.S. to relieve Capt. DIXON who returns to Headquarters.	
July 6th. 1916. COUTURELLE.	Hospital at LARBRET shelled at 3 P.M., five H.E. shells bursting in the hospital & about twelve others	

Army Form C. 2118.

WAR DIARY
or
INTELLIGENCE SUMMARY.
(Erase heading not required.)

Instructions regarding War Diaries and Intelligence Summaries are contained in F. S. Regs., Part II. and the Staff Manual respectively. Title pages will be prepared in manuscript.

Hour, Date, Place	Summary of Events and Information	Remarks and references to Appendices
July 3rd. 1916. GAUDIEMPRÉ.	In morning rode to PAS to see A.D.M.S. the unit to take over Advanced Dressing Station at BIENVILLIERS & main dressing station at LARBRET to-morrow. In afternoon rode to LARBRET to inspect dressing station. Pau. Capt. DIXON R.A.M.C. with 1 N.C.O. & ten men proceeded to A.D.S. at BIENVILLIERS. Remaining personnel returned from FONCQUEVILLERS.	
July 4th 1916. LARBRET.	Captain YATES R.A.M.C. with 40 O.R's most exhausted men proceeded to LARBRET in motor ambulances at 9 A.M. Capt. MANFIELD with 4 N.C.O's + 20 men proceeded to BIENVILLIERS at 10.30 A.M. At 11.A.M. remainder of unit with all transport proceeded to LARBRET arriving at 12.30 P.M. Dressing station in huts capable of accommodating 1,800 patients, & is shelled daily. In afternoon visited to BIENVILLIERS & inspected A.D.S., dug-outs, & regimental aid posts.	
July 5th. 1916. LARBRET	Men resting & mending & cleaning clothing & kit. No. 2383 Pte. C. DEPLEDGE, 6th Sea-forth's killed by a shell near main dressing station this morning. Body brought to dressing station & C.O. informed.	
July 6th. 1916. COUTURELLE.	Capt. YATES R.A.M.C. proceeded to A.D.S. to relieve Capt. DIXON who return to Headquarters. Hospital at LARBRET shelled at 3 P.M. five H.E. shells bursting in the hospital & about twelve other	

WAR DIARY or INTELLIGENCE SUMMARY

Army Form C. 2118

Place	Date	Hour	Summary of Events and Information	Remarks and references to Appendices
COUTURELLE	July	7 A.	In the immediate neighbourhood. Casualties as follows:- **WOUNDED.** 2857 Pte. TALBOT 9. 8 R. Shropshires } 43758 Pte. WINSTONE F. 2nd R.M. & Amb. } Since died of wounds 1713 Pte. WINSTONE 9. 2nd R.M. & Amb. 7/957 Dr. CATTELL H. A.S.C. attached 2nd R.M. & Amb. P.S. All patients were transferred to 1st R.M. & Amb. Personnel & equipment followed later arriving at COUTURELLE at 11.30 P.M. In morning visited A.D.M.S. & will. Rew inspected was site for hospital in huts near BAVINCOURT. In afternoon Capt. PERRY with 2 N.C.O's & 20 men proceeded by route march to BAVINCOURT & Captain DIXON R.A.M.C. detailed for duty with 7 F. Scouts.	
"	July	8 A.	In morning motored to BAVINCOURT, then to D.D.M.S. VIII Corps together with Capt. DIXON R.A.M.C. & Lieut. FRASER R.A.M.C. mental specialist from G.H.Q. Went proceeded at 2.30 P.M. MYERS, mental specialist from G.H.Q. Lieut. CROSS & proceeded by route march to BAVINCOURT. On arrival orders were received from A.D.M.S. to return to COUTURELLE	
"	July	9 A.	Hospital established under canvas at COUTURELLE; accommodation 80.	
"	July	10 A.	In morning called on A.D.M.S. for conference. In afternoon D.D.M.S. VIII Corps & A.D.M.S. called to inspect hospital. Capt. W.T. WOOD R.A.M.C. (??) joined for duty with this unit from 1st R.M. & Amb.	
"	July	11 A.	Captains YATES & MANFIELD with Rew party returned from Advanced Dressing Station at BIENVILLIERS which had been taken over by 34th Division	

Army Form C. 2118

WAR DIARY or INTELLIGENCE SUMMARY

(Erase heading not required.)

Instructions regarding War Diaries and Intelligence Summaries are contained in F. S. Regs., Part II. and the Staff Manual respectively. Title Pages will be prepared in manuscript.

Place	Date	Hour	Summary of Events and Information	Remarks and references to Appendices
COUTURELLE	July	12th	Large number of cases of fever N.Y.D. are being admitted to Hospital, most of them with temperatures of 102°–104°. Several cases of diphtheria.	
"	July	13th	One hut brought from LARBRET for erection at COUTURELLE.	
"	July	14th	Captain YATES + PERRY with 3 N.C.O.s & 30 men proceeded to BIENVILLIERS to take over Advanced Dressing Station there. By order of A.D.M.S. all sick & wounded (152) returned to Ordnance.	
"	July	15th	Inspection of unit by Major General THWAITES, the new G.O.C.	
"	July	17th	Visited A.D.M.S. for conference; subsequently proceeded to BIENVILLIERS to inspect Advanced dressing station. Twenty five patients sent to D.A.C. for light duty.	
"	July	18th	Vapour baths + second hut erected.	
"	July	19th	D.D.M.S., VII th Corps called.	
"	July	20th	Lieut. FRASER proceeded to Adv. Dressing Station to relieve Capt. PERRY who returns to Rdqrs. In afternoon visited BIENVILLIERS to inspect A.D.S. In evening A.D.M.S. called. Second hut erected.	
"	July	21st	Advanced Dressing Station shelled at 8.15 A.M., two H.E. shells bursting in ward for patients, & completely wrecking it. No casualties. The band being empty at the time. In afternoon received order from A.D.M.S. to withdraw personnel from A.D.S. except 1 N.C.O. & 8 men who are to work under orders of M.O. of battalion in BIENVILLIERS.	
"	July	22nd	Proceeded to BIENVILLIERS to inspect Adv. Dressing Station. Hut from LARBRET erected in grounds of 1st K.M. & Amb.	

WAR DIARY
or
INTELLIGENCE SUMMARY

(Erase heading not required.)

Army Form C. 2118

Instructions regarding War Diaries and Intelligence Summaries are contained in F.S. Regs., Part II. and the Staff Manual respectively. Title Pages will be prepared in manuscript.

Place	Date	Hour	Summary of Events and Information	Remarks and references to Appendices
COUTURELLE	July 24		Visited ADMS for conference. Roads in shelled area to be kept in order as possible by motor traffic during day. Arranged for Horsed Ambulance waggon to be stationed at LATBAZEQUE to evacuate sick from TOM on BIENVILLIERS during day. Men returning to duty to be conveyed to LAHERLIERE Church of Same walks to their respective Brigades. Charge of an orderly.	
"	July 25		Visited ADMS & with him went to C.R.E. to arrange for dug outs for new dressing station at BIENVILLIERS	
"	July 26		Attended as witness F.G.C.M. on 1372 Pr. COLEMAN, held 2 nd times.	
"	July 27		Gave Lecture on water purification at Div. Sanitary Section.	
"	July 29		Lieut. T.D. MORGAN RAMC (T.C) joined for duty from France. Lieut. W.E. FRASER RAMC (T.C) detailed for duty with 45 & Heavy Artillery Group.	
"	July 30		Capt. W.T. WOOD RAMC (T.F) detailed for duty with 45 & Heavy Artillery Group to replace Lieut. FRASER recalled by order of ADMS.	
"	July 31		Visited ADMS for conference.	

1/2nd cp. M. F. A.

Aug. 1916.

COMMITTEE FOR THE
MEDICAL HISTORY OF THE WAR
Date -5 OCT 1915

ADMS, 46th Div.

Herewith War Diary for
August 1916, amended
according to instructions.

A C Turner Major
1.9.16
           COMDG.
2nd North Mid. Fd. Amb. R.A.M.C.

To A.D.M.S. 46th Div.

Herewith War Diary for
August 1916 of
1/2nd N. Mid. F. Amb.

A. C. Turner Major
LT. COL. COMDG.
2nd North Mid. Fd. Amb. R.A.M.C.

31.8.16

O.C. 2nd N.M.F. Amb.

Please sign your War
Diary — also give a short
account of what measures
you adopted on receipt
of warning of Gas operations
to Record Col
A.D.M.S.

31.8.16

MEDICAL

WAR DIARY
or
INTELLIGENCE SUMMARY
(Erase heading not required.)

Army Form C. 2118.

Hour, Date, Place	Summary of Events and Information	Remarks and references to Appendices
August 2nd 1916 COUTURELLE	Capt. T. GRAHAM RAMC returned from leave & reported for duty. Party of 3 NCO's & 22 men of this unit returned from duty at no. 19 CCS.	
3rd "		
4th "	Visited ADMS together with Capt. PERRY & Lieut. FRASER	
5th "	Capt. PERRY RAMC detailed for duty with 4TH Leicesters to relieve Lieut. DOUGLAS who is attending course at Pulh. Sanitary School. One NCO & eight men sent to 5TH Leicester for temporary duty as stretcher bearers.	
6th "	Lieut. FRASER detailed for duty with 5TH Leicesters to relieve Capt. BARTON who has been accidentally wounded. Party of 1 NCO & 8 men returned from 6TH Leicester.	
7th "	Visited ADMS for conference. B section took over hospital from A section.	
8th "	Extract from LONDON GAZETTE:- Capt. G.H.H. MANFIELD awarded Military Cross 2324 Sergt. POWELL " " D.C.M.	

Army Form C. 2118.

WAR DIARY
or
INTELLIGENCE SUMMARY.
(Erase heading not required.)

Hour, Date, Place	Summary of Events and Information	Remarks and references to Appendices
August 9th 1916 COUTURELLE	Heavy Bombardment of BIENVILLIERS in morning; two H.E. shells striking Q.D.S. About 40 casualties, no R.A.M.C. men hit. Evacuated BIENVILLIERS in evening; all quiet.	
" 10th "	Wet day; 139 patients in Hospital.	
" 11th "	Attended F.G.C.M. at POMMIER on 1864 Pte. G. GEE of this unit charged with stealing money the property of a comrade, & 2270 Pte. C. CHALLONER of this unit charged with attempting to evade it. Censorship by means of a test code. Proceeded to BIENVILLIERS in evening together with Capt. YATES, 3 N.C.O's, & 36 stretcher bearers in anticipation of casualties to carrying party. Only one casualty. Returned 2.30 A.M.	
" 12th "	Capt. PERRY proceeds to 4th Lincolns to relieve Lieut. COETZEE who is to attend Sanitary School.	
" 13th "	No. 2270 Pte. C. CHALLONER of this unit sentenced by F.G.C.M. to two months F.P. no 2. No. 1864 Pte. G. GEE of this unit sentenced by F.G.C.M. to 9 months imprisonment with hard labour, sentence being deferred for.	

Army Form C. 2118.

WAR DIARY
or
INTELLIGENCE SUMMARY.
(Erase heading not required.)

Instructions regarding War Diaries and Intelligence Summaries are contained in F.S. Regs., Part II. and the Staff Manual respectively. Title pages will be prepared in manuscript.

Hour, Date, Place	Summary of Events and Information	Remarks and references to Appendices
August 14th 1916. COUTURELLE.	a month in order that he may be kept under medical observation. Sentence promulgated on parade. In morning visited ADMS for conference. Later ADMS 3rd Army, together with ODMS, ADMS & Major LEGGE called to inspect horses & mules. Capt. J.H. ASKIN RAMC (T.C) reported for duty from Base. One motor ambulance returned from workshop armour-plated.	
August 15th.	ADMS VIIth Corps called & inspected hospital. At 4.30 P.M. received orders to know reserve trenches at BIENVILLERS at 6.30 P.M. Went up, together with Capt. ASKIN & 39 % CO's & men; all quiet. Returned at 10 P.M. & sent Capt. GRAHAM to relieve Capt. ASKIN & withdraw 32 % CO's & men.	
" 16th "	G.O.C. VIIth Corps called & inspected hospital	
" 17th "	Orders received from 46th Division to construct immediately permanent horse standings for winter	

WAR DIARY
or
INTELLIGENCE SUMMARY.
(Erase heading not required.)

Army Form C. 2118.

Hour, Date, Place	Summary of Events and Information	Remarks and references to Appendices
August 18th 1916 COUTURELLE	Two G.S. waggon loads of chalk & flint drawn for Horse standings. G.O.C. 46th Division called. Capt. GRAHAM returned from BIENVILLIERS.	
" 19th "	Horse standings marked out	
" 21st "	Visited A.D.M.S. for conference	
" 22nd "	A.D.M.S. 3rd Army called & inspected Hospital. Lieut. T.D. MORGAN detailed for duty with 5th Leicesters to relieve Lieut. FRASER.	
" 23rd "	Visited A.D.M.S. together with Colonel WRAITH. Accommodation of this Hospital to be reduced to 100 & patients not to be kept more than 48 hours. The 1st H.M. F. Amb. are to run Div. Rest Station	
" 24th "	One marquee & two bell tents returned to 1st H.M. F.A.	
" 25th "	Capt. MANFIELD & Sergt. POWELL attended investiture by G.O.C. VII th Corps. Capt. PERRY returned to unit.	
" 26th "	Rough timber drawn for Horse standings. Colonel MYERS, mental specialist, called to examine 1864 Pte. G. GEE. Party of 20 men detailed for duty with Div. Sanitary Section	

WAR DIARY or INTELLIGENCE SUMMARY.

(Erase heading not required.)

Army Form C. 2118.

Hour, Date, Place	Summary of Events and Information	Remarks and references to Appendices
August 28. 1916. COUTURELLE	Visited A.D.M.S. in morning for conference. Lieut. FRASER R.A.M.C. evacuated to No. 20 C.C.S. suffering from myalgia. Yorkes for myalgia & neuritis force standings drawn from 1st R.M. & and Capt. PETRY R.A.M.C. detailed for duty with 48'''. Heavy Artillery Group to relieve Capt. WOOD. He subsequently returned to this unit as Capt. WOOD to remain with the Heavy Artillery. Captain GRAHAM proceeded to 4th Leinsters and Capt. ASKIN to 5th Lincolns to relieve Lieut. DOUGLAS & Capt. SINCLAIR who are to attend Anti-Gas School. At 10.30 p.m. D.A.D.M.S called.	
" 29 "	Visited A.D.M.S. in morning together with Capt. PERRY.	
" 30 "	Wire received from A.D.M.S at 8.15 p.m. saying an gas attack to be delivered on our front at 10.10 p.m. Capt. YATES with 1 N.C.O & 6 stretcher bearers with one extra motor ambulance proceed to BIENVILLERS. One N.C.O & one stretcher bearer took up position in trenches between 91 street & MONCHY Road in anticipation of casualties to gas poisoning. Only one casualty dealt with by them.	

Army Form C. 2118.

WAR DIARY
or
INTELLIGENCE SUMMARY.
(Erase heading not required.)

Instructions regarding War Diaries and Intelligence Summaries are contained in F.S. Regs., Part II. and the Staff Manual respectively. Title pages will be prepared in manuscript.

Hour, Date, Place	Summary of Events and Information	Remarks and references to Appendices
August 31st, 1916. COUTURELLE.	At 8.20 P.M. received message from A.D.M.S. warning of raid on enemy trenches at 11.30 P.M. Six extra stretcher bearers & another motor ambulance were despatched to BIENVILLIERS & Capt. GRAHAM was ordered to remain at A.D.S. until raid was over. Lieut. DOUGLAS returned to H.Q. Leicesters on conclusion of gas course.	A.C. Younin Meyer Lieut. Col. R.G. 2nd North Mid. Fd Amb. R.A.M.C.

46th 10...

Sep 1916

COMMITTEE FOR THE
MEDICAL HISTORY OF THE WAR
Date 26 OCT 1916

Army Form C. 2118

WAR DIARY
or
INTELLIGENCE SUMMARY
(Erase heading not required.)

1/2nd NORTH MIDLAND FIELD AMBULANCE R.A.M.T.F.
46th DIVISION
B.E.F.

MEDICAL

Vol 19

Instructions regarding War Diaries and Intelligence Summaries are contained in F.S. Regs., Part II. and the Staff Manual respectively. Title Pages will be prepared in manuscript.

Place	Date	Hour	Summary of Events and Information	Remarks and references to Appendices
COUTURELLE FRANCE	Sept 1. 1916.		Section of this Unit at Advanced Dressing Station at BIENVILLIERS returned to COUTURELLE, being relieved by the 3rd N. Mid. Field Ambulance.	
	Sept 2.		Sentence of 9 months imprisonment awarded on Aug. 11th by F.G.C.M. to 1864 Pte. GEE, of this Unit, quashed by Army Commander on ground of insanity. Capt. HANNAH RAMC (T.C.) reported for duty from 3rd N. Mid Field Ambulance.	
	Sept 3.		G.O.C. VIIth Corps inspected Hospital.	
	Sept 4.		A.D.M.S. Conference.	
	Sept 7.		D.D.M.S. VIIth Corps inspected Hospital.	
	Sept 11.		A.D.M.S. Conference. Scabies Hospital established at HUMBERCOURT, in charge of Capt YATES, of this Unit. Capt MANFIELD, with 2 N.C.O.s and 24 men, proceeded this evening to BIENVILLIERS, to deal with any casualties occurring to carrying party. No casualties. Capt HANNAH, RAMC, proceeded to 230th Bde. R.F.A, to relieve Capt. ARMITAGE, RAMC, detailed to attend Gas-course.	
	Sept 12.		Capt. PERRY, with 1 N.C.O and 24 men, proceeded this evening to BIENVILLIERS, to deal with casualties occurring to carrying party: no casualties.	
	Sept 14.		G.O.C. 46th Division inspected Hospital. Capt HANNAH, RAMC reported for duty from 230th Bde. R.F.A. Capt MANFIELD, with a party, proceeded to BERLES, in anticipation of operations developing there. Nothing having occurred, he returned here at midnight, leaving 1 N.C.O. and 20 men on duty with Capt YATES at Scabies Hospital.	
	Sept 15.		Capt. HANNAH detailed for duty with Capt YATES at Scabies Hospital. Capt MANFIELD, with a party, proceeded to BERLES, as yesterday. Returned at midnight, nothing having occurred.	

R.M. West
LIEUT. COL. COMDG.
1/2nd North Mid. Fd. Amb. R.A.M.C.

Army Form C. 2118

2nd NORTH MIDLAND FIELD AMBULANCE. R.A.M.C. T.F.
46th Division
B.E.F.

MEDICAL

WAR DIARY
or
INTELLIGENCE SUMMARY
(Erase heading not required.)

Instructions regarding War Diaries and Intelligence Summaries are contained in F.S. Regs., Part II. and the Staff Manual respectively. Title Pages will be prepared in manuscript.

Place	Date	Hour	Summary of Events and Information	Remarks and references to Appendices
COUTURELLE. FRANCE.	Sept 16 1916		In anticipation of arrival of wounded, 52 patients evacuated to No 3 M.A.C.	
	Sept 17		A.D.M.S. Conference. Capt MANFIELD, with party, proceeded to BERLES, returning L.A.M., nothing having occurred. Detailed Sergt KEOGH for duty at Divl Laundry.	
	Sept 19		D.M.S. 3rd Army inspected Seabies Hospital.	
MONDICOURT FRANCE	Sept 20		The Unit, less the Section on duty at the Seabies Hospital, proceeded by route march to new billets at MONDICOURT, where it took over billets and Hospital from 52nd Field Ambulance. The Hospital here will be run as a Divisional Rest Station, and will accommodate 200 patients. Accommodation consists of large Country House for Officers, Rest Stable and Hut. Marquees and Bell Tents for NCO's and men. The Huts require considerable alteration before cold weather sets in.	
	Sept 21		A.D.M.S. inspected Seabies Hospital	
	Sept 23		Capt HANNAH proceeds on leave. D.A.D.M.S. VIIth Corps inspected Hospital	
	Sept 25		A.D.M.S. Conference, 1 NCO and 20 men wheeled from BERLES, having been relieved by 1st N Mid Field Ambulance.	
	Sept 26		Lieut Col. WEST returned from sick leave, resumes command of the Unit. Established Laundry for patients clothing and Russian Vapour Bath in Hospital.	
	Sept 27		Reported arrival to A.D.M.S	
	Sept 28		Gas Alert.	
	Sept 29		Gas Alert ended.	
	Sept 30		G.O.C. inspected Hospital.	

A. M. WEST
LIEUT. COL. COMDG.
2nd North Mid Fd. Amb. R.A.M.O.

140/1/58

46th Div

2nd. A.M. Field Ambulance

Oct 1916

MEDICAL

Army Form C. 2118

WAR DIARY
or
INTELLIGENCE SUMMARY
(Erase heading not required.)

2nd North Midland Field Ambulance R.A.M.C.
46th Division BEF

Wt 20

Place	Date	Hour	Summary of Events and Information	Remarks and references to Appendices
MONDICOURT FRANCE	Oct. 1st 1916		Unit assuming Rest Station and Officers Hospital for 46th Division. Time put back 1 hour today. Reported to A.D.M.S.	
GOUY-EN-ARTOIS FRANCE	Oct 2nd		Unit marched from MONDICOURT to GOUY-EN-ARTOIS to take over new billets, handing over Divisional Rest Station at MONDICOURT to Field Ambulance of 4th Division; and relieving Field Ambulance of 17th Division at GOUY, where Jetenham Divisional Rest Station. Capt PERRY, R.A.M.C., of this Unit, detailed for duty with 2nd Lincoln Regiment, vice Lieut COETZEE proceeding on leave.	
"	Oct 3rd		Heavy rain all day. Reported to A.D.M.S. Lieut PIERY, R.A.M.C., reported for duty from Home Service.	
"	Oct 4th		Acting ADMS for ADMS (Lt. W. BEEVOR. C.B) (who proceeded on leave today), until return from leave of Lieut Col WRAITH of 1st N Midland.	
"	Oct 5th		Inspected Seabies Hospital at HUMBERCOURT. D.A.D.M.S. inspected camp at GOUY. — Gas-helmet Inspection and drill	
"	Oct 7th		Capt LUDOLF, R.A.M.C. reported for duty with the Unit from leave. Gas Helmet Inspection: One P.H. helmet withdrawn from each N.C.O and men, and replaced by a P.H.G. helmet. Inspection of camp by G.O.C. Gouy Transport Vehicle has been fitted with a 2 Gall. Petrol tin, for water for each Animal.	
"	Oct 9th		Conference at ADMS Headquarters. Gas-Helmet Inspection and drill	
"	Oct 10th		D.D.M.S. III Army, inspected camp. Divisional Sanitary Officer inspected camp. Major TURNER, R.A.M.C.T. proceeded on leave. Capt LUDOLF, R.A.M.C. detailed for duty with 2nd Lincoln Regiment, vice Capt PERRY, R.A.M.C.T. who is detailed to N Irish Horse. Inspection of Transport, by D.C. A.S.C.	
"	Oct 11th		Capt HANNAH, R.A.M.C. reported for duty from leave, and proceeded to Seabies Camp at HUMBERCOURT. Gas Helmet Inspection and drill.	

Army Form C. 2118

2nd North Midland Field Ambulance
R.A.M.C.T.
46th Division. B.E.F.

WAR DIARY
or
INTELLIGENCE SUMMARY
(Erase heading not required.)

Instructions regarding War Diaries and Intelligence Summaries are contained in F.S. Regs., Part II. and the Staff Manual respectively. Title Pages will be prepared in manuscript.

Place	Date	Hour	Summary of Events and Information	Remarks and references to Appendices
GOUY-EN-ARTOIS FRANCE	Oct 13th 1916		Inspected Scabies Camp at HUMBERCOURT. Sanitary Officer III Army inspected Scabies Camp at HUMBERCOURT.	
"	Oct 14th		Lieut. W. WRAITH, O.C. 1st N.M.F.A. having returned from leave, to be acting A.D.M.S. Proceeded with acting A.D.M.S. to LARBRET, to inspect Huts, with a view of removing them for use at Divisional Scabies Camp, but found them too dilapidated. Rest. Station case/full : Accommodation 130. Number of patients 170.	
"	Oct 16		A.D.M.S. Conference. Gas helmet inspection and drill.	
"	Oct 19th		Proceeded with acting A.D.M.S. to inspect Scabies Camp at HUMBERCOURT. Major TURNER, R.A.M.C.T. reported for duty from leave.	
"	Oct 21st		Lieut. PIERY, R.A.M.C.T.C. detailed for temporary duty with 6th North Stafford Battalion. Proceeded with acting A.D.M.S. to SOMBRIN and COUTURELLE, to prospect for building for Hospital in the event of this Unit moving to new billets. Gas alert.	
COUTURELLE FRANCE	Oct 22		Unit proceeded from GOUY to new billets at COUTURELLE.	
"	Oct 23		A.D.M.S. Conference. All Personnel of Unit anew inoculated with T.A.B. Gas Alert Off. Iodin : Gas alert.	
"	Oct 24		Capt. GRAHAM, R.A.M.C.T. with 1 N.C.O. and 8 men, detailed for duty at 43 C.C.S.	
"	Oct 25		D.D.M.S. III Army inspected Camp. Inspected Scabies Camp at HUMBERCOURT. Gas alert off.	
"	Oct 26		Gas helmet inspection and drill. In evening, Major TURNER, R.A.M.C.T. with 2 N.C.O's and 24 men, proceeded to BIENVILLERS, in anticipation of casualties to Gas cylinder carrying party. Returned 2 A.M. Oct. 27. — no casualties.	W. M. Wraith O/C 2nd N.M.F.A. O/C 2/1 N.M. F. Amb.

1875 Wt. W593/826 1,000,000 4/15 J.B.C. & A. A.D.S.S./Forms/C. 2118.

WAR DIARY
or
INTELLIGENCE SUMMARY

(Erase heading not required.)

Army Form C. 2118

2nd/West Midland Field Ambulance
R.A.M.C.
46th Division
B.E.F.

Place	Date	Hour	Summary of Events and Information	Remarks and references to Appendices
COUTURELLE FRANCE	Oct 28 1916		Orders received that, on moving from COUTURELLE to new area, all extra equipment is to be handed over to incoming field Ambulance. Wagon loads will conform to scale laid down in F.S. Regs. Lieut. PIRIE, R.A.M.C.T.C. reported for duty from 6th/North Stafford Battalion. The division will shortly move to new area. Field Ambulances will be attached to their respective Brigades.	
"	Oct 29 1916		Now arranged for a horsed Ambulance to follow 3 of the 4 Battalions on the march to pick up casualties; and for sick unable to march, to be collected each day by motor Ambulances, and carried to their new billets. One officer, with advance party, from 98th Field Ambulance (30th Division) reported to take over Camp and billets. Capt. HANFIELD, R.A.M.C., proceeded to GRENAS with advance party, to take over billets for this Unit, which arrives tomorrow.	
GRENAS FRANCE	Oct 30		Unit moved out from COUTURELLE, proceeding by route march to GRENAS, where billets were taken over. 27 patients were left at COUTURELLE, with the 98th Field Ambulance. Capt. FLAXMAN, R.A.M.C., reported for duty from leave. Capts. YATES, R.A.M.C. and Capt. HANNAH, R.A.M.C.T.C. with 34 men from the Scottish Hospital at HUNGERFORD, reported for duty with the Unit. A detachment from the 98th Field Ambulance, having taken over the Scottish Hospital, remained on all day.	
"	Oct 31		Capt. GRAHAM, R.A.M.C., with personnel from No 43 C.C.S., reported for duty, with the Unit. The Unit moves tomorrow to new billeting area at WAVANS.	

R. M. West
Lieut. Colonel R.A.M.C.
O/C 2nd/West Midland Field Ambulance
46 Division

140/1849

46th Div.

Nov. 1916

1/3rd N.M. Field Ambulance

COMMITTEE FOR THE
MEDICAL HISTORY OF THE WAR
Date -3 JAN. 1917

MEDICAL

WAR DIARY or INTELLIGENCE SUMMARY

(Erase heading not required.)

Army Form C. 2118

November 1916.
2nd North Midland Field Ambulance
R.A.M.C.
46th Division   B.E.F.

Place	Date	Hour	Summary of Events and Information	Remarks and references to Appendices
WAVANS. FRANCE	Nov. 1 1916		Unit marched from GRENAS to WAVANS (16 miles), on the way to Training Area for Division	
MAISON-PONTHIEU	Nov. 2 1916		Unit marched from WAVANS to MAISON-PONTHIEU (9 miles).	
LE PLESSIEL	Nov. 3 1916		Unit marched from MAISON-PONTHIEU to LE PLESSIEL (15 miles), arriving at Divisional Training Area. Established Hospital for 35 patients. During above march, detailed horsed ambulances to follow battalions to pick up men falling out on the march, and transported men unable to march from one billeting area to another.	
"	Nov. 6 1916		Training begins. A.D.M.S. weekly conference.	
"	Nov. 7 1916		A.D.M.S. inspected Hospital	
FROYELLES	Nov. 8 1916		Unit marched to new billets at FROYELLES (6 miles). Detailed Capts. YATES and HANNAH to open Hospital at DOMVAAST, 1½ mile from FROYELLES — for 80 patients.	
"	Nov. 9 1916		G.O.C. inspected arrangements at FROYELLES	
OUVILLE	Nov. 11 1916		Unit, less section at DOMVAAST, moved to new billets at OUVILLE (7 miles). Established hospital in empty farm, to accommodate 130 patients. G.O.C. inspected hospital at DOMVAAST.	
"	Nov. 12 1916		Training proceeding. Inspected Hospital at DOMVAAST.	
"	Nov. 13 1916		Evacuated Hospital at DOMVAAST, which was taken over by 3rd N.M.F.A., for a Scabies Hospital. Inspection of the 3 Field Ambulances, under command of A.D.M.S., by G.O.C.	
"	Nov. 14 1916		Capts. YATES and HANNAH, with personnel, reported for duty, from hospital at DOMVAAST.	
"	Nov. 15 1916		A.D.M.S. inspected hospital. Several cases of Diphtheria in Division.	

R.M. West
LIEUT. COL. COMDG.
2nd North Mid. Fd. Amb. R.A.M.C.

Army Form C. 2118

WAR DIARY
or
INTELLIGENCE SUMMARY

(Erase heading not required.)

2nd North Midland Field Ambulance
R.A.M.C.
46th Division
B.E.F.

November 1916

Instructions regarding War Diaries and Intelligence Summaries are contained in F. S. Regs., Part II. and the Staff Manual respectively. Title Pages will be prepared in manuscript.

Place	Date	Hour	Summary of Events and Information	Remarks and references to Appendices
OUVILLE FRANCE	Nov. 18 1916		Lecture to officers by ADMS at St RIQUIER. — 100% unit inoculated with T.A.B.	
"	Nov. 19 1916		In anticipation of a move from the training area, 18 patients transferred to HÉNU, by order of ADMS.	
"	Nov. 20 1916		Lecture at St RIQUIER by Col. WEBER, G.S.O.1, 30th Division. Attended, with Major TURNER, R.A.M.C.	
			Capt YATES detailed to attend GAS-SCHOOL at St POL.	
			Capt HANNAH detailed for permanent duty with 6th N. Staffs. Battalion, vice Capt V. GRAVES, evacuated sick.	
			Capt FLAXMAN detailed for temporary duty with 5th Lincoln Battalion.	
"	Nov. 21 1916		ADMS conference.	
			Transferred temporarily 70 cases from Hospital to 1st S. African General Hospital, ABBEVILLE, until arrival in new area.	
			New censor stamp issued - N° 2519. Old stamp destroyed.	
RIBAUDCOURT	Nov 22 1916		Unit proceeded with Division to march to new billeting area, marres factory to RIBAUDCOURT (17 miles). Small Hospital for 30 cases opened here. Arrangements for picking up men falling out used for transport of men unable to march to new area, similar to those made on the march down.	
VILLERS L'HOPITAL	Nov 23 1916		Unit marched with Division to billets at VILLERS L'HOPITAL (12 miles). Opened small Hospital on arrival. A.D.M.S. called to inspect arrangements. G.O.C. called to inspect arrangements.	
CAUMESNIL	Nov. 25 1916		Unit marched with Brigade to billets in new area at CAUMESNIL (France 1:40000 57D). B 29 A central). (12 miles). No accommodation in Village for Hospital, took over 12 Huts at HALLOY, ½ mile N of CAUMESNIL, capable of accommodating 230-250 patients. Detailed Capt. GRAHAM and Lieut. PIRIE for duty with Hospital.	
"	Nov. 27 1916		Undermentioned N.C.O.'s and men have been awarded the Military Medal, in this Unit :—	
			N° 2369 L. Cpl. C.H. WELLS.	
			2372 Cpl. D.G. ASHLIN.	
			049226 L. Cpl. A.E. BONIFACE. (A.S.C. M.T. attached)	
			2237 Pte. T.H. NEWBERRY	

LIEUT. COL. COMDG.
2nd North Mid. Fd. Amb. R.A.M.C.

Army Form C. 2118

1st November 1916

2nd North Midland Field Ambulance
NANET.
46 Division
B.E.F.

WAR DIARY
or
INTELLIGENCE SUMMARY
(Erase heading not required.)

Place	Date	Hour	Summary of Events and Information	Remarks and references to Appendices
AUMESNIL FRANCE	Nov 27 1916 (continued)		A.D.M.S. Conference at LUCHEUX. Capt MANFIELD, R.A.M.C. detailed for temporary duty with 5th Lincoln Battalion, vice Capt FLAXMAN R.A.M.C., who reports for duty with this Unit. The patients transferred temporarily to ABBEVILLE (No. 3 Stationary General Hospital) on Nov 21st returned to this Hospital today.	
"	Nov 28 1916		Capt YATES, R.A.M.C., reports for duty from Gas School at ST POL. G.O.C. inspected hospital at HALLOY. Box-Respirators issued to Unit.	
"	Nov 29 1916		G.O.C. 138th Infantry Brigade inspected Hospital at HALLOY.	
			Weather during month of November has on the whole been wet, and latterly cold, frost, foggy.	

J. Millet
LIEUT. COL. COMDG.
2nd North Mid. Fd. Amb. R.A.M.C.

War diary for
November 1916
of
2⁰ West Mntd F amb
RAMC T

140/1900

COMMITTEE FOR THE
MEDICAL HISTORY OF THE WAR

Date 31 JAN. 1917

Army Form C. 2118

WAR DIARY
or
INTELLIGENCE SUMMARY

(Erase heading not required.)

No 2 MEDICAL

War Diary for December 1916
of 1/2nd N.M.F. Amb. RAMC (T.F.)

[Stamp: 1/2nd N. MID. FIELD AMBULANCE]

WAR DIARY or INTELLIGENCE SUMMARY

Army Form C. 2118

Place	Date	Hour	Summary of Events and Information	Remarks and references to Appendices
CAUMESNIL	Dec 1st		Inspected hospital at HALLOY; 150 patients in hospital. Called on A.D.M.S. in morning to report.	
"	2nd		A.D.M.S. inspected hospital at HALLOY. Rode to GAUDIEMPRÉ in afternoon & inspected dressing station there, now being run by 3rd W. Riding F.A. Lieut. 29th CROSS proceeded to ST POL for lecture at School of Cookery, returning in evening. Box respirators tested in gas chamber; results satisfactory. Instructions received A.D.M.S. 'C' section to proceed to move to GAUDIEMPRÉ to relieve a section of the 13th W. Riding F. Amb., the remainder of the unit following on the 6th inst.	
"	3rd			
"	4th		Attended A.D.M.S. conference in morning. Major TURNER & Capt. FLAYMAN with C section proceeded by route march to GAUDIEMPRÉ to take over from 3rd W. Riding F. Amb.	
"	5th		All patients from HALLOY hospital evacuated to dressing station at GAUDIEMPRÉ & to dressing station of 142 M.M. F.Amb. near COUIN. All sick less patients sent to GAUDIEMPRÉ.	
GAUDIEMPRÉ			Lieut. W.C.C. EASTON R.A.M.C. (S.R.) from 21st Divn. F. Amb. reported for duty with the Unit moved to take over dressing station at GAUDIEMPRÉ. Leaving CAUMESNIL at 10 A.M. & arriving at GAUDIEMPRÉ at 12 noon. A.D.M.S. called & inspected dressing station.	
"	7th		Hospital to be run by B & C sections. By order of A.D.M.S. Lieut. PIRIE R.A.M.C. (S.R.) detailed for duty with the Sherwood Foresters.	
"	8th		A.D.M.S. called & inspected hospital. Corpl. MULLINS detailed for duty at Divisional Baths. BIENVILLIERS, & Pte. BUTLER to Brigade Baths at ST AMAND.	

Army Form C. 2118

WAR DIARY
or
INTELLIGENCE SUMMARY
(Erase heading not required.)

Instructions regarding War Diaries and Intelligence Summaries are contained in F.S. Regs., Part II. and the Staff Manual respectively. Title Pages will be prepared in manuscript.

Place	Date	Hour	Summary of Events and Information	Remarks and references to Appendices
GAUDIEMPRÉ	Dec. 9th	—	ADMS VIITH Corps & ADMS called.	
"	10th		GOC VIITH Corps inspected camp. Capt. MANFIELD reports for duty from 57th Inf. Bde. Several reported for duty with this unit.	
"	11th		Attended ADMS conference; arrangements to be made in anticipation of artillery battle in a day or two. Four huts at GAUDIEMPRÉ to be cleared & got ready for wounded. Fifty beavers to be ready & at the disposal of O.C. 3rd F.Amb. for any wounded who will do the collecting. An Myron & 3 suspects to be detailed to reconnoitre the best way across country from ST AMAND to BIENVILLIERS – HANNESCAMPS road. All foot sick cases to be sent to 1st F.M. & Amb.	
"	12th		GOC 46th Division inspected camp.	
"	13th		ADMS inspected arrangements for wounded. Capt. YATES proceeds on leave. Heavy artillery bombardment in afternoon. Twenty nine wounded, chiefly shell wounds admitted during night.	
"	14th		Capt. BARTON RAMC (T) & Capt. WORMOLD RAMC (TC) reported for duty.	
"	15th		Capt. BARTON RAMC (T) ordered to report to O.C. 3rd F.M. & Amb. for duty.	
"	16th		GOC VIITH Corps inspected dressing station; ADMS inspected dressing station.	
"	17th		Capt. WORMOLD RAMC (TC) ordered by ADMS to report to O.C. 1st F.M. & Amb. for duty.	
"	18th		Attended ADMS conference. Capt. FLAXMAN detailed for temporary duty at Corps hq at PAS. Lieut. PIRIE RAMC (TC) to be attached for permanent duty to 7th Seaforth Foresters. Seven cases of trench foot admitted to-day, chiefly from 4th Lincoln. 1st F.M. & Amb. are to take over treatment of sick cases; I want rank detailed for duty with 1st F.M.&A.	

Army Form C. 2118

WAR DIARY
or
INTELLIGENCE SUMMARY
(Erase heading not required.)

Instructions regarding War Diaries and Intelligence Summaries are contained in F. S. Regs., Part II. and the Staff Manual respectively. Title Pages will be prepared in manuscript.

Place	Date	Hour	Summary of Events and Information	Remarks and references to Appendices
GAUDIEMPRE	Dec. 19th 1916	—	GOC 46th Division inspected drawing station. Capt. FLAXMAN RAMC proceeded to PAS to take charge of Corps Laundry.	
"	20th	—	ADMS & Sanitary Officer 3rd Army inspected drawing station. All soldiers evacuated to 1st M. & Amb. with Flannelets, Malay mats, one day rations, & Harken Zenuk.	
"	21st	—	Instructed by ADMS to send G.S. waggon to SAULTY to draw elephant hut and transport same to VIENNA dump, FONQUEVILLIERS. Waggon returned in evening having failed to find VIENNA dump.	
"	23rd	—	Requested elephant hut to VIENNA dump, BIENVILLIERS. A party of 24 NCO's & men under Lieut. EASTON detailed to attend funeral of Major LLOYD JONES, RAMC M.S. 46th Div. who was killed by a shell yesterday.	
"	24th	—	Lieut. Col. R.M. WEST proceeded on leave. A second elephant hut drawn from SAULTY & conveyed to BIENVILLIERS, as the first hut was deficient. Deficient hut brought back to GAUDIEMPRÉ.	
"	25th	—	ADMS called. Lce Sergt. ASHLIN, Lce Corpl. WELLS, Lce Corpl. BONIFACE, & Pte NEWBERRY invested with Military Medal by G.O.C. 46th Div. Concert for patients & personnel in evening.	
"	26th	—	GOC VIIth Corps called & inspected hospital. Elephant hut returned to SAULTY.	
"	27th	—	Capt. T. GRAHAM RAMC detailed for temporary duty with 6 G.S. Staff. Lieut. EASTON with 30 NCO's & men proceed through Gas Chamber. Corpl. CLACK detailed for duty at Field Baths, BIENVILLIERS.	

Army Form C. 2118

WAR DIARY
or
INTELLIGENCE SUMMARY
(Erase heading not required.)

Instructions regarding War Diaries and Intelligence Summaries are contained in F.S. Regs., Part II. and the Staff Manual respectively. Title Pages will be prepared in manuscript.

Place	Date	Hour	Summary of Events and Information	Remarks and references to Appendices
GAUDIEMPRE	Dec. 27th	—	to relieve Capt. MULLINS who returns to unit. ADMS & Divl. San. Officer called.	
"	28th		ADMS VIIth Corps called & inspected camp. Capt. MULLINS detailed for duty with 1st. Monmouths; Pte. WILLBOND reported for duty with from 1st. Monmouths.	
"	29th.		GOC 46th Division called.	
"	30th.		Party of 10 NCO's & men passed through gas chamber	
"	31st.		Inspection of small box respirators.	

A C .... Major
LIEUT. COL. COMDG
2nd North Mid. Fd. Amb. R.A.M.C.

[Stamp: 1/2nd N. MID. FIELD AMBULANCE Date 1.1.17]

140/1941.

2nd M.M. Field Ambulance.

COMMITTEE FOR THE
ICAL HISTORY OF THE WAR
Date **13 MAR. 1917**

CONFIDENTIAL

MEDICAL
Army Form C. 2118

2nd NORTH MIDLAND FIELD AMBULANCE. R.A.M.C.
46th Div'sion. BEF France

Vol 23

WAR DIARY or INTELLIGENCE SUMMARY
(Erase heading not required.)

Instructions regarding War Diaries and Intelligence Summaries are contained in F.S. Regs., Part II and the Staff Manual respectively. Title Pages will be prepared in manuscript.

Place	Date	Hour	Summary of Events and Information	Remarks and references to Appendices
GAUDIEMPRE	Jan 1st 1917		ADMS Conference. — Lieut W.C. EASTON, R.A.M.C., attached for duty with 4th Leicester Battalion, vice Lieut H.T. DOUGLAS, R.A.M.C., evacuated sick. — Capt T.G. GRAHAM, R.A.M.C., reports for duty from 6th S. Stafford. Augt. D.A.Q.M.G., VIIIth Corps, inspected hospital.	
"	Jan 2		Capts. L.H. TERRY, R.A.M.C., M.H. PATERSON, R.A.M.C., and H.W.B. DANAHER, R.A.M.C., report for duty from base.	
"	Jan 3		Capt. L.H. TERRY, R.A.M.C., attached for temporary duty with 5th Leicesters.	
"	Jan 4		Lt Colonel R.M. WEST, returns from short leave.	
"	Jan 5		Capt PATERSON R.A.M.C., attached for duty with 2nd Lincolns, vice Capt LUDOLF, R.A.M.C., sick.	
"	Jan 6		Capt. MANFIELD, R.A.M.C., proceeds on short leave.	
"	Jan 7		Corps Commands. (VIIIth Corps), inspected dressing station.	
"	Jan 8		ADMS Conference.	
"	Jan 10		Lecture by ADMS at Divl School, on "Trench Discipline". — Capt DANAHER, R.A.M.C., proceeds to St POL, for course at 3rd Army Sanitary School.	
"	Jan 12		Following D.R.O. issued: "The Corps commander is much pleased with the effort which has been made by the Field Ambulance at GAUDIEMPRE to increase comfort, and improve conditions at GAUDIEMPRE." — The G.O.C. is much gratified to receive this report, and wishes it to be communicated to the Unit."	
"	Jan 14		G.O.C. Division inspected dressing station. — Capt DANAHER, R.A.M.C., reports for duty, from 3rd Army Sanitary School.	
"	Jan 15		ADMS Conference. — ADMS 55th Division inspected hospital station.	
"	Jan 16		Capt. Rev. BEECHER, C.F. (Wesleyan) reports for duty with this Unit — Capt DANAHER, R.A.M.C. detached for duty with A.S.C., vice Capt BROGDEN, R.A.M.C., sick.	
"	Jan 17		Capt. TERRY, R.A.M.C., reports for duty, from 5th Leicesters.	

Army Form C. 2118

2nd North Midland Field Ambulance
BAMCT
46th Division BEF France

WAR DIARY
or
INTELLIGENCE SUMMARY
(Erase heading not required.)

Instructions regarding War Diaries and Intelligence Summaries are contained in F.S. Regs., Part II and the Staff Manual respectively. Title Pages will be prepared in manuscript.

Place	Date	Hour	Summary of Events and Information	Remarks and references to Appendices
GAUDIEMPRÉ	Jan 19 1917		Capt. DANAHER, RAMCT.C., from Emergency duets with A.S.C., reports for duty.	
"	Jan 20		Headquarters VIIth Corps removed to FOSSEUX. Headquarters XVIIIth Corps established at PAS. This Unit transferred to XVIIIth Corps.	
"			DDMS XVIIIth Corps inspected dressing station.	
"	Jan 22		Capt. HANFIELD, RAMCT, reports for duty from 40th Division	
"			Capt. DANAHER, RAMCT.C., detailed for duty with 5th N Staffords Battalion.	
"	Jan 22		ADMS Conference. - Established Medical Inspection Post at S'AMAND, for troops of 138th Infantry Brigade Depot	
"	Jan 23		Very cold - 15° Fahr. - DDMS XVIIIth Corps inspected dressing station.	
"	Jan 24		Capt. TERRY, RAMCT.C., proceeds to S'ARMY Sanitary School at S'POL, for course of Sanitation	
"	Jan 27		Capt. TERRY, RAMCTC., from 3rd Division School of Instruction, reports for duty.	
"	Jan 29		ADMS Conference.	
"	Jan 31		Very Cold - 18° front.	

R.M. West
Lieut-Colonel RAMCT
O/C 2nd NMFA
BEF

140/1994

46 Divn.

2nd/1st N.M. Field Ambulance.

Feb. 1917

COMMITTEE FOR THE
MEDICAL HISTORY OF THE WAR
Date 4 - APR 1917

WAR DIARY or **INTELLIGENCE SUMMARY** 1/2nd N. Mid. F. Amb. RAMC (T.F.)

Army Form C. 2118

MEDICAL

Vol 24

Place	Date	Hour	Summary of Events and Information	Remarks and references to Appendices
GAUDIEMPRÉ	Feb. 1st	1917.	Twenty R.C.O's & men of B section proceeded to A.D.S at BIENVILLIERS under Capt. YATES. Twenty R.C.O's & men of C section proceeded to A.D.S. at FONQUEVILLIERS under Capt. MANFIELD	
"	2nd.		Remainder of B section proceeded to BIENVILLIERS under Capt. GRAHAM. Remainder of C section proceeded to FONQUEVILLIERS under Major TURNER	
ST AMAND	3rd.		Headquarters of unit moved to new billets at ST AMAND. Lt. Colonel R.M.WEST remained at GAUDIEMPRÉ as he was too ill to be moved.	
"	4 "		Lt. Colonel R.M. WEST evacuated to 20 C.C.S suffering from bronchitis. Major TURNER assumed temporary command of unit. Capt. TERRY RAMC (T.C) left for England, his contract having expired.	
"	5 "		Capt. DANAHER RAMC (T.C) reported for duty with this unit from 5 N. S. Staffs Reg.	
"	6 "		Visited A.D.S at BIENVILLIERS.	
"	7 "		Order received from A.D.M.S. to send 4 stretchers to each battalion of 135 Brigade	
"	9 "		Major TURNER ordered by A.D.M.S to return to ST AMAND. Capt. DANAHER proceeded to A.D.S. FONQUEVILLIERS to replace him. Capt. YATES RAMC (T.F) reported sick with myalgia.	
"	10 "		Motor ambulance sent to convey Lt. Colonel R.M. WEST from LUCHEUX to AMIENS en route for CAP. MARTIN. Visited A.D.S at BIENVILLIERS.	
"	12 "		Attended A.D.M.S's conference. Capt. DANAHER RAMC (T.F) left for England. His contract having expired. Visited A.D.S at BIENVILLIERS & went round bearer posts. Capt. FOSTER RAMC (T.F) from 466 D. de L. laundry reported for duty with this unit & proceeded to A.D.S. FONQUEVILLIERS.	
"	13 "		Visited A.D.S at FONQUEVILLIERS. Capt. YATES RAMC (T.F) reported fit for duty. No. M2/048759 Pte. A. FULLER A.S.C (M.T) attached to 1/2 N. M. F. Amb. admitted to hospital suffering from burns of left hand (accidental, self inflicted)	

WAR DIARY
or
INTELLIGENCE SUMMARY

Army Form C. 2118

Place	Date	Hour	Summary of Events and Information	Remarks and references to Appendices
ST AMAND	Feb 15th 1917		Visited ADS at BIENVILLIERS. Two THOMAS's splints sent to each Regt. Aid Post by order of ADMS	
	17th		About 1 A.M. working parties of Sherwoods & of 2/11th London Regt were shelled with gas shells in FONQUEVILLIERS near SNIPERS SQUARE. Their way back from the front line trenches. Five cases of shell gas poisoning were treated at ADS FONQUEVILLIERS about 2 A.M. At 8.30 A.M. more cases began to arrive until twenty in all had been brought in. On 9.30 A.M. a message was received at ADS FONQUEVILLIERS asking for an M.O. to go to CHATEAU LA HAIE to see a sergeant who was not feeling well. On arriving there at 10.20 A.M. Capt. FOSTER RAMC (T.F) found three men dying from the effects of the gas, & fifty three more or less seriously gassed. The chief symptoms noted were cyanosis in some patients but not at all. There being marked pallor in the worst cases. Pulse feeble & rapid cough present in most cases. The patients after a time began to cough up small amounts of frothy tenacious mucus. Many of the patients complained of pain in the stomach. Treatment. Oxygen administered for ten minutes at a time through a nitrous oxide inhaler gave distinct relief. Ammonium Carbonate ampoules proved useless. Hypodermic injections of strychnine gr 1/30 & administration of hot drinks containing brandy caused considerable improvement in the Pulse. Blankets, hot bottles, & hot kitchen were applied, & all cases evacuated as speedily as possible to 20 C.C.S. The evacuation was accomplished without difficulty as the day was fifty 4 motor ambulances were able to proceed right up to FONQUEVILLIERS & CHATEAU LA HAIE. In all, nine men died from the effects of the gas & eighty one were evacuated to 20 CCS. The nine bodies were also sent to 28 CCS for post mortem examination.	

WAR DIARY or INTELLIGENCE SUMMARY

Army Form C. 2118

(Erase heading not required.)

Instructions regarding War Diaries and Intelligence Summaries are contained in F.S. Regs., Part II. and the Staff Manual respectively. Title Pages will be prepared in manuscript.

Place	Date	Hour	Summary of Events and Information	Remarks and references to Appendices
ST AMAND	Feb. 17th	(continued)	The delayed effect of the gas was well shown by the cases which occurred at CHATEAU LA HAIE; many of these men had attended the ordinary parade in the morning & did not complain of feeling ill till afterwards. All these men had had a march of about two miles after being gassed. Both Captains MANFIELD & FOSTER describe the odour of the gas as resembling that of hydrochloric acid. Visited CHATEAU LA HAIE & Adv Dressing Stations at FONQUEVILLERS & at BIENVILLERS. No casualties from gas poisoning at the last place.	
"	18th		Seven more cases of gas poisoning treated at A.D.S. FONQUEVILLERS. Two Limbers sent to 1st. M. & Amb.	
"	19th		Attended A.D.M.S. conference. One G.S. waggon sent to 1st. M. & Amb. as Flanders waggon. Capt. FLAXMAN R.A.M.C. reported for duty from PREVENT & was detailed to A.D.S. FONQUEVILLERS to replace Capt. FOSTER who returned to R.E.s. Capt. V.E. Lloyd R.A.M.C. (T.C) reported for duty from there. Four cases of delayed shell gas poisoning treated at A.D.S. FONQUEVILLERS.	
"	20th		Headquarters of 46th Division move to new area this morning. Two units coming under command of A.D.M.S. 58th Division. Visited Adv Dressing Stations & known posts G.S. waggon & limbers return from 1st. M. M. & Amb.	
"	21st		Two cases of shell gas poisoning treated at A.D.S. BIENVILLERS.	
"	22nd		A.D.M.S. 58th Division called. Four cases of shell gas poisoning treated at A.D.S.	
"	23rd 24th		BIENVILLERS. Visited Adv Dressing Stations & known posts. Lieut G.H. CORBETT R.A.M.C. (T.C) reported for duty from base. Visited A.D.S. FONQUEVILLERS.	

Army Form C. 2118

WAR DIARY
or
INTELLIGENCE SUMMARY

(Erase heading not required.)

Instructions regarding War Diaries and Intelligence Summaries are contained in F.S. Regs., Part II. and the Staff Manual respectively. Title Pages will be prepared in manuscript.

Place	Date	Hour	Summary of Events and Information	Remarks and references to Appendices
ST AMAND	Feb. 26th		Capt. FLAXMAN R.A.M.C. with 1 N.C.O. & 10 men proceeded to 46th Divnl. Laundry at HUMBERCOURT. No. M2/048759 Pte. A. FULLER A.S.C.(MT) attached to 1/2nd. N.M.Fd.Amb. tried by F.G.C.M. ft. conduct to the prejudice of good order & military discipline in that he on 13.2.17 did negligently burn some of the bands. (vide A.D.S., BIENVILLIERS.	
"	27th		Proceeded to A.D.S., FONQUEVILLIERS with ten stretcher bearers, all available stretcher stations (four), & extra dressings, medical comforts, & stretchers. Called on O.C. 4th. Leicester Regt. to discuss medical arrangements with him, in view of proposed heavy casualties. Two N.C.O's & twenty stretcher bearers lent to 4th. Leicester Regt.	
FONQUE-VILLIERS	28th		At 4.30 A.M. two companies of 4th. Leicester Regt. advanced & occupied GOMMECOURT without any casualties. Called on A.D.M.S. 58th Division. By his orders Headquarters of this unit were moved to FONQUEVILLIERS. Heavy shelling of FONQUEVILLIERS & GOMMECOURT during afternoon & evening. No. M2/048759 Pte. A.FULLER A.S.C.(MT) attached to 1/2nd. N.M.Fd.Amb. sentenced by F.G.C.M. to 42 days F.P. no. 2. Sentence promulgated on parade.	

A.C. Turner Meyer
LIEUT. COL. CO. R.A.M.C.
1/2nd. North Mid. Fd. Amb. R.A.M.C.

[Stamp: 1/2nd N. MID. FIELD AMBULANCE No. Date]

1875 Wt. W593/826 1,000,000 4/15 J.B.C. & A. A.D.S.S./Forms/C. 2118.

COMMITTEE FOR THE
MEDICAL HISTORY OF THE WAR
Date   11 MAY 1917

To A.D.M.S., 46th Division

Herewith War Diary of
1/2nd. N. Mid. F. Amb. for
March 1917.

A.C. Turner Major

1.4.17.
~~LIEUT.COL.~~ COMDG.
2nd North Mid. Fd. Amb. R.A.M.C.

WAR DIARY
or
INTELLIGENCE SUMMARY
(Erase heading not required.)

Army Form C. 2118

Instructions regarding War Diaries and Intelligence Summaries are contained in F.S. Regs., Part II. and the Staff Manual respectively. Title Pages will be prepared in manuscript.

1/2nd N. MID. FIELD AMBULANCE
No. ....
Date 1.4.17

MEDICAL
Vol 25

Place	Date	Hour	Summary of Events and Information	Remarks and references to Appendices
FONQUE-VILLIERS	March 1st	—	Hdqrs. 46th Division returned.	All map references are to Sheet 57 D (1/40,000)
"	2nd		Visited GOMMECOURT. Tested sample of water from well in GOMMECOURT. Lieut. & 2nd P.T. CROSS proceeds on leave.	
"	4th		5th, 6th & 8th Sherwood Forester advancing beyond GOMMECOURT. Visited R.M.O.'s three battalions to arrange evacuation of wounded. Advanced bearer post established in GOMMECOURT at E.28.c.6.4.	
"	5th		Bearer post established in dug-outs on ESSARTS ROAD at E.29.a.6.0	
"	6th		Bearer post established at K.6.d.8.8. Sergt. PERRY with 9 men returned from 46th Divl. Laundry.	
"	7th		Many cases of shell gas poisoning treated at A.D.S. BIENVILLIERS. two men of this unit evacuated to 20 C.C.S. suffering from shell gas poisoning :— 2370 Pte. ALLEN H. & 2367 Pte. TAILBY E. Two divisions transferred to V P.R. Corps.	
"	8th		One R.C.O. & 10 stretcher bearers from 1st F.M. & Amb. reported for temporary duty at A.D.S. BIENVILLIERS.	
"	10th		The undermentioned casualties to men of this unit occurred at BIENVILLIERS :— 2721 Sergt. ATKINS J. GSW Shoulder L. } Both remain at duty. 2309 Pte. BURRELL G. GSW Head.	
"	11th		A.D.S. at FONQUEVILLIERS heavily shelled from 2.30 P.M. to 4 P.M. Large dug-out for personnel struck by H.E. shell. The central portion being blown in & the undermentioned men buried in the débris :— 40678 Pte. KALLAWAY A.F. 2282 Pte. VEASEY A. They were evacuated to 3rd N. M. F. Amb. suffering	

WAR DIARY
or
INTELLIGENCE SUMMARY

(Erase heading not required.)

Army Form C. 2118

Place	Date	Hour	Summary of Events and Information	Remarks and references to Appendices
FONQUE-VILLIERS	March 11th.		from wounds of head & shell shock. Heavy shelling of GOMMECOURT Road during evening caused the following casualties to men of this unit who were bringing down wounded:- 2399 Pte. HICKLING J. S.W. Head & arm L. Shell gas poisoning 2392 Pte. FLETCHER A.P. S.W. Face 2460 Pte. POTTER E.S. Shell gas poisoning 2698 Pte. SHARPE C. Shell gas poisoning 2231 L/Cpl. STORER S. Shell gas poisoning	
"	12th.		Visited A.D.S. for conference on impending operations. Beaver post established at K.12.b.4.6.	
"	13th.		Seventy Bearers from 3rd. H.M. F. Amb. & thirty from 1st. H.M. F. Amb reported for temporary duty with this unit. B section was withdrawn from BIENVILLIERS & FONQUEVILLIERS, the A.D.S. at BIENVILLIERS being handed over to a field amb. of 58th Division. A.D.S. at FONQUEVILLIERS struck & slightly damaged by a shell about 8.30 P.M. At 11. P.M. a Beaver post of 24 men under Capt. GRAHAM was established in trench at E.29.b.10.3. in anticipation of heavy casualties.	
"	14th.		At 1 A.M. two Battalions of 137th Bgde. attacked enemy positions West of BUCQUOY. At 4.30 A.M. I was informed that casualties of Staffords on left sector were trifling, whilst those of Staffords on right were severe. Fifty extra bearers were despatched to BIEZ WOOD under Capt. GRAHAM & the work of clearing the wounded was completed shortly after mid-day. The carry was a long one (5,000 yards) over very bad ground the roads being thigh deep in mud & water. Seventy five stretcher cases were dealt with at A.D.S. FONQUEVILLIERS during day; walking cases were directed to a temporary A.D.S. on the SOUASTRE-FONQUEVILLIERS road, staffed by 3rd. H.M. F. Amb. No. 2339 Pte. G. BALL of this unit was killed by a shell at RETTEMOY FARM.	
"	15th.		Lieut. & 2/Lt. CROSS reported for duty from leave. Capt. S.C.R. FLAXMAN RAMC reported for duty from laundry.	

Army Form C. 2118

WAR DIARY
or
INTELLIGENCE SUMMARY
(Erase heading not required.)

Instructions regarding War Diaries and Intelligence Summaries are contained in F.S. Regs., Part II. and the Staff Manual respectively. Title Pages will be prepared in manuscript.

Place	Date	Hour	Summary of Events and Information	Remarks and references to Appendices
FONQUE-VILLIERS	March 16th		Lieut. G.H. CORBETT RAMC (T.C) detailed for temporary duty with 4th Leicester Regt. Sentence of 42 days F.P. no 2 passed on M2/048759 Pte A. FULLER by FGCM on 28.2.17 reduced to 14 days F.P. no 2 by order of G.O.C. XVIII Corps.	
	17th		Our bearer post established in former enemy ADS at ESSARTS at F.19.C.4.6.	
	18th		Enemy retreating rapidly. In company with ADMS visited ESSARTS & BUCQUOY. The ADS at ESSARTS is a large dug-out capable of accommodating thirty stretchers. One M.O. with fifty stretcher bearers detailed to occupy it. Bearer posts at TRETTEMOY FARM, ROSSIGNOL WOOD, & at W.S.d.8.8 given up, & bearers withdrawn from them. Transport & stores with all remaining personnel of the unit moved to FONQUEVILLIERS.	
	19th		Bearer posts established at QUESNOY FARM (F.14.a.3.6) & at DOUCHY.	
VAUCHELLES	20th		Unit left FONQUEVILLIERS at 10.45 A.M. & proceeded to VAUCHELLES arriving at 3.15 P.M. Took over VR Corps Rest Station from 21st F. Amb.	
	22nd		Capt. R.B.M. YATES RAMC (T.F) evacuated to 47 CCS suffering from Bronchitis.	
	23rd		Party from 35th F. Amb. arrived to take over Rest Station.	
SEPTONVILLE	24th		Rest Camp handed over to 35th F. Amb. Unit left VAUCHELLES at 11.30 A.M. & proceeded by route march to SEPTONVILLE, arriving 5.30 P.M. Roads very bad.	
PETIT CAGNY	26th		Unit left SEPTONVILLE at noon & marched to VILLERS BOCAGE where it was conveyed by motor buses to DURY. From DURY proceeded to new billets at PETIT CAGNY arriving at 4.30 P.M. Transport left SEPTONVILLE at 2 P.M. & proceeded independently to PETIT CAGNY via AMIENS arriving at 7.30 P.M.	
VERS	27th		At 1 P.M. received orders to entrain immediately. Unit left PETIT CAGNY at 1.55 P.M. & proceeded to SALEUX where final orders were received not to entrain but to proceed to VERS. Arrived at VERS at 3.30 P.M.	

Army Form C. 2118

WAR DIARY
or
INTELLIGENCE SUMMARY
(Erase heading not required.)

Instructions regarding War Diaries and Intelligence Summaries are contained in F. S. Regs., Part II. and the Staff Manual respectively. Title Pages will be prepared in manuscript.

Place	Date	Hour	Summary of Events and Information	Remarks and references to Appendices
IN THE TRAIN	March 28th	—	Unit left VERS at 1.30 P.M. & proceeded to SALEUX where it entrained. Train departed at 5.25 P.M.	
LIVOSSART.	29th		Train arrived at LILLERS at 4 P.M. Unit detrained & at 5.50 P.M. proceeded by route march to LIVOSSART (12 miles) arriving at 11 P.M.	
"	30th		Hospital arranged in empty farm house. Accommodation 50.	
"	31st			

A. C. Turner, Major
COMDG. 2nd North Mid. Fd. Amb. R.A.M.C.

140/2326

12nd North Midland F.A.

COMMITTEE FOR THE
MEDICAL HISTORY OF THE WAR
Date - 6 JUN. 1917

WAR DIARY or INTELLIGENCE SUMMARY

Army Form C. 2118

1/2nd North Midland Field Ambulance R.A.M.C.T.F. 46th Division B.E.F. FRANCE

Vol 26

Place	Date	Hour	Summary of Events and Information	Remarks and references to Appendices
LIVOSSART FRANCE	April 1 1917		Capt. HANFIELD, M.C. goes on short leave to England. — Division in Rest. — Unit running small Divisional Hospital in a barn.	
"	April 2		Capt. V. E. LLOYD. RAMC. detailed for temporary duty with 46th Div. Train	
"	April 3		Lieut. G. H. CORBETT. RAMC.T.C., reported for duty from 4th Leicester Regiment. — Heavy snowfall.	
"	April 4		Capt. FLAXMAN, RAMC T.C., with 11 O.R. sent to 23 C.C.S. for temporary duty. — ADMS called. — 36 cases of Scabies sent to Divisional Scabies Hospital, near NORRENT-FONTES *	* France 40000 36 A O. 31. Central
"	April 5		Lieut. Col. R. M. WEST, RAMC T., reports for duty from sick leave at Cap MARTIN, and resumes command of Unit.	
"	April 7		Attended ADMS conference.	
"	April 8		DDMS. 11 Corps orders 3 motor Ambulances from each Field Ambulance in the Division, to be stationed at ST HILAIRE, for supplementary service to C.C.S. if needed. Attended ADMS conference. Inspected billets, Misies cottages at AUCHY, (to be used if necessary) for overflow from C.C.S. Estimated accommodation 500.	
"	April 9		Snow and hail. Divisional route march, and inspection by Corps Commander. Orders received for Unit to be prepared to move at short notice, and travel light. New organisation of Motor section for use in case of advance over ground impassable for wagons. Consisting of 2 Officers, 36 bearers, and 4 mules with improvised pack saddles, each pair of mules carrying 1 and 2 F.M. Panniers. 2 boxes filled with Bully-beef and biscuits, a primus stove, tin of paraffin, 4 tins of water, and blankets. Attended tactical scheme of E.O.E. at ESTREES BLANCHE. Very cold. Some snow.	* France 40000 36 A. P. 27 A 87
"	April 10			
"	April 11		Box dispensers inspection. Sergt POWELL, of this Unit, proceeds to England to take up a Commission.	
"	April 12		Snow, snow, with deep drifts.	
BUSNES FRANCE	April 13		Unit proceeded to BUSNES. To take over Scabies Hospital from 1/3 N.M.F.A. RAMC. Reported arrival to ADMS. *	
"	April 15		Division in reserve into the line E and S of BETHUNE. Transported sick of Units unable to march to new area. New Unit's glands sent. — Capt T. GRAHAM, RAMC, awarded medallion, from S of E, for good work in February advance at GOMMECOURT. 11 N.C.Os and men sent to 23 C.C.S. on April 4. (All T.F. men) relieved to Unit, being replaced by a similar number of New Army men.	R. M. West, Lieut Colonel, RAMC, O/C 2nd NMFA

1875 Wt. W593/826 1,000,000 4/15 J.B.C. & A. A.D.S.S./Forms/C. 2118.

WAR DIARY or INTELLIGENCE SUMMARY

Army Form C. 2118

1/2 North Midland Field Ambulance BEF France
46 Division BEF France

Place	Date	Hour	Summary of Events and Information	Remarks and references to Appendices
BUSNES FRANCE	April 16 1917		A.D.M.S. Conference.— 3 Motor ambulances stationed at St HILAIRE (April 13th). What hrs for duty with Unit.	
"	April 17		A.D.M.S. Headquarters moved to LA BEUVRIERE.	
"	April 19		Lieut DOWLING, R.A.M.C., reports for duty with unit, from England. Orders from ADMS: The Unit to proceed on 20th to LA BEUVRIERE, to take over A Section, 1 Corps Rest Station. One Section to proceed to Advanced Dressing Station at BULLY-GRENAY* (4 miles W. of LENS) to relieve Field Ambulance 24th Division. Capt MANFIELD, M.C., with B Section for her duty. Proceeded to BULLY-GRENAY, to inspect Advanced Dressing Station. Capt MANFIELD takes over ADS transfer.	*France Sheet 36B R.W.P. 27.
"	April 20		Unit proceeded A Section under command of Major TURNER, R.A.M.C., proceeded to LA BEUVRIERE. To take over Corps Rest Station from 72nd Field Ambulance.	
LA BEUVRIERE FRANCE	April 22		Remainder of Unit, with Headquarters, under command of Lt.Col. WEST, R.A.M.C., proceeded to 1 Corps Rest Station *LA BEUVRIERE. By order of ADMS, sent all available bearers to Advanced Dressing Station at BULLY-GRENAY. Division now in 1 Corps 1 Army.	*France Sheet 36B R.W.P. 2:B:67
"	April 23		DDMS 1 Corps inspected Rest Station. This is an Monastery, and with 3 large Huts will accommodate 300 patients — on an emergency, 700. Patients are employed at work on Rest Station: all available ground to be planted with vegetables. Assistance to be given to civilian inhabitants in ploughing, etc.; bi-weekly entertainment of patients by Divisional troops, etc.	
"	April 24		Inspected Advanced Dressing Station, and reported to ADMS, wire headquarters have been moved from NOEUX-LES-MINES to Tom 10*, near BULLY-GRENAY, on account of NOEUX being heavily shelled. Detailed Lieut DOWLING for duty with Capt. MANFIELD, M.C. at Advanced Dressing Station. Last night, 14-5"-42 shells over Rest Station, exploded in yard at back	*K 16 B 2.6 *R 2:B:3:2:6
"	April 25		G.O.C. Division inspected Rest Station. — 720 patients in Rest Station.	
"	April 26		Reported to DDMS at Corps Headquarters, LA BUSSIÈRE.* Capt MANFIELD, M.C. detailed for duty with the Divisional Vice Lieut CORBETT, R.A.M.C., evacuated sick.	
"	April 27		Detailed Capt GRAHAM, M.C. to proceed to Advanced Dressing Station, vice Capt MANFIELD, M.C. with V. G. Division. Lieut DOWLING, and one blanket, with Same.	
"	April 28		Reported to DDMS at Corps Headquarters	

W. Wyllie
Lieut Colonel R.A.M.C.
O/C 2/1 N.M.F.A.

WAR DIARY 1/2ⁿᵈ NORTH MIDLAND FIELD AMBULANCE Army Form C. 2118
or
INTELLIGENCE SUMMARY 46ᵗʰ Division BEF France

(Erase heading not required.)

Instructions regarding War Diaries and Intelligence Summaries are contained in F.S. Regs., Part II and the Staff Manual respectively. Title Pages will be prepared in manuscript.

Place	Date	Hour	Summary of Events and Information	Remarks and references to Appendices
LA BEUVRIÈRE FRANCE	April 29 1917		Major A.C. TURNER, R.A.M.C., of this Unit, awarded D.S.O. for good work and gallant conduct in taking of BUCQUOY, in March. G.O.C. Division presented ribbon at ceremonial parade at Rest Station.	
	April 30		ADMS and AMC Corps inspected Rest Station. — ADMS inspected Rest Station. A.D.M.S. conference. Inspected Advanced dressing Station, and RAMC posts* at PONT DE GRENAY and CITE MAROT, near LIEVIN. District constantly under heavy shell fire: a large mining district, bath knocked about.	* F. form 20000 36C. M.I.D.B.2. † F. form 20000 36C. M.3. A, B, and C.
			Remarks: A. The Corps, consisting of VI ᵗʰ and 46ᵗʰ Divisions is now holding the line from LOOS, South to S.E. of LENS.	
			B. The shortage of Medical Officers is causing some inconvenience: This Field Ambulance at present has 4: Lieut. Col WEST and Major TURNER, DSO at the Corps Rest Station; and Capt GRAHAM, M.C. and Lieut DOWLING at the Advanced Dressing Station. Their shortage involves very strenuous work, and, in the case of an advance, with many casualties, might prove serious.	
			C. Strength of Unit at beginning of month: R.A.M.C. 176 H.T. 46 M.T. 12 TOTAL 234 " " End " : 174 43 13 230.	

NWWest
Lieut Colonel RAMCT
O/C 2ⁿᵈ NMFA

B.E.F.

SUMMARY OF MEDICAL WAR DIARIES FOR 1/2nd N. Mid. F.A. 46th Divn. 2nd Corps.
1st Corps 22/4/17.
1st Army.
WESTERN FRONT April-May. '17.

O.C. Lt. Col. R.M. West.

SUMMARISED UNDER THE FOLLOWING HEADINGS.

Phase "B" Battle of Arras April- May. '17.

1st Period Attack on Vimy Ridge April.

2nd Period Capture of Siegfried Line May.

B.E.F.

1/2nd N. Mid. F.A. 46th Divn. 2nd Corps. WESTERN FRONT.

O.C. Lt. Col. R.M. West. April. '17.

1st Army.

1st Corps from 22/4/17.

Phase "B" Battle of Arras April.- May. '17.
1st Period Attack on Vimy Ridge April.

1917.	Headquarters. At Livossart.
April 1st.	Division in Rest.
4th.	Moves Detachment: 1 and 11 to No. 23 C.C.S. returned on 15th and replaced by new army men.
	Scabies. 36 cases of Scabies were sent to Divisional Scabies Hospital near Norrent Fontes- Map 36s O.31.central.
8th.	Transport. 3 motor ambulances stationed at St. Hilaire-
	Accommodation. Empty Miners' Cottages at Auchy for overflow from C.C.S. accommodated 500:-
13th.	Moves: To Busnes- P.27.A.8.7..
	Moves Detachment: "A" Section proceeded to Norrent Fontes and took over Scabies Hospital from 1/3rd N. Mid. F.A.
15th.	Decoration. Capt. T. Graham awarded M.C. for good work in Feb. advance at Gommecourt.
22nd.	Moves: To La Beuvriere- D.17.a.4.4..
	Transfer. Division now in 1st Corps.

B.E.F.

1/2nd N. Mid. F.A. 46th Divn. 1st Corps.   WESTERN FRONT.
   O.C. Lt. Col. R.M. West.   April. '17.
   1st Army.

Phase "B" Battle of Arras April- May. '17.
1st Period Attack on Vimy Ridge April.

1917.

April. 22nd.   Transfer. Division now in 1st Corps.

Location Field Ambulances. 1st Corps Rest Station- in a monastery and with 3 large huts accommodated 300- or on emergency 700-

A.D.S. at Bully Grenay- R.11.a.7.7.

24th.   Operations Enemy. During night 23rd/24th 14-5.4 shells exploded in field at back of Rest Station.

29th.   Decoration. Major A.C. Turner- awarded D.S.O. for good work and gallant conduct in taking of Bucquoy in March-

30th.   Operations Enemy. Pont De Grenay- M.1.d.8.2. and Cité Maroc-M.3.a.b.c.

This district was constantly under shell fire. A large mining district- badly knocked about.

The 1st Corps consisting of 6th and 46th Divisions held the line from Loos- S. to. S.E. of Lens.

b,e,f

B.E.F.

1/2nd N. Mid. F.A. 46th Divn. 2nd Corps. WESTERN FRONT.
O.C. Lt. Col. R.H. West. April. '17.
1st Army. 1.
1st Corps from 22/4/17.

Phase "B" Battle of Arras April.- May. '17.
1st Period Attack on Vimy Ridge April.

1917.	Headquarters. At Livossart.
April 1st.	Division in Rest.
4th.	Moves Detachment: 1 and 11 to No. 23 C.C.S. returned on 15th and replaced by new army men.
	Scabies. 36 cases of Scabies were sent to Divisional Scabies Hospital near Norrent Fontes- Map 36s O.31.central
8th.	Transport. 3 motor ambulances stationed at St. Hilaire-
	Accommodation. Empty Miners' Cottages at Auchy for overflow from C.C.S. accommodated 500:-
13th.	Moves: To Busnes- P.27.A.8.7..
	Moves Detachment: "A" Section proceeded to Norrent Fontes and took over Scabies Hospital from 1/3rd N. Mid. F.A.
15th.	Decoration. Capt. T. Graham awarded M.C. for good work in Feb. advance at Gommecourt.
22nd.	Moves: To La Beuvriere- D.17.a.4.4..
	Transfer. Division now in 1st Corps.

B.E.F.

1/2nd N. Mid. F.A. 46th Divn. 1st Corps.   WESTERN FRONT.
O.C. Lt. Col. R.M. West.   April. '17.
1st Army.

Phase "B" Battle of Arras April- May. '17.
1st Period Attack on Vimy Ridge April.

1917.	
April. 22nd.	**Transfer.** Division now in 1st Corps.
	Location Field Ambulances. 1st Corps Rest Station- in a monastery and with 5 large huts accommodated 300- or on emergency 700-
	A.D.S. at Bully Grenay- R.11.a.7.7.
24th.	**Operations Enemy.** During night 23rd/24th 14-5.4 shells exploded in field at back of Rest Station.
29th.	**Decoration.** Major A.C. Turner- awarded D.S.O. for good work and gallant conduct in taking of Bucquoy in March-
30th.	**Operations Enemy.** Pont De Grenay- M.1.d.8.2. and Cite Maroc-M.3.a.b.c.

This district was constantly under shell fire. A large mining district- badly knocked about.

The 1st Corps consisting of 6th and 46th Divisions held the line from Loos- S. to. S.E. of Lens.

Major Mark Method F.O.

COMMITTEE FOR THE
MEDICAL HISTORY OF THE WAR
Date -7 AUG.1917

1/2" NORTH MIDLAND FIELD AMBULANCE
R.A.M.C.T.F.
46th Division

Army Form C. 2118.

WAR DIARY
or
INTELLIGENCE SUMMARY.
(Erase heading not required.)

Instructions regarding War Diaries and Intelligence Summaries are contained in F.S. Regs., Part II. and the Staff Manual respectively. Title pages will be prepared in manuscript.

Place	Date	Hour	Summary of Events and Information	Remarks and references to Appendices
LABEUVRIERE Ref. France 40000 BETHUNE (enclosed sheet)	May 1 1917		Unit forming A Section 1 Corps Rest Camp — Reported to A.D.M.S. Received instructions to detail all available bearers to report to Capt GRAHAM M.C. of this Unit, in command of Advanced Dressing Station at BULLY-GRENAY. Also one Motor Ambulance — the whole to be under the command of Lt. Col. WRAITH, ½ NORTH MID. F. Amb.ce	Fine. Warm
do.	May 2		D.D.M.S. and Sanitary Officer I Corps inspected Corps Rest Station. Instructions received from D.D.M.S. to arrange for reception of overflow of patients from Corps Scabies Station at ALLOUAGNE — up to 50 patients	Fine. Warm
do.	May 3		O.C. 46th Divisional Train inspected Transport. — 4 reinforcements report for duty	Very fine - Warm.
do.	May 4		Capt. HEGRA, R.A.M.C.T.F., 1/3 NORTH MID. F. Amb.ce detailed by A.D.M.S. to assist Capt GRAHAM at Advanced Dressing Station	Very fine - Warm.
do.	May 5		D.D.M.S. 1 Corps inspected Rest Station.	Hot. Thunder.
do.	May 6		Administration of C.R.S. allotted to A.D.M.S. — A.D.M.S. inspected C.R.S. this afternoon	Fine. Cool
do.	May 7		A.D.M.S. Conference. Attended and later inspected Advanced Dressing Station at BULLY-GRENAY.	Fine. Rain in night.
do.	May 8		R.A.M.C. Post at LOOS, under Lieut. DOWLING to be under command of VIst Division. — Entertainment for patients in Evening. 1 Charger and 3 mules (re-inforcement) received. All available land space about C.R.S. being cultivated, chiefly potatoes.	Rain; Fine later.
do.	May 9		Recommended following N.C.O. and men for decoration for gallantry and devotion to duty under Shell fire: Staff-Sergeant NEALE H., Pte BROWN J., Pte GANDY H.	

J. M. Moor

1/2 North Midland Field Ambulance
RAMC T.F.
46' Division

Army Form C. 2118.

WAR DIARY
or
INTELLIGENCE SUMMARY.
(Erase heading not required.)

Instructions regarding War Diaries and Intelligence Summaries are contained in F.S. Regs., Part II. and the Staff Manual respectively. Title pages will be prepared in manuscript.

Place	Date	Hour	Summary of Events and Information	Remarks and references to Appendices
LA BEUVRIERE FRANCE	May 10		Inspected advanced Dressing Station at BULLY-GRENAY. Capt SPRAWSON, RAMC T.C. and Lieut CARROLL	See diary app
			RAMC T.C. from Tunnelling Company R.E. report for duty. - Inspecting Cinema entertainment for patients	
			Following casualties to Unit in action on May 9th: 419012 Pte ALLEN E.A. Killed; 419140 Pte CLARKE J.H. Killed;	
			2448 Pte GRAHAM C. Died of Wounds; 2696 Pte BRANLEY H. Severely Wounded.	
do	May 11		DDMS 1 Corps inspected C.R.S. - Capt MANFIELD M.C. reports for duty at A.D.S. BULLY GRENAY.	See diary app
			duty with 4th Leicesters	
do	May 13		ADMS inspected C.R.S.	See diary app
do	May 14		ADMS conference. - Inspected A.D.S. BULLY-GRENAY.	
			Capt GRAHAM M.C. proceeds on short leave; Capt SPRAWSON RAMC T.C. detailed for duty at A.D.S. vice Capt MANFIELD	
			Capt FLAXMAN RAMC T.C. with 11 N.C.O.s and men who were detailed for temporary duty with 23 C.C.S. on April 4	
			reports for duty; Lt Col NIGHTINGALE, RAMC T. o/c B Section 1 Corps Rest Station inspected C.R.S.	
do	May 15		Rode to FOUQUIERES to inspect B Section 1 C.R.S. in accordance with instructions received from DDMS	See diary app
			Instructed to cease admitting Scabies cases to C.R.S.	
do	May 16		Lieut DOWLING, RAMC T.C. from RAMC POST LOOS reports for duty.	See diary app
			ADMS 9th Cavalry Brigade killed in Village, inspected C.R.S. - The A.D.S. at BULLY-GRENAY to be known	
			1/1 NORTH MID F AMB" Capt MANFIELD M.C. detailed for duty at A.D.S. NORTH MAROC	

Army Form C. 2118.

2/1 North Midland Field Ambulance
N.A.M.C.T
R.A.M.C. 46 Div.

WAR DIARY
INTELLIGENCE SUMMARY.
(Erase heading not required.)

Instructions regarding War Diaries and Intelligence Summaries are contained in F.S. Regs., Part II. and the Staff Manual respectively. Title pages will be prepared in manuscript.

Place	Date	Hour	Summary of Events and Information	Remarks and references to Appendices
LA BEUVRIERE	May 17		Major TURNER D.S.O. R.A.M.C. detailed for duty tonight at CITÉ St PIERRE for special gas duty. Two motor Ambulances to be stationed at BULLY-GRENAY, and all R.A.M.C Posts strengthened by 50%.	Cool Rain
			Concert for patients in Evening.	
do	May 18		Major TURNER reported for duty from CITÉ St PIERRE.	Dull clear.
			Capt. FLAXMAN R.A.M.C.T.C. detailed for duty with 5th N. STAFFS.	
			Capt. Rev. PUTTOCK, U.B. appointed for attachment to unit	
do	May 19		A.D.M.S. inspected Rest Station.	Fine warm
do	May 21		A.D.M.S. conference. D.D.M.S. I Corps inspected Rest Station - Entertainment for patients in Evening.	
do	May 22		Instructions received to change over with 1/3 N. Mid F.Amb.ce, relieving them by May 26th at AIX NOULETTE.	Rain
			and they taking over 1 Corps Rest Station. Visited to AIX NOULETTE and inspected Dressing Station. - D.D.M.S. called.	
do	May 25		Inspection of C.R.S. by A.A. and Q.M.G. 1st Army. In evening reported to A.D.M.S. proceeded to LIÉVIN to inspect A.D.S.	Fine Warm.
			Major TURNER D.S.O. to be in charge. In addition to the A.D.S. there are 3 R.A.M.C. posts in the town, which will be taken	
			over by the unit Tomorrow	
AIX NOULETTE	May 26		Unit marched from LABEUVRIERE to AIX NOULETTE and took over Dressing Station from 1/3 N. Mid F. Amb.ce - Reported	
			to A.D.M.S. This Dressing Station receives sick and wounded evacuated from A.D.S. at LIÉVIN. Evacuation are carried	
			out at night. 1 Ford Motor Ambulance is stationed all day in outskirts of LIÉVIN for cases of great urgency. N.M. Hibbet	

1/2nd North Midland Field Ambulance
R.A.M.C.T.
46th Division

Army Form C. 2118.

WAR DIARY
INTELLIGENCE SUMMARY
(Erase heading not required.)

Place	Date	Hour	Summary of Events and Information	Remarks and references to Appendices
AIX NOULETTE	May 27		Capt GRAHAM, M.C. R.A.M.C.T., reports for duty from leave.	Fine. Warm
do			Lieut DOWLING R.A.M.C.T., detailed for duty with 1/1st Lincolns.	do
			In evening, with Col. GRAHAM and Lieut. CROSS, Q.Ms., proceeded to LIÉVIN and inspected A.D.S. and R.A.M.C. posts. These are located in cellars, and in old German Dug-outs. The A.D.S. is in charge of Major TURNER, and Capt SPRAWSON. Each R.A.M.C. post is in charge of a N.C.O. Heavy and constant shelling at LIÉVIN.	
do	May 28		A.D.M.S. Conference.	Fine Warm
do	May 29		Inspected dressing Station.	Cool, cloudy
do	May 30		Capt CONDY R.A.M.C.T., reported for duty from England.	Fine Warm
			Following mentioned in F.M. Sir D. HAIG'S despatches: Lieut Col. R.N. WEST R.A.M.C. O/C Unit; and No. — Staff Sergeant.	
			WAKELING, H. R.A.M.C.T. of this Unit.	
			Proceeded with A.D.M.S. to inspect ground W. of LIÉVIN and ANGRES, for an alternative route for evacuation of sick.	
			Wounded, should main road prove impassable through barrage, etc.	
do	May 31		In Evening, proceeded to LIÉVIN to inspect A.D.S. and R.A.M.C. Posts.	
			With A.D.M.S. proceeded this afternoon to inspect the ground W. of LIÉVIN and ANGRES. Two light railways	Fine warm
			run from BULLY GRENAY to ANGRES and LIÉVIN respectively, which ought to be used for evacuation of wounded	

1/2 North Midland Field Ambulance
RANET
46 Division

Army Form C. 2118.

WAR DIARY
or
INTELLIGENCE SUMMARY.
(Erase heading not required.)

Instructions regarding War Diaries and Intelligence Summaries are contained in F.S. Regs., Part II. and the Staff Manual respectively. Title pages will be prepared in manuscript.

Place	Date	Hour	Summary of Events and Information	Remarks and references to Appendices

Wounded of sort was impassable. There are also several tracks leading on to the BULLY-GRENAY-AIX-NOULETTE Road, but the easy is a long one - nearly 3½ miles - and the tracks lead over the old German lines.

Inspected A.D.S. and RAMC Posts at LIEVIN. In evening reported to A.D.M.S.

MAP REFERENCES:—

LA BEUVRIÈRE (FRANCE 1/20000 36B) D.17.A.4.4.
FOUQUIÈRES (FRANCE 1/20000 36B) E.15.D.1.3
AIX-NOULETTE (FRANCE 1/20000 36B) R.22
BULLY GRENAY (FRANCE 1/20000 36B) R.11.A.7.7
LIEVIN (FRANCE 1/20000 36B) M.28
CITÉ MAROC (FRANCE 1/20000 36C) M.3.B.1.5.
ANGRES (FRANCE 1/20000 36C) M.27.C.5.2

Strength of Unit at beginning of month: Officers 5 RAMC Personnel and ASC 234 = Total 239
End   "   "   9   "   "   232   "   "   241.

R. M. West.
LIEUT. COL. COMDG.
2nd North Mid. Fd. Amb. R.A.M.C.

Secret.

WAR DIARY
of
1/2- North Mid. Field Amb.
RAMET
from March 1 to May 31.
1917

B.E.F.

SUMMARY OF MEDICAL WAR DIARIES FOR 1/2nd N. Mid. F.A. 46th Divn. 2nd Corps

1st Corps 22/4/17.

1st Army.

WESTERN FRONT April-May. '17.

O.C. Lt. Col. R.M. West.

SUMMARISED UNDER THE FOLLOWING HEADINGS.

Phase "B" Battle of Arras April- May. '17.

1st Period Attack on Vimy Ridge April.

2nd Period Capture of Siegfried Line May.

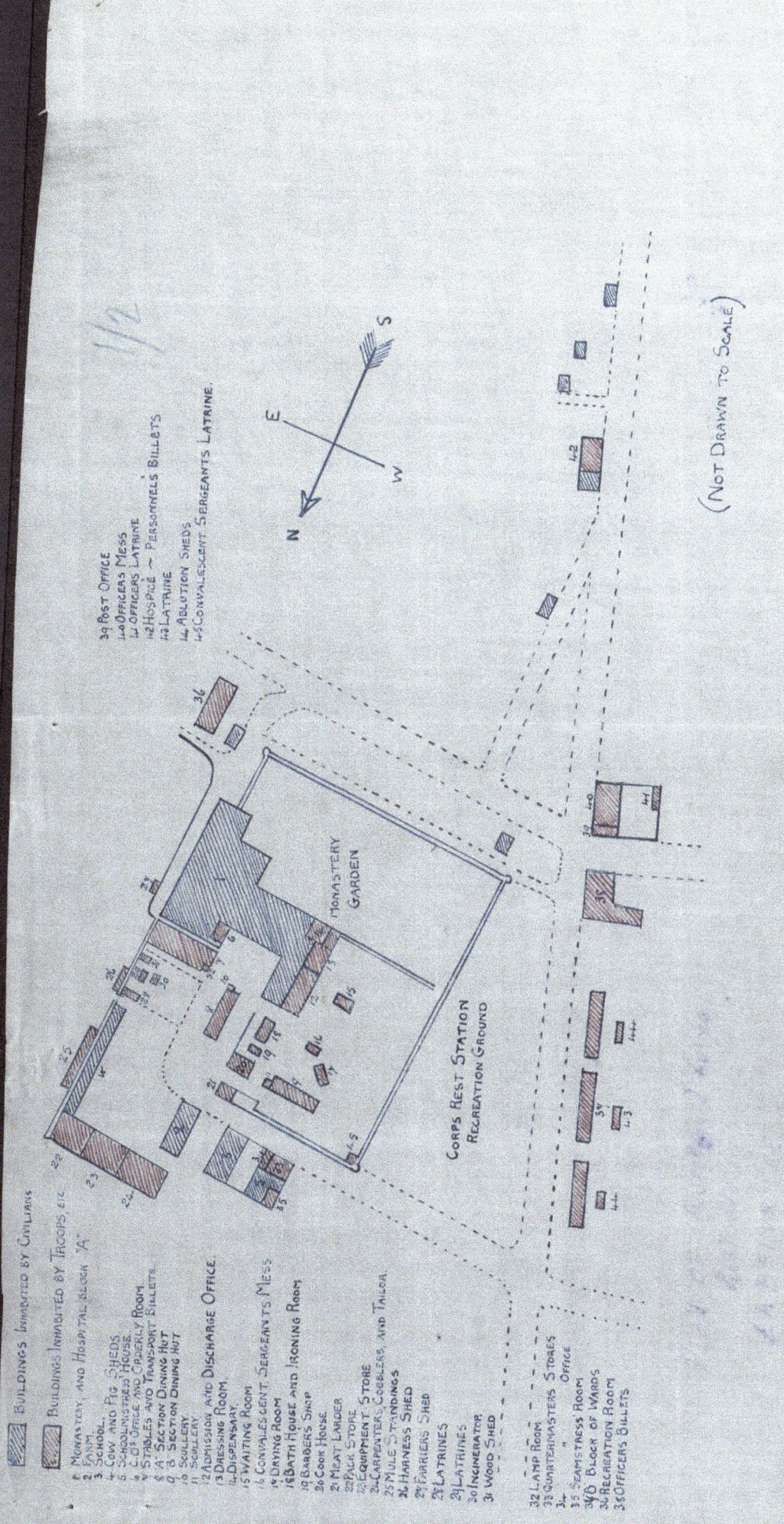

B.E.F.

1/2nd N.. Mid. F.A. 46th Divn. 1st Corps.   WESTERN FRONT.
O.C. Lt. Col. R.M. West.   May. '17.
1st Army.

Phase "B" Battle of Arras April.- May. '17.
2nd Period Capture of Siegfried Line May.

1917.
May. 2nd.   Scabies. Accommodation: Corps Scabies Station at Allouagne was arranged to receive additional 50 cases.

9th.   Casualties R.A.M.C. 0 and 2 killed 0 and 2 wounded, 0 and 1 Died of wounds.

10th-25th.   Nothing of interest.

26th.   Moves: To Aix Noulette Map 36b R.22 and took over D.S. from 1/3rd N. Mid. F.A.

27th.   Operations Enemy. Liévin shelled constantly.

B.E.F.

1/2nd N. Mid. F.A. 46th Divn. 1st Corps.   WESTERN FRONT.
O.C. Lt. Col. R.H. West.   May. '17.
    1st Army.   1.

Phase "B" Battle of Arras April.- May. '17.
2nd Period Capture of Siegfried Line May.

1917.
May. 2nd.   Scabies. Accommodation: Corps Scabies Station at
               Allouagne was arranged to receive additional 50 cases.
   9th.   Casualties R.A.M.C. 0 and 2 killed 0 and 2 wounded, 0 and 1
               Died of wounds.
10th-25th.   Nothing of interest.
   26th.   Moves: To Aix Noulette Map 36b R.22 and took over
               D.S. from 1/3rd N. Mid. F.A.
   27th.   Operations Enemy. Liévin shelled constantly.

110/250

1/1st North Midland F.A.

June 1917.

COMMITTEE FOR THE
MEDICAL HISTORY OF THE WAR
Date -7 AUG. 1917

WAR DIARY
or
INTELLIGENCE SUMMARY

Army Form C. 2118.

1/2· North Midland Field Ambulance
Name.T.F
46' Division
B.E.F

Place	Date	Hour	Summary of Events and Information	Remarks and references to Appendices
AIX NOULETTE FRANCE	June 1 1917		D.D.M.S. I Corps inspected dressing Station at AIX NOULETTE.	
	June 2		A.D.M.S conference. Visited A.D.S. at LIÉVIN.	
	June 4		A.D.M.S conference, with reference to proposed Operations on front of LENS, on night 5-9 June. Visited A.D.S. LIÉVIN and RAMC Posts.	
	June 5		Birthday Honours list :- Lt Col. R.H. WEST, RAMC, O/C 1/2 NMFA, awarded D.S.O. Visited A.D.S. LIÉVIN.	
	June 6		Capt TREW, CF R.C. reports for attachment to Unit Visited A.D.S. LIÉVIN, and R.A.M.C. Posts	
	June 7		D.D.M.S. I Corps inspected main dressing Station, AIX NOULETTE Capt FLAXMAN, R.A.M.C T.F. reports for duty from Temporary duty with 1/3 NMFA. Visited A.D.S, LIÉVIN, to arrange for medical arrangements in connection with raid on German front trenches night by 138 E Infantry Brigade. Proceeded to A.D.S LIÉVIN, and made following arrangements for tonight's operation.	
	June 8		Proposed Operations:- (West LIÉVIN LENS 10000 36 c. S.W.) A raid on enemy's position by 1/5 Lincolns Batallion. (Left subdivision) and 1/5 Leicester Battalion (Right subdivision), returning to our lines. Our lines SUEZ CANAL in charge of capturing prisoners and destroying dug-outs and Munitions. From positions - to prisoners to be evacuated with exception of Trench line M.30.D.22.40 — M.30.D.20.80 — M.30.B.02.73 in walking cases to be held by 1/5 Leicester Batallion. Medical Arrangements. The A.D.S. late WHITE HOUSE, LIÉVIN (M.75 E.7.2.) to remain open. 2 officers and 36 O.R., to be reinforced from overnight by 20 stretcher from other Field Ambulances.	

WAR DIARY or INTELLIGENCE SUMMARY

Army Form C. 2118.

1/2 NORTH MIDLAND FIELD AMBULANCE
N.M.C.T.F.
46th Division
B.E.F.

Place	Date	Hour	Summary of Events and Information	Remarks and references to Appendices
AIX NOULETTE FRANCE	June 8 1917 (continued)		O.C.'s 1/1 and 1/3 N.M.F.A. to hold a reserve of 40 bearers each for despatch to ADS of LIEVIN. 1st 40 bearers of 1/1 N.M.F.A. despatch when sent for at 7 P.M., as arranged; but the bearers of the 1/3 N.M.F.A. were not available. — Capt FOSTER, M.C. R.A.M.C., M.O. R.E., and Capt HERGA, R.A.M.C., 1/3 N.M.F.A. detailed for duty, expecting with reserve bearers to work with 1/5 Leicesters and 1/5 Lincoln Battalions. HQ Adv Dres[s]t established at M. 27. B.4.1., M. 23. A. 2.4., and M. 27. B.1.1. (LIEVIN), with N.C.O. and Bearers. Operation to commence 8.30 P.M. At A.D.S., following officers for duty: Lieut. Col WEST, D.S.O (Major TURNER, D.S.O. Army M.R.) Capt. BRAHAM, M.C.; Capt. SPRAWSON; and Lieut. CARROLL; 36 bearers detailed with Capt. HERGA; and 50 with Capt. FOSTER, R.M.C. 8 same bearers detailed to work with R.S.B.s of each Battalion. Walking cases to report to A.D.S., whence they will be taken by Motor Ambulance to AIX NOULETTE. Lying cases to be evacuated from A.D.S. to Fosse 10. (1/1 N.M.F.A. Main dressing Station). All wounded to be fed at A.D.S. before evacuation. Evacuation proceeded smoothly. There being at no time any congestion at either A.D.S., or Main dressing Station. The first Military casualties arrived at A.D.S. at 10 P.M., from 1/5 Leicesters; others from 1/5 Lincolns arrived later. Scarcely been held up by Bossing — 50 stretcher cases and 180 walking wounded from Tonys A.D.S., and by 10 A.M. June 9th all cases, no farther as were at contaminated, had been collected. Majority of wounds shrapnel, and machine gun bullet wounds.

J Mullen Lt Colonel R.A.M.C.T
O/C 1/2 N.M.F.A.

WAR DIARY or INTELLIGENCE SUMMARY

1/2 North Midland Field Ambulance
Name of 46 Division
B.E.F.
Army Form C. 2118.

(Erase heading not required.)

Place	Date	Hour	Summary of Events and Information	Remarks and references to Appendices
AIX NOULETTE FRANCE	June 8 1917 (continued)		Following Casualties to personnel of Unit :- 249083 Pt. DALEY. S KILLED. 249454. Pte FOXON. S Wounded. 249103 " CREMORN. G.T. " 2413 " WARD. G " 249158 " BURRELL. G NYDN. 249145 " STEPHENS A.E NYDN. 423066 " BRADBURY T ?NYDN.	
	June 9		Capt. GRAHAM R.C. attached for duty at A.D.S. vice Major TURNER. D.S.O. R.R D.D.M.S. 1 Corps. inspected Main Dressing Station G.O.C. Division called, and started out for reasons on which remains of recovered and were carried out last night. Capt. FLAXMAN R.A.M.C. T.F. evacuated to C.C.S. (Diphtheria).	
			Visited A.D.S. LIÉVIN.	
	June 10		Visited A.D.S. LIÉVIN. Lieut. CARROLL proceeded on short leave.	
	June 11		Visited A.D.S. and R.A.M.C Posts, LIÉVIN.	
	June 12		Find by 1 Company 1/5 Lincoln Battalion on German trenches just north of RIVER SOUCHEZ 2:55 p.m. Proceeded to A.D.S. LIÉVIN, with 30 horses at 7 A.M. Retired Capt SPRAWSON to M. Main Office, with 20 horses: to be stationed in Issuer, S.W. of BOIS DE RIAUMONT. 8 horses retained at present R.S.B of 1/5 Lincoln Battalion. All remainder to be evacuated to MAIN DRESSING Station at AIX NOULETTE.	

W. Whitney Last Lieut. R.A.M.C.
O.C. 1/2 N.M.F.A.

1/2 N MIDLAND FIELD AMBULANCE
R.A.M.C.T.F.
46 Division
B.E.F.

Army Form C. 2118.

WAR DIARY
or
INTELLIGENCE SUMMARY
(Erase heading not required.)

Instructions regarding War Diaries and Intelligence Summaries are contained in F.S. Regs., Part II. and the Staff Manual respectively. Title Pages will be prepared in manuscript.

Place	Date	Hour	Summary of Events and Information	Remarks and references to Appendices
AIX NOULETTE FRANCE	June 12 1917		Officers detailed for duty at A.D.S.: Lt Col WEST, D.S.O. and Capt GRAHAM, M.C. Officers detailed for duty at Main Dressing Station: Capt MANFIELD, M.C. and Capt RONDY. Evacuation working smoothly; 19 wounded having passed through A.D.S. by 1 p.m., the delay having caused by enemy shelling. Officers off rail returned.	
	June 13		Capt B. SIMMONDS, R.A.M.C.T.C., reports for duty from Base. Capt CRAWSON R.A.M.C.T.C., transferred to 1/1 N. Mid. Field Ambulance. 10 O.R. reinforcements report from Base.	
	June 14		Shell last night on German position at CITÉ ST PIERRE. Before sunrise 10 Walking and 8 lying were evacuated to C.C.S. Visited A.D.S. LIEVIN, and NAME DAME.	
	June 16		Capt. MANFIELD, M.C. detailed for temporary duty with 1/5 Lincoln Battalion, vice Capt. DALY, R.A.M.C.T.C., who reports for temporary duty with this Unit – pending completion of the exchange.	
	June 17		Visited A.D.S. LIEVIN. A.D.M.S. inspection.	
	June 18		Attack on TOSH 3, LENS, tomorrow - by 2 companies of 1/5 Lincolns. Medical Arrangements were made as under: All wounded cases – to the number of about 70 – to be evacuated to the regimental reserves as A.D.S. and farther. After closing the night 18-19 June. Half Bear. House to be placed in Trinity S.W. of Bois de Rimmont, under Sergt Aspt. WEALE, R.A.M.C. 16 bearers detailed to report to R.H.O. 1/5 Lincolns, for duty with R.S.B. Officers detailed for duty at A.D.S.: Lieut Col WEST D.S.O.; Capt. GRAHAM. M.C.; and Lieut RONDY.	

R Miller
Lt Colonel RAMCT
O/C 1/2 N MID F.A.

1/2 NORTH MIDLAND FIELD AMBULANCE
RAMC
16 Division
BEF

Army Form C. 2118.

WAR DIARY
or
INTELLIGENCE SUMMARY
(Erase heading not required.)

Place	Date	Hour	Summary of Events and Information	Remarks and references to Appendices
AIX NOULETTE	June 18 1917 (continued)		Officers for duty at Main Dressing Station, AIX NOULETTE: (Capt. SIMMONDS, RAMC TC.) and Capt. DALY, RAMC TC. Evacuation of wounded along ASSIGN trench by Motors, as far as necessary & from there to ADS by or with stretcher ; and to MDS by Motor Ambulance. 247 inspected & passed to A.N. NOULETTE. Major TURNER, D.S.O., Inspector of that area.	
	June 19		Attack by 2 companies of 1/5 North Staffs Battalion on Post 3, LEWIS took place at 9.30 P.M. After several attacks gained Post. Ground held. 28 prisoners. Started at 2 PM to A.D.S. LIEVIN. (Williams) to M.R.S. at 5.30 P.M. Returned to A.D.S. LIEVIN at 8.30 P.M. Evacuation of wounded was/not directly ; 52 pass through A.D.S. LIEVIN to A.D.S. VIS-EN-ARTOIS. Visited A.D.S. LIEVIN.	
	June 20			
	June 21		At 2 AM through an ESSM gas cylinder from our right front was projected into a trench held by 1/5 Gloucester regiment (1 Company). By morning 52 cases had been evacuated through ADS LIEVIN. Of these 18 died in hospital or on arrival at CCS. Pte GOODE, of this Unit awarded Military Medal for gallantry in organising & supervising ST from 43 such gassed cases from 1/5 Leicester, passed through ADS. DDMS and ADMS inspected Dressing Station at AIX NOULETTE.	
	June 22		Major CARROLL reported for duty from leave.	

[signature]
Lt.Col.
O/c 1/2 N. M. F. A.

Army Form C. 2118.

WAR DIARY
or
INTELLIGENCE SUMMARY
(Erase heading not required.)

1/2 NINTH MIDLAND FIELD AMBULANCE
A.A.M.C.
1.6 Division
B.E.F.

Place	Date	Hour	Summary of Events and Information	Remarks and references to Appendices
AIX NOULETTE	June 23 1917		A.D.M.S. Inspected Dressing Station, AIX NOULETTE. 5 Fresh gassed cases, all acute victims from 1/5th Lincolns Battalion. The chief action of the gas employed on these cases appears to be on the Cardiac Centre - cases dying without from Heart Failure. Other symptoms are Headache, Vomiting, prostration, depression, and Cough. Visited A.D.S. LIEVIN.	
	June 24		Part Strength of 139 Infantry Brigade on Garrison duty with object of holding part of the trenches visited, instructions obtained. Sent up 50 reinforcement horses to A.D.S. under Lieut. CARROLL for Man Passettes. In evening, proceeded to A.D.S., LIEVIN, to superintend medical arrangements, which worked smoothly. 57 wounded passed through A.D.S., of whom 30 were 1/5" South Staffords.	
	June 25		A.D.M.S. Conference. Visited A.D.S., LIEVIN. Capt. SIMMONDS, A.A.M.C., evacuated sick to CCS - P.U.O. Visited A.D.S., LIEVIN.	
	June 26		D.D.M.S. I Corps. inspected Main Dressing Station.	
	June 27		Relieved tomorrow: attack by 1/2S Division on German lines on S.W. outskirt of LENS. Medical arrangements similar to those made for operations on June 8 & 9th: the officers for duty at Main Dressing Station: Capts DALY and HERIA (from 1/3 N.M.F.A.), and Lieut. CARROLL at A.D.S. LIEVIN. Lt. Col. WEST, D.S.O., Capt GRAHAM, M.C., Capt CONDY, Capt SHARP, Capt STRAWSON, the one extra officer from the 1/1 N.M.F.A. - Bearer officers: Capt FOSTER, M.C., and Capt SUTTIE, M.C. - from 1/3 N.M.F.A. - Walking Wounded to be evacuated from A.D.S. by Motor Ambulance to Main Dressing. Station AIX NOULETTE.	

WAR DIARY or INTELLIGENCE SUMMARY

Army Form C. 2118.

1/2 North Midland Field Ambulance
R.A.M.C.
46th Division
B.E.F.

Place	Date	Hour	Summary of Events and Information	Remarks and references to Appendices
AIX NOULETTE	June 27 1917 continued		Motor cars from A.D.S. to Main Dressing Station (Fosse 10) of 1/1 N.M.F.A. The attacking force to consist of 1/4 and 1/5 Amwick Battalions; the 1/5 South Stafford, and the 1/5 North Stafford Battalions. Proceeded in Evening to A.D.S., LIÉVIN. Attack opened at 7.10 P.M. with heavy barrage. Attack was a great success. [struck through] First wounded reported at A.D.S. at 8.10 P.M. From then until 8.10 A.M. June 29, 3 officers and 165 O.R. passed through A.D.S.	
	June 28		Visited A.D.S., LIÉVIN in early morning. A.D.M.S. and D.D.M.S. Iº Corps inspected main Dressing Station. Capt. FOSTER, M.C. R.A.M.C. T.F. R.E. awarded bar to Military Cross for gallantry in action on June 8 and 9th. Capt. HEREA, R.A.M.C.T.F. 1/3 N.M.F.A. successful the Military Cross, and Staff Sergeant WAKELING, 2/1 N.M.F.A. the D.C.M. for gallant conduct on same occasion. A.D.M.S. Conference tonight.	
	June 29		Recovered body of M. SERGE BASSET, a French Journalist, Killed during the attack on June 28. Conveyed it to the Mairie at PETIT SAINS, where it was handed over to 46th French Mission. Tonight, attack on LENS by 46th Division; troops engaged:- 137th, 138th, 139th Infantry Brigades and 1/2 N.M.F.A. Medical arrangements as for previous operations - the same officers being detailed for the various stations, &c.	
	June 30		Proceeded in afternoon to A.D.S. LIÉVIN. Attack opened at 7.43 P.M., assisted along whole section.
J. M. Rst? Colonel A.D.M.S. O/c 1/2 N.M.F.A.	

1/2 NORTH MIDLAND FIELD AMBULANCE
R.A.M.C. T.F.
46' Division
B E F

WAR DIARY
or
INTELLIGENCE SUMMARY
(Erase heading not required.)

Army Form C. 2118.

Instructions regarding War Diaries and Intelligence Summaries are contained in F. S. Regs., Part II. and the Staff Manual respectively. Title Pages will be prepared in manuscript.

Place	Date	Hour	Summary of Events and Information	Remarks and references to Appendices
AIX NOULETTE FRANCE	June 30 1917 (continued)		First wounded lifted at A.D.S. at 8.30 P.M. Collection of Wounded during stations weather well. We had to practically crawl out down, on account of enemy aircraft machine gun fire. 12 Be infantrymen O.R. Affected by shell. Total Wounded through A.D.S. during June 29-30 : Walking: Officers 11, O.R. 160. - Stretcher cases. Officers 9 ; O.R. 147 ; Total Officers 20 ; O.R. 307. Pte. J. Brown, of this Unit killed. The 46' Division to be relieved by the 2nd Canadian Division. (11th and) Total Number of Wounded treated at Major Grassey Station, AIX NOULETTE, since June 25 : Sick 1170 ; Wounded 1493. The casualties during the months has been very heavy, with little rest, and some Tours.	

R. M. West
Lieut Colonel R.A.M.C.
O/C 1/2 North Midland Field Ambulance
46' Division
B E F

WAR DIARY
of
1/2 N. Mid. Field Amb⁶
JAMET
46' Division
BEF

From
June 1 1917
to
June 30 1917

W Herbert
Major
O.C.

140/298

1/2st M.M. Field Ambulance

COMMITTEE FOR THE
MEDICAL HISTORY OF THE WAR
Date   10 SEP. 1917

½ North Midland Field Ambulance
R A M C T F
26th Division
BEF FRANCE

Army Form C. 2118.

WAR DIARY
or
INTELLIGENCE SUMMARY.
(Erase heading not required.)

Instructions regarding War Diaries and Intelligence Summaries are contained in F.S. Regs., Part II. and the Staff Manual respectively. Title pages will be prepared in manuscript.

MEDICAL

Place	Date	Hour	Summary of Events and Information	Remarks and references to Appendices
AIX NOULETTE FRANCE.	July 1st 1917		Instructed to move from AIX NOULETTE on 2nd to billets in dept area. This Dressing Station was taken over A.D.S. LIEVIN to be taken over by 6th Canadian Field Ambulance (2nd Canadian Division) where advanced party reported today. ADMS called. Divisional Commander called. — Major A. C. TURNER D.S.O. of this Unit ――― ― from ――― ――― Lieut or Captain	
			Pte. J. BROWN, of this Unit, Killed at LIEVIN last night.	
HOUDAIN FRANCE	July 2nd		Unit moved from AIX NOULETTE to HOUDAIN, where it billets for the night. Tents, Kitchens. Lieut Col WEST, D.S.O., O/C this Unit, to be acting ADMS; Lt BEEVOR, O.B.ENS, ADMS, to be acting DDMS 1 Corps.	
			Major TURNER, D.S.O. of this Unit, to have temporary command of the Unit.	
HOUCHY-LE-BRETON July 3rd			Unit marched from HOUDAIN, to billets in and area at MONCHY BRETON. Hospital established under canvas. Summer establishments.	
FRANCE			Colonel BEEVOR, C.B.E.N.G., acting DDMS 1 Corps inspected Ambulance.	
do.	July 4		O/ADMS inspected Ambulance — Capt LUDOLF, RAMCT. reported for duty with Unit, from Base	
do	July 5		O/ADMS inspected Hospital. — ADMS 1 Corps and DADVS 26 Division inspected these transport	
do	July 6		O/ADMS inspected Unit. — Capt LUDOLF, RAMCT. detached for duty with ½ N. Midland Battalion	
do	July 9		Capt DOWLING, RAMCT, reported for duty with Unit, from the N. Midland Battalion	
			Capt CONDY, RAMCT, detached for duty with 1/5 Lincoln Battalion	
			Capt MANFIELD, RAMCT, reported for duty with Unit from 1/5 N. Midld. Battalion	
			Undermentioned N.C.O. and men awarded Military Medal for work at Colonment Dressing Station LIEVIN	
			No 419008 S/Sergt NEAL H.W. ½ NMFA RAMCT.	
			419402 Pte JOHNSON R.E. " "	
			419413 " ROBERTS H. " "	
			419224 " JOHNSON W. " "	

(A 7092) Wt. W12899/M1293. 75,000. 1/17. D. D. & L., Ltd. Forms/C.2118-14.

Army Form C. 2118.

½ NHFamb? NMITE
46th Division
BEF
FRANCE

WAR DIARY
or
INTELLIGENCE SUMMARY.
(Erase heading not required.)

Instructions regarding War Diaries and Intelligence Summaries are contained in F.S. Regs., Part II. and the Staff Manual respectively. Title pages will be prepared in manuscript.

Place	Date	Hour	Summary of Events and Information	Remarks and references to Appendices
MONCHY BRETON FRANCE	July 10 1917		Capt. MANSFIELD, M.C. RAMC., transferred to 54 C.C.S. for duty	
do	July 13		Capt. I.H. LLOYD WILLIAMS transferred from 54 C.C.S. for duty with this Unit	
do	July 14		1st Lieut A. FLORIAN, U.S.M.C., reports for attachment to this Unit, from base. Capt DOWLING RAMC, proceeds on leave	
do	July 15		Lieut Col WEST, D.S.O. proceeded on leave to England.	
do	July 16		D.D.M.S. 1 Corps called.	
do	July 18		A.D.M.S. conference at OURTON.	
do	July 19		Capt. GRAHAM, M.C., RAMC, proceeds to MITCHELHAM CONVALESCENT HOME, DIEPPE,- sick.	
do	July 20		Division to move back into Rest: proceeded to inspect A.D.S. VERMELLES, which this Unit will take over.	
do	July 21		Advance party, with Capt. LLOYD WILLIAMS RAMC. proceeded to A.D.S. VERMELLES, to take over. Advance party of 17th Field Ambulance, 6th Division, reported here to take over from this Unit.	
do			Advance party proceeded to BETHUNE, to take over billets for Headquarters of Unit, where will establish a Hospital there in the ECOLE JULES FERRY.	
do	July 22		Inspected A.D.S. VERMELLES. - Reported to A.D.M.S.	
BETHUNE	July 23		Unit marched from MONCHY BRETON, to new billets in BETHUNE.	
do	July 25		Lt Col WEST, D.S.O. returned from leave, and resumed command of the Unit. Took over ECOLE JULES FERRY from Canadian Field Ambulance	

1/2 NORTH MIDLAND FIELD AMBULANCE.

Army Form C. 2118.

R.A.M.C.T.F.
46' Division
B.E.F. FRANCE

WAR DIARY
or
INTELLIGENCE SUMMARY.

(Erase heading not required.)

Instructions regarding War Diaries and Intelligence Summaries are contained in F. S. Regs., Part II. and the Staff Manual respectively. Title pages will be prepared in manuscript.

Place	Date	Hour	Summary of Events and Information	Remarks and references to Appendices
BETHUNE	July 26 1917		Inspected A.D.S. VERMELLES. Reported to A.D.M.S. Capt LANG, R.A.M.C.T.F., from No. 1 C.C.S., reports for duty with this Unit.	
do	July 27		A.D.M.S. conference at SAILLY-LABOURSE. Last night, 12 bombs dropped on BETHUNE: no damage.	
do	July 28		Inspected A.D.S., VERMELLES. Reported to A.D.M.S. Capt DOWLING, R.A.M.C.T.C., reports for duty from leave.	
do	July 30		A.D.M.S. conference at SAILLY LABOURSE. — Inspected A.D.S., VERMELLES. D.D.M.S. & Capt. inspected M.D.S., BETHUNE. Capt LANG, R.A.M.C.T.F., detailed for temporary duty with 1/5 Lincolns Battalion.	
			Strength of Unit at beginning of month:	
			Reinforcements	

J.M. West
Lieut Colonel R.A.M.C.T.F.
O/C 1/2 N.M.F.A.

140/23 64.

1/2nd No. th Midland F.A.

Aug 1917

COMMITTEE FOR THE
MEDICAL HISTORY OF THE WAR
Date -1 OCT.1917

1/2 NORTH MIDLAND FIELD AMBULANCE
R.A.M.C. T.F.
46th Division
B.E.F. France

Army Form C. 2118.

WAR DIARY
or
INTELLIGENCE SUMMARY.
(Erase heading not required.)

Instructions regarding War Diaries and Intelligence Summaries are contained in F.S. Regs., Part II. and the Staff Manual respectively. Title pages will be prepared in manuscript.

Place	Date	Hour	Summary of Events and Information	Remarks and references to Appendices
BETHUNE FRANCE	Aug 1. 1917		Took over A.D.S. VERMELLES, which has up to this, been shared with 16th T.A.	
"	Aug 2		Capt. Dowling, R.A.M.C.T.F., detailed for temporary duty with 1/5 Sherwood Foresters.	
"	Aug 4		Lieut and QMr. CROSS proceeds to ENGLAND on leave.	
"			Lieut CARROLL, R.A.M.C.T.F. proceeds to ENGLAND, on expiration of contract.	
"			Raid carried by 6th N. and 6th South Stafford Battalions near LOOS: detailed 20 extra bearers to proceed to A.D.S. VERMELLES. Wounded from last night's raid, through A.D.S. VERMELLES: 13.	
"	Aug 5		Capt. GRAHAM, M.C., R.A.M.C.T.F. of this Unit, returns from MITCHELHAM HOME, DIEPPE, for duty.	
"	Aug 6		A.D.M.S. weekly conference at SAILLY-LABOURSE. Proceeded to A.D.S. VERMELLES, and inspected R.A.M.C. Post and R.A.P.s in trenches.	
"			G.O.C. Division inspected Main Dressing Station, BETHUNE.	
"	Aug 7		Capt. LLOYD WILLIAMS, R.A.M.C.T.F, proceeds on leave to ENGLAND, and is replaced at A.D.S. by Capt. GRAHAM, M.C. R.A.M.C.T.F. A.D.M.S. inspected Main Dressing Station.	
"	Aug 8		Main Dressing Station inspected by D.M.S., FIRST ARMY, D.D.M.S I Corps, and A.D.M.S 46 Division.	
"	Aug 9		Inspected A.D.S. VERMELLES. — 14 aeroplanes bombs dropped on BETHUNE at 4.30 A.M.	
"			Inspected A.D.S. VERMELLES.	
"	Aug 10		Major TURNER, D.S.O. R.A.M.C.T.F., inspected A.D.S. and R.A.M.C. Posts. Instructed to claim to remount Depot, 6 of my 11 Chargers.	
"	Aug 11		Transport horses inspected by A.D.V.S. with a view to testing.	
"			A.D.M.S. weekly conference. Inspected A.D.S. VERMELLES.	
"	Aug 13		Major TURNER, D.S.O. Divisional Gas expert, proceeds to A.D.S. VERMELLES. in view of gas alert, and attached LENS, during next 3 days. In addition, detailed 30 bearers to proceed to A.D.S. as reserve bearers	

1/2 NORTH MIDLAND FIELD AMBULANCE.
R.A.M.C.F.
46th Division
B.E.F.
France

Army Form C. 2118.

WAR DIARY
or
INTELLIGENCE SUMMARY.
(Erase heading not required.)

Instructions regarding War Diaries and Intelligence Summaries are contained in F. S. Regs., Part II. and the Staff Manual respectively. Title pages will be prepared in manuscript.

Place	Date	Hour	Summary of Events and Information	Remarks and references to Appendices
BETHUNE FRANCE	Aug 14 1917		Inspected ADS, RAMC posts and R.A.P.'s in Bethune. Reported to ADMS.	
	Aug 15		Canadian attack on LENS this morning: all objectives gained and positions consolidated. In afternoon visited ADS, VERMELLES. Reported to ADMS.	
	Aug 16		Capt DOWLING, RAMC, from temporary duty with 1/8 Sherwood Foresters, reports for duty. Visited ADS, VERMELLES. Major TURNER, DSO. with 30 Reserve teams. Reports for duty from ADS, VERMELLES.	
	Aug 17		Lieut FLORIAN, U.S.M.C. attached for instruction to ADS, VERMELLES. Capt J.LANG, from temporary duty with 1/5 Berwick Battalion, reports for duty. BETHUNE shelled this afternoon with 9" H.V. shells.	
	Aug 18		Major TURNER, D.S.O., detailed for duty in trenches tonight, during transport of gas cylinders. Capt J.LANG, RAMC, proceeds on leave to ENGLAND.	
	Aug 19		Capt LLOYD WILLIAMS, RAMC, reports for duty, from leave. Major TURNER, DSO, detailed for duty in trenches tonight, during transport of gas cylinders. ADMS weekly conference. Proceeded to VERMELLES, to inspect A.D.S.	
	Aug 20		Major TURNER, D.S.O. detailed for duty in trenches tonight, during transport of gas cylinders. BETHUNE shelled this morning by 9" H.V. shells.	
	Aug 22		With Major TURNER, D.S.O. and Capt GRAHAM, M.C. proceeded to trenches and inspected 3.A.M.C. posts and R.A.P.'s VERMELLES heavily shelled. Major TURNER D.S.O. detailed for duty in trenches tonight, during transport of gas cylinders.	

1/2 NORTH MIDLAND FIELD AMBULANCE
BANCTF
46th DIVISION
B.E.F.
FRANCE

Army Form C. 2118.

WAR DIARY
or
INTELLIGENCE SUMMARY.
(Erase heading not required.)

Instructions regarding War Diaries and Intelligence Summaries are contained in F. S. Regs., Part II. and the Staff Manual respectively. Title pages will be prepared in manuscript.

Place	Date	Hour	Summary of Events and Information	Remarks and references to Appendices
BETHUNE. FRANCE	Aug 23 1917		Orders received to move Transport to FOUQUIÈRES, and take over B Section 1 Corps Field Station, from 1/1 N. Mid F Amb'ce; This Unit to take over ECOLE JULES FERRY, BETHUNE, from same. — Also to hand over A.D.S. VERQUELLES to 1/1 N Mid F Amb'ce, and take over A.D.S. at PHILOSOPHE from 1/3 N.Mid F Amb'y — The 1/3 N Mid F Amb'y to establish a C.ofH. Main Dressing station at LABOURSE. — The A.D.S. PHILOSOPHE will be administered by A.D.M.S. 6th Division and to be shared by one of that Division's Field Ambulances. — BETHUNE again shelled this morning	
FOUQUIÈRES FRANCE	Aug 24		Took over B Section 1 Corps Rest Station, at FOUQUIÈRES the morning Accommodation 300 patients. 1/Lieut FLORIAN, U.S.M.C. reported for duty from A.D.S.	
"	Aug 25		A.D.M.S. called D.D.M.S. 1 Corps, inspected C.R.S. 1/Lieut FLORIAN U.S.M.C. detailed for temporary duty with 18th C.C.S. LAPUGNOY Capt LLOYD WILLIAMS, RAMC TF, with 32 O.R., proceeds to A.D.S. PHILOSOPHE in view of 6 Div'n on Sussex trenches	
"	Aug 26			
"	Aug 27		A.D.M.S. weekly conference	
"	Aug 28		Inspected A.D.S. PHILOSOPHE	
"	Aug 29		Capt LLOYD WILLIAMS, RAMC TF. with 32 O.R. reports for duty, from detached duty at A.D.S	
"	Aug 30		A.D.M.S. inspected C.R.S.	
"	Aug 31		Relief at ECOLE JULES FERRY, BETHUNE, by Col. WALLACE, A.M.S. forwarding surgeon to Third Army on Typhus fever. (Capt J LANE, RAMC TF reports for duty from leave.	

R. M WEST
Lieut. Colonel R.A.M.C TF
O/C 1/2 N MID FLD AMB

Confidential

WAR DIARY
OF
1/2 NORTH MIDLAND FIELD AMBULANCE
RAMC TF
46th Division
BEF
France

From
August 1. 1917
to
August 31. 1917

A.M. West
Lieut Colonel
1/2 NMFT
Officer Commanding

COMMITTEE FOR THE
MEDICAL HISTORY OF THE WAR
Date -8 DEC. 1917

WAR DIARY

INTELLIGENCE SUMMARY.

1/2 - North Midland Field Ambulance
N.M.F.F.
46 Div. B.E.F.
FRANCE

Army Form C. 2118.

Place	Date	Hour	Summary of Events and Information	Remarks and references to Appendices
FOUQUIERES (Regt Station, 1 Corps) FRANCE.	Sept 1. 1917		D.M.S. First Army, and D.D.M.S. 1 Corps inspected Rest Station. Instructed by A.D.M.S. 46th Division to hand over A.D.S. Philosophe, and R.A.M.C. Pers connected with it, to 17th Field Ambulance, 6th Division: accordingly, established Capt. GRAHAM, M.C. and personnel.	
	Sept 2		D.D.M.S. 1 Corps inspected Rest Station.	
	Sept 3		A.D.M.S. Conference at Montgomaries, SAILLY LABOURSE. Capt DOWLING, R.A.M.C.T.C., detached for permanent duty with 231 Bde R.F.A.	
	Sept 5		Col. W BEEVOR, C.B. C.M.G., who is proceeding to England, made Officers' Mess farewell to Mess on present. D.D.M.S. 1 Corps inspected Rest Station. 10 P.B. men suffering for duty on return, was 10 A.S.C. men to report to A.S.C. Batt.	
	Sept 6		A and Q.M.G. 1 Corps, and D.D.M.S. 1 Corps, inspected Rest Station.	
	Sept 7		Capt. GRAHAM, H.C., detached for temporary duty with 1/1 North Mid. Field Amb.ce at A.D.S., VERMELLES. Capt. LANG, R.A.M.C.T.C. detached for permanent duty with 231 Bde R.F.A., vice Capt. DOWLING, R.A.M.C.T.C. Nursing sord on Convoy Excursion. Capt. LLOYD WILLIAMS, R.A.M.C.T.F., attached to this unit for training.	
	Sept 8		Lieut GODPASTER, U.S.M.C., attached to this Unit for training. S.N.C.O. and 14 O.R. detached for temporary duty with 230 Bde A.F.A.	
	Sept 9		Capt. GRAHAM, M.C. reports for duty from A.D.S., VERMELLES. Capt DOWLING, R.A.M.C. detached for temporary duty as 1 Corps Solvent, GOSNAY.	

Army Form C. 2118.

WAR DIARY
or
INTELLIGENCE SUMMARY.
(Erase heading not required.)

1/2 North Midland Field Ambulance
RAMETT
46 Division
BEF
FRANCE

Instructions regarding War Diaries and Intelligence Summaries are contained in F. S. Regs., Part II. and the Staff Manual respectively. Title pages will be prepared in manuscript.

Place	Date	Hour	Summary of Events and Information	Remarks and references to Appendices
FOURIÈRES (Aid Station 1 Coy) FRANCE	Sept 10 1917		ADMS Conference at Headquarters. SAILLY LABOURSE. 30 patients sent today to Noeny Rest Camp, BOULOGNE.	
	Sept 11		Capt GRAHAM, R.C., detached for temporary duty at 1 Coy. Lieut ROSANY, now Capt ROWLING, is now in charge for temporary duty with 1/5 N Midland Ambulance.	
	Sept 12		DDMS 1 Coy inspected Corps Rest Station this morning. 50 patients from 95th Division admitted - the Division Keep men in 1 Coy. Major GOODPASTER, USMC, detached to relieve Yieut FLORIAN, USMC, at 18 C.C.S. Lieut FLORIAN, USMC, detained for duty with 1/5 N Midland Toronto.	
	Sept 15		D.D.M.S. 1 Coy. inspected Rest Station.	
	Sept 17		A.D.M.S. Conference at Headquarters. SAILLY-LABOURSE.	
	Sept 19		A and Q.M.G. and D.D.M.S. 1 Coy. inspected Rest Station.	
			Capt FOSTER, M.C. RAMCTF, returned R.C., detached to duty with the above inspections - returned west. Lieut Hastings.	
	Sept 21		Capt BURNHAM, M.C. RAMCTF, reported for duty from Reserve and to No. 1 Coy. Lieut.	
			Capt LLOYD-WILLIAMS RAMCTF, reports for many duty, from temporary duty with No. Div. MED.	
	Sept 22		Hy Kay reported ADMS 46 Division, via lot BELSON R.C. CME. Reception + Station.	
			DDMS, Corps and ADMS 46 Division inspected Rest Station. 20 patients sent to Noeny Rest Camp, BOULOGNE.	
			Capt FOSTER, R.C. RAMCTF, attached O.E., return to the west for duty.	

1/2 North Midlands Field Ambulance
MMCTF
46 Division
BEF FRANCE

Army Form C. 2118.

WAR DIARY
or
INTELLIGENCE SUMMARY.
(Erase heading not required.)

Army Form C. 2118.

Instructions regarding War Diaries and Intelligence Summaries are contained in F.S. Regs., Part II. and the Staff Manual respectively. Title pages will be prepared in manuscript.

Place	Date	Hour	Summary of Events and Information	Remarks and references to Appendices
FOUQUEREUIL (1 Corps Rest Station) FRANCE	Sept 25		ADMS Conference at Montgomerie. SAILLY LABOURSE. Capt LLOYD MMCTF detailed for temporary duty with 1/6 North Staffordshire Battalion.	
	Sept 26		ADMS inspected personnel Details at FOUQUIERES this morning. Capt DOWLING AMCTF left for duty from temporary duty with 1/5 Lincolns	
	Sept 27		ADMS inspected Rest Station	
	Sept 29		DDMS 1 Corps inspected Rest Station. Average numbers of patients in Corps Rest Station - 240. Average numbers of moderate effects at Corps Rest Station - 3.	

R.M.Wright
Lieut Colonel AMCTF
O/C 1/2 North Mid. Field Amb?

Confidential

WAR DIARY
of
1/2 N. Mid Field Amb
R.A.M.C. T.F.
46th Division

from
September 1st 1917
to
September 30th 1917

N Wilbert
H Coland
R.A.M.C.
O/C 1/2 NMFA

140/578

1/2st North midland F.A.

COMMITTEE FOR THE
MEDICAL HISTORY OF THE WAR
Date 17 JAN. 1918

Army Form C. 2118.

WAR DIARY
or
INTELLIGENCE SUMMARY.
(Erase heading not required.)

Instructions regarding War Diaries and Intelligence Summaries are contained in F.S. Regs., Part II. and the Staff Manual respectively. Title pages will be prepared in manuscript.

1/2 N.M. 2d [?]

Place	Date	Hour	Summary of Events and Information	Remarks and references to Appendices
Longuenesse	1/10/17		O.C. attended conference at A.D.M.S. Capt Graham. I.O. proceeded on leave. 5 Aeroplane bombs dropped at Longuenesse this evening	
	4/10/17		A.D.M.S. I Corps inspected Corps Rest Station. By order of A.D.M.S. Ireland. 1 N.C.O & 24 men to report to O.C. 1/3 N. Mid. Fd Amb for duty during a Gas attack	
	5/10/17		The above Telephone party returned this morning. Attended Lecture at Noeux-les-Mines by Col. Beebee concerning Surgeon I Corps. Subject Thomas' Splint.	
	9/10/17		G.O.C. & A.D.M.S. 46th Div. inspected Corps Rest Station in which there is at present 308 patients	
	10/10/17		Attended conference at A.D.M.S. Capt Forster R.A.M.C. (T.C) detailed for duty with 1/5 North Staffs. D.D.M.S. I Corps inspected C.P.S.	
	12/10/17		Major Parker I.S.O. proceeded on 6 months leave.	
	13/10/17		Capt Lloyd Billiards rejoined unit after temporary duty with 1/6 N. Staffs	

Army Form C. 2118.

WAR DIARY
or
INTELLIGENCE SUMMARY.
(Erase heading not required.)

Instructions regarding War Diaries and Intelligence Summaries are contained in F. S. Regs., Part II. and the Staff Manual respectively. Title pages will be prepared in manuscript.

Place	Date	Hour	Summary of Events and Information	Remarks and references to Appendices
Dunquerre	13/10/17		ADMS inspects CRS & instructs me to arrange for the admissions & treatment of scabies patients	
	16/10/17		DDMS I Corps visits hospital. 60 patients sent to I Army Rest Camp Boulogne. Patients have been instructed & are taking Sibbald Thoiry Rub for the troops in rotation	
	17/10/17		Attended ADMS' conference	
	19/10/17		ADMS inspects CRS. 67 scabies patients in CRS	
	20/10/17	10:15 am	Hostile aeroplane disguised as a British dropped 3 bombs, one of which landed in CRS injuring 3 personal & 11 patients most seriously. As a result 2 RAMC & 2 patients died up to this evening. Most of the wounds were abdomen, head & chest. ADMS SMSH 16th Div called to inspect damage. SMO GOC and DDMS I Corps also called. Capt Graham RC demobilised and sent home for the purpose of attending civil population in England	
	23/10/17		DADMS I Corps visits CRS	

A6945 Wt W14422/M1160 35,000 12/16 D. D. & I. Forms/C./2118/14.

Army Form C. 2118.

WAR DIARY
or
INTELLIGENCE SUMMARY.
(Erase heading not required.)

Instructions regarding War Diaries and Intelligence Summaries are contained in F. S. Regs., Part II. and the Staff Manual respectively. Title pages will be prepared in manuscript.

Place	Date	Hour	Summary of Events and Information	Remarks and references to Appendices
Jonquin	28/10/17		ADMS & DDMS visits CRS & sent orders to meet Sick & patients. There are no at present in CRS	
	29/10/17		DDMS I Corps visits CRS. Capt Gowtin R.A.M.C (S.R) reports for duty and was detailed for duty with 1/5 Lincolns	
	30/10/17		Attended ADMS Conference. Lt Col Best to proceed to England Nov 1, 1917. Major L. Barron R.A.M.C I/S. Iud S.B. and to take Temporary Command	

J. C. Barron
Major R.A.M.C (S.R)
Commanding
1/2 North Midland Field Amb.

1/2nd North Midland F.A.

COMMITTEE FOR THE
MEDICAL HISTORY OF THE WAR
Date 17 JAN.1918

Army Form C. 2118.

WAR DIARY
or
INTELLIGENCE SUMMARY.

(Erase heading not required.)

Instructions regarding War Diaries and Intelligence Summaries are contained in F.S. Regs., Part II. and the Staff Manual respectively. Title pages will be prepared in manuscript.

Place	Date	Hour	Summary of Events and Information	Remarks and references to Appendices
Jacqueue	1/11/17		Lt. Col. Kent proceeds to England and Major J. McBarron 1/1 N. Fus. So Comd assumes temp. command. Lieuts W.A. McHugh & E.J. McCormick U.S. M.O.R.C. reports for duty. S.O./G.H.S. I Corps visits Hospital	
	2/11/17		S.O./G.H.S. I Corps visits Hospital	
	3/11/17		A.D.M.S. 46th Div visits Hospital. 17 cases of empetigo remaining after scabies arrived from I Corps Scabies Hospital Allouagne	
	5/11/17		A.D.M.S. 46th Div visits Hospital. Recd R.A.M.C. Garrison Order 129 address. 1/2 N Fus So Comd to relieve 5 Lorks 1/3 N Fus So Comd at Laborure. A.D.S's Philosophe & Lort Platz & attached Garen took Capt. G.S. Brown taken on the strength from Nov 1.17.	
	6/11/17		Div Quartermaster proceeds to Philosophe, Lort Platz, Laborure	
	8/11/17		Attended conference at A.D.M.S. Office. Capt. J. Fuller Quartermaster 2/3 N Fus So Comd came to look over B sec. I Corps R.S. Lorgueises with Capt Fuller. Drew up scheme for the approaching relief.	

Army Form C. 2118.

WAR DIARY
or
INTELLIGENCE SUMMARY.
(Erase heading not required.)

Instructions regarding War Diaries and Intelligence Summaries are contained in F. S. Regs., Part II. and the Staff Manual respectively. Title pages will be prepared in manuscript.

Place	Date	Hour	Summary of Events and Information	Remarks and references to Appendices
Jaqures	9/11/17		Despatched 4 N.C.O's & 20 men to A.D.S. Philosophe to G. Distributers Store at Lost Gats & Transport at an advance party	
	10/11/17		Detailed Lt. McCormick U.S. M.O.R.C. to proceed to Lost Gats. Capt Lloyd Williams to proceed to Philosophe. Relay of our A.D.S. & Transport was completed as regards personel & Equipment by 6 p.m.	
	11/11/17		Detailed Lt. Knight U.S. M.O.R.C. to proceed to A.D.S. Philosophe. Lieut C. Read R.A.M.C. (T.C.) from 58 Gen. Hospital taken on the strength	
	12/11/17		Lieut C. Read Detached for temporary duty at 18 CCS vice Lieut Goodpaster U.S. M.O.R.C. struck off the strength. Two officers sent to this unit by 1/3 N. Mid. Fd Amb. viz Capt Horsa to remain at Lost Gats & Capt Ellman U.S. M.O.R.C. at M.D.S. Labourse	
Labourse	13/11/17	9 p.m.	The ambulance proceeded to new Headquarters in the Schools Labourse Major K.C.I. Farmer returned from leave A.D.M.S. visits Hospital	

Army Form C. 2118.

WAR DIARY
or
INTELLIGENCE SUMMARY.

(Erase heading not required.)

Instructions regarding War Diaries and Intelligence Summaries are contained in F. S. Regs., Part II. and the Staff Manual respectively. Title pages will be prepared in manuscript.

Place	Date	Hour	Summary of Events and Information	Remarks and references to Appendices
Lillers	18/11/17	9.30 am	Proceeded to Philosophe which was visited by D.D.M.S. I Corps & D.D.M.S. 46 Div. Visit Capt Lloyd Williams (visits Hollywood Horse, S.T. Georges, Post Shed	
			Also to Check Pit Alley, Post Resp, Post Glab	
			Lt. McCormick returned to HdQrs. Lt. McVrigh proceeded from R.S.	
			Philosophe to Medical School 33 C.C.S. Bethune	
	16/11/17		Capt. I.S. Ullman proceeded to Lys & with 1/5 Lincs	
	17/11/17		Went to Post Glab & visits all Bearer posts in Chat sector	
	18/11/17		Went to D.M.S. visits Philosophe, Post Glab & all Bearer posts except	
			New Street, Laurel & Natal	
			A.A. & Q.M.G. 46th Div. visits Hospitals	
	20/11/17		Major Joscan proceed to Philosophe & visits Hollywood Horse, St Georges, R.A.P.	
	21/11/17		Attend conference A.D.M.S's office	
	22/11/17		Sent Lt McCormick to report for duty with 1/5 Sherwood Foresters	
	20/11/17		Lt. McCormick rejoined unit	

Army Form C. 2118

WAR DIARY
or
INTELLIGENCE SUMMARY
(Erase heading not required.)

Place	Date	Hour	Summary of Events and Information	Remarks and references to Appendices
Labourse	24/11/17		Lt. F.C. Hayt returned from T. Army Medical School Bethune. Recd R.A.M.C. Operation Order 131 saying that the Cambrin Sector would be taken over by 46th Div. about Dec 1 and that we were to relieve by 35 So Amb XI Div at Gorre Glatz & allied relay post. Made all necessary arrangements with F.O. i/c Gorre Glatz for this relief.	
	25/11/17	9.30	Proceeded to Cambrin & met O.C. 35th Do Amb 25th Div. Saw A.D.S's Harley St & Cambrin Church & discussed the means of evacuation & positions of relay posts. Reports the same to A.D.M.S. 46th Div.	
		2.30	Met A.D.M.S. 46th Div & so proceeded to H.Q. 6 1/3 N. Md Fd Amb.	
	26/11/17	10 am	With O.C. H.N. Md Fd Amb proceeded to A.D.S. Vermelles then to Bart's was post and then to a new post Paris constructed by 75th I.A. Map ref 36c G 30 a 7.5. This is to replace the old post Georges G 30 a 3 8. R. found that Patients could easily be conveyed from this new post to Bart post & so all casualties from the Cambrin sector could pass through Vermelles A.D.S.	

Army Form C. 2118.

WAR DIARY
or
INTELLIGENCE SUMMARY.
(Erase heading not required.)

Instructions regarding War Diaries and Intelligence Summaries are contained in F.S. Regs., Part II. and the Staff Manual respectively. Title pages will be prepared in manuscript.

Place	Date	Hour	Summary of Events and Information	Remarks and references to Appendices
	26/11/17		Reports recd of our reconnaissance to GHQ 46th Div	
		6 p.m.	Capt Horse & all personnel arrived from Lut Gheb & relief posts. Its relief by 35th Scot Bord Regiers been completed at 4 p.m.	
	27/11/17		Capt Horse proceeds to H.Q. 7th Div 26 Corps	
	28/11/17		Attended conference at 7th Div Hyder	
			Lt. E. J. McCormick 2nd Lt Breen and Cpl Boggs have proceeded to 7 Corps Medical School Bethune	
	29/11/17		Capt G.S. Breen R.A.M.C. (TC) reported for duty from leave	
			The relieve of the Transport complete with the exception of one Lewis mail received for inspection & trenches posts G.O.C of T Div. The relief was truth commended on its smart & efficient appearance by G.O.C	
	30/11/17		Proceeded to R.B.S Philosophe & Coss Staff were known St Pierres Lost St French Astillery Activity both ours & hostile	
			J.J. Raney Major Commanding	
			H.M. This to Conf	

COMMITTEE FOR THE
MEDICAL HISTORY OF THE WAR
Date -1 FEB. 1918

Army Form C. 2118.

14   1/2 WM 2nd Dec 1917

WAR DIARY
or
INTELLIGENCE SUMMARY.
(Erase heading not required.)

Instructions regarding War Diaries and Intelligence Summaries are contained in F.S. Regs., Part II. and the Staff Manual respectively. Title pages will be prepared in manuscript.

Place	Date	Hour	Summary of Events and Information	Remarks and references to Appendices
Lebanon			**MEDICAL**	
	1/12/17		Recd operation orders Re the No 132 describing one to take over Cambrin sector. Detailed Capt. G.S. Brown & a party of 10 men to proceed to R.B.S. Cambrin Church & relay posts	
	2/12/17	9 a.m.	Detailed a party of 17 men with equipment of a A.D.S. to proceed to Cambrin also 1 motor amb. to the Stationed Crew	
		1 a.m.	Lieut Colonel J. MILLER R.A.M.C. reports for duty and took over command of the Field Ambulance. — MAJOR BARRON R.A.M.C. relinquishes the 1/North Midland Field Amb. for duty.	
	3/12/17		Visited the ADS and been park at CAMBRIN, RAP in full working order and OR 35. The new RAP Humanity Trench were opened by ME in tunnel Dug out is already finished. The reserve water supply being fixed & and is nearly completed. and water to draw out	
	4/12/17		Visited ADS PHILOSOPHE and the 3 bearer posts attached to it. All in good condition. The Section Office is being installed at the ADS, and a portion built for the engine. Personnel examined by IMO R 42 OR 1 water cart + 2 mules	

WAR DIARY
or
INTELLIGENCE SUMMARY.
(Erase heading not required.)

Army Form C. 2118.

Place	Date	Hour	Summary of Events and Information	Remarks and references to Appendices
LABOURSE	4/12/17		ADS PHILOSOPHE had heavy traffic (gas?) also in good condition. No shelter	
	5/12/17		Repts. being received in ADS. Visited by our patrol surgeon.	
			Attended COs conference with ADMS.	
	7/12/17		Visited ADS CAMBRIN and became posted. Red cross car "Humber" filled to its door R.RAYS	
			WEEP under turnley & steelwire. 38 min RAP (Humanity Post) occupied by RMO	
			It is not familiar for M.P. + Personnel. The bield. The road with limbered	
			Sent 4 O.R. & ack as a fatigue party for improving ADS VERMELLES	
	8/12/17		Lt. Dr. CORMIER returned from RMC School 33 CCS BETHUNE in July	
			Visited ADS + BEARER POSTS PHILOSOPHE	
			Still crowding out parties of HUMANE M.D.S LABOURSE. Room for not improved—	
	10/12/17		Visited ADS CAMBRIN + took lunch	
	11/12/17		GERMAN Gas shell attack on CAMBRIN 2.45 enemies Rum (Phos + HBr Lichy	
			Scene —— 8 cases that to ADS.VERMELLES as extra heavy	
			Lt. Dr. CORMIER v.s. MRC went to RAP CAMBRIN 16 wound CAPT DEVELIN & Paris	
			from 8.30AM to 5pm	
			at 3.40pm a daylight raid on GERMAN Trenches 1st 2nd + 3rd lines 9900 rounds	

A6915 Wt. W14422/M1160 35,000 12/16 D. D. & L. Forms/C./2118/14.

Army Form C. 2118.

WAR DIARY
or
INTELLIGENCE SUMMARY.
(Erase heading not required.)

Instructions regarding War Diaries and Intelligence Summaries are contained in F. S. Regs., Part II. and the Staff Manual respectively. Title pages will be prepared in manuscript.

Place	Date	Hour	Summary of Events and Information	Remarks and references to Appendices
LABOURSE	12.12.17		SHERWOOD FORESTERS sent four ADS VERMELLES. ADS-in-Rillieux 3 Kelly.	
			Wounded. Our two front MDS sent 8 stops wounded GERMANS told MO	
			Officers returning to wound. No wounded on return. Success the raid by our RAP.	
			2 Rep[?] fatalities and new hut ½ P. Belfield	
			Lieut M.R. HUGH R.G.M.R.C. returned from UK after sick leave.	
	14.12.17		Lecture to Unit on War Savings by Major Turner D.S.O.	
			Conducted two American Officers consisting of one Colonel and two Majors of	
			the American Army Medical services round the CAMBRIN Sector & saw both	
			their round the front line. ADS and RAP the through MUNSTER TUNNEL	
			to front line and along the line of evacuation of wounded to ADS at	
			CAMBRIN. Took them over MDS. LABOURSE and lunched them afterwards.	
			Then left on motors Bruay.	
	16.12.17		Visited PHILOSOPHE ADS + been parts also RAP all in good order. Very quiet.	
			Very few casualties coming through.	
	17.12.17		Visited CAMBRIN ADS + been parts all in good condition. In the RAP the	
			Gas curtain was not from RAP reported this to ADMS 46 Div.	

A6915 Wt.W11422,M1160 35,000 12/16 D.D.&L. Forms/C/2118/14.

WAR DIARY
INTELLIGENCE SUMMARY

Army Form C. 2118.

Place	Date	Hour	Summary of Events and Information	Remarks and references to Appendices
LABOURSE	17.12.17		Our late RAP the only unit for MO & RAMC personnel are now quite finished and there are no stretcher cases up. Lieut. McCORMICK goes to ADS PHILOSOPHE for duty. Capt G.H.H. MANSFIELD and Capt. B.H. PALMER joined the Unit from 54. C.C.S. for duty	
	18.12.17		CAPT G.H.H. MANSFIELD returned Capt. I.H. LLOYD WILLIAMS at the ADS PHILOSOPHE the latter proceeding on 14 days leave.	
	19.12.17		Conducted Classes & P.M.O. to inspect 457 & 458 amb ASC at NOEUX LES MINES every Saturday at 2.15 & 3.45. Conferences at ADMS office. Was visited by ADMS who brought up American Medical Officers to see Horse Lines, the Wheel transport and the complete equipment of our section of a Field Ambulance.	
	21.12.17		Cpl King RAMC left for England to take up to Commission. One ASC driver for party proceeding to BOULOGNE for demount. Visited PHILOSOPHE ADS & been posts, all correct.	
	22.12.17		Visited CAMBRIN ADS & been posts	
	23.12.17		Lieut McHUGH to 1st Corps School GOSNAY to relieve Capt. STRANGE presently on Sphere line	
	24.12.17		Visited CAMBRIN ADS & teams posts also New ADS. Gas curtains finished	

WAR DIARY
or
INTELLIGENCE SUMMARY.

Army Form C. 2118.

Place	Date	Hour	Summary of Events and Information	Remarks and references to Appendices
LABOURSE	25.12.17		CAPT MANFIELD proceeded to ENGLAND 14 days leave. SOUS PHILOSOPHE ADS + CAMBRIN ADS + lorry park all order. Sad News from Tuly Palm-putting taken	
	27.12.17		With 2 m/s Platoon of Civil Rifles on the salvate work. Very little shelling. Had 10 Grand Corps from 125" Siege Bat. S.A.H.A. Gas Plugged. 3 cases severe, the other of slight nature. When seen were evacuated straight from ADS to CCS	
	28.12.17		Visited PHILOSOPHE ADS + lorry park. Capt + QM CROSS returned from leave	
	31.12.17		Visited CAMBRIN ADS + Beaver park. The new RAP HUMANITY POST is now finished. Gas door complete and good. RMOs discreet finished. Stretcher Racks on Gun frames. Day out for present Stretcher bearers and RAMC bearers complete. under 10 lines Good work done R.e.D D Expedients.	

John Walter
LIEUT. COL. Comdg
1/2nd North Mid Fd Amb RAMC

1/2nd North Midland F. A.

WAR DIARY
or
INTELLIGENCE SUMMARY.
(Erase heading not required.)

Army Form C. 2118.

1/2 N M 3rd Army

Place	Date	Hour	Summary of Events and Information	Remarks and references to Appendices
LABOURSE	1.1.18		Capt T GRAHAM. RAMC. rejoined the Unit from ENGLAND	
	2.1.18		Conference at ADMS. Visited PHILOSOPHE ADS + mean pale extra ADS all places in order	
	4.1.18		Capt. Lloyd Williams RAMC Returned from short leave. On Duty	
	5.1.18		Capt. B.H. PALMER returned at VERQUIN to act as T/MO to 24 Sultan group in place of	
			Lt. W PROUNIER proceeding on 14 days leave. Lt Col J MILLER awarded A.M.S.	
			Visited CAMBRIN ADS and mean pale also the new RAP which is near finished	
	7.1.18		Joined both ADSs at PHILOSOPHE + CAMBRIN, means of selling the letter from	
			and near ADS.	
	8.1.18		Lt Col J MILLER proceeded on 14 days leave	
	9.1.18		Attended ADMS Conference. QMS (Acting S.S.E Major) T. WHEWAY awarded the M.S.M. 1st Lieut	
			McHUGH returned for duty from No Corps Schools	
	10.1.18		1st Lieut. McHUGH detailed for duty at No 18 CCS. Capt MANSFIELD MC. returned from Leave	
			for duty. Visited ADS CAMBRIN. Slopes	
	12.1.18		ADMS AcA Div + DMS called. Visited CAMBRIN ADS. PHILOSOPHE Recently ALS in influence	
			constructive one SOYERS. STOVE.	
	13.1.18		Visited PHILOSOPHE with DADMS visited new billeting area and called on 132 Bde. HQ.	

Army Form C. 2118.

WAR DIARY
or
INTELLIGENCE SUMMARY.
(Erase heading not required.)

Instructions regarding War Diaries and Intelligence Summaries are contained in F. S. Regs., Part II. and the Staff Manual respectively. Title pages will be prepared in manuscript.

Place	Date	Hour	Summary of Events and Information	Remarks and references to Appendices
LABOURSE	13.1.18		Concluded arrangements for forthcoming course.	
	14.1.18		With ADMS went over crest Infantry area. Billets quite insufficient on pass starting.	
	16.1.18		Snow postponed until further orders.	
	17.1.18		Visited CAMBRIN + brown funks, trenches bad and falling in in many places.	
	18.1.18		Visited PHILOSOPHE and town hall. In evening received orders. Ambulances to be relieved tomorrow.	
	19.1.18		At noon received orders to stand fast. Move postponed.	
	22.1.18		Visited PHILOSOPHE + CAMBRIN	
	23.1.18		With ADMS went to CANTRAINNE and inspected new billets for Regt.	
	24.1.18		Relieved by 35th Fd Ambc 11th Divn at LABOURSE M.D.S. and took over at CAMBRIN + PHILOSOPHE	
			8th Hants moved from the M.D.S + ADSs marched by separate routes to new billets at CANTRAINNE	
			arriving about 3.45 pm in good condition. Lt Col J Miller MC. detained by duty from Regt.	
CANTRAINNE	24.1.18	4 pm	The sanitary condition of this village on arrival billets for troops is bad. No public latrines built.	
			All our places are inaccessible. It is impossible to dig deeper than 12 inches on account of water	
			from an estate in some walls from 6-10 inches of water fairly clean and rain water, the Lesses	
			in various sheds and subways in tired school farm. No barrack rooms. Officers billets four	
			the one around billet club in small courtyard. Water supply autumn wells. Two Case troops.	

A6945 Wt. W14422/M1160 35,000 12/16 D. D. & L. Forms/C./2118/14.

Army Form C. 2118.

WAR DIARY
or
INTELLIGENCE SUMMARY.
(Erase heading not required.)

Instructions regarding War Diaries and Intelligence Summaries are contained in F. S. Regs., Part II. and the Staff Manual respectively. Title pages will be prepared in manuscript.

Place	Date	Hour	Summary of Events and Information	Remarks and references to Appendices
CANTRAINE	24.1.18		Special Corps Bokrooms and incinerators found for collection refuse. Cook houses in that order Eng.	
	25.1.18		and training started. All further orders to boss quarter orderly. Capt. R. ROWE RAMC 15 Corps duty on MO 1/1 Leices Regt in place of Capt MASON in leave.	
			1st Lieut McCORMICK US MRC 15 Corps duty as MO 1/1 Staffs Regt. Capt LAMB R.A.M.C in place. Men employed in general clean up of billet and bivouac. Two Extra baths and disinfectors mth of eb. 138 Inf Bde. daily. bringing them to the demand level of ANZAC MOB. BATH.	
	26.1.18		Men are washed and examined 15 N.C.Os. & other LR Corps Reg Schm. Series IV Anroos Scheme Boys 15.4.18 Ex Brad 136 Bde.	
	27.1.18		1/1/4/23 said Pte HOGART J transferred to 38 Div Train.	
	28.1.18		Recent clean trains to keep best on back of the 213 billet. Route march for personnel in morning. Physical exercises in afternoon.	
	31.1.18		Arranged for weekly inspection for Scabies of 138 & 139 Inf. Bde. and DHQ	

J. ....
LIEUT. COL. COMDG.
1/2nd North Mid. Fd. Amb. R. A. M. C:

1/24 N.M. T.O.

COMMITTEE FOR THE
~~DICAL HISTORY O~ THE WA~

Date -8 APR.1918

Army Form C. 2118.

WAR DIARY
or
INTELLIGENCE SUMMARY.
(Erase heading not required.)

1/2 N M Fd A YA 36

Place	Date	Hour	Summary of Events and Information	Remarks and references to Appendices
CANTRAINNE	1.2.18		General training of the Unit continued. Chiefly Physical exercises and route marches	
	3.2.18		Inspection of whole unit and church parade at 3.15 pm.	
	4.2.18		Lieut. W.A. McHUGH U.S. M.R.C. transferred to No 58 C.C.S. and is struck off the strength of the Unit. Until the Unit in the 138 Inf Bde cares being R.M.O.	
	6.2.18		Sent 2 riding horses with saddles and bridles with groom to R.A.M.C. school at BRAY for duty in riding school.	
	7.2.18		CAPT. A.H. DONALDSON. at present at R.A.M.C. school is placed on the strength of the Unit. CAPT LLOYD WILLIAMS. R.A.M.C. to act as M.O. to 46 DAC. while CAPT WOOD is a month leave attended a conference of O.C's of 138 Inf Bde. under the Bns, Comdr 138 Inf Bde. at H.Q Qrs. 138 Inf Bde, regarding the pending move of the Bde	
	8.2.18		Marched from CANTRAINNE "Rawley House" our billet and Car store to area Concentration to starting point M.G. 45.70 Sheets 36 A & 36 B. Post Bayolier 138 Inf Bde at starting point at 11.38 a.m. following 452 Coy A.S.C. Distance between Units 500 yards. Route: LILLERS. HURIONVILLE BELLERY ANNETTES NADON to NEDONCHELLE arrived at billets place 2.15 pm No man of the Ambulance fell out.	

Army Form C. 2118.

WAR DIARY
or
INTELLIGENCE SUMMARY.
(Erase heading not required.)

Instructions regarding War Diaries and Intelligence Summaries are contained in F. S. Regs., Part II. and the Staff Manual respectively. Title pages will be prepared in manuscript.

Place	Date	Hour	Summary of Events and Information	Remarks and references to Appendices
NEDONCHELLE	8.2.18		No mid day halt, only the 10 minute halts at each hour allowed. Why the R Ambulances carried 33 men unable to march and the Horse Ambulances following the Brigade picked up 15 men fallen out during the march of the Brigade.	
	9.2.18		Left NEDONCHELLE 10-45 am.; passed starting point, road junction S.28.e.3.0., which was passed at 11.45 am., followed 139 Inf. Bde. to FEBVIN PALFART, 90 yards distance between all Units. Between FEBVIN PALFART and FLECHIN we passed in column of route the G.O.C. the Division & 1st CORPS Commander. Salutes were given. Shortly after this marching halt was ordered. Watered and fed animals, men mid day ration on resuming march towards FLECHIN. I received orders to proceed direct to AUDINCTHUN. Route FLECHIN, LAIRES, BEAUMETZ-LES-AIRES, RECLINGHEM, DENNEBROEUCQ to AUDINCTHUN, arriving at 5.15 pm. No R.A.M.C. men fell out. Horse Ambulances picked up 13 men on the route.	
AUDINCTHUN	9.2.18		Billets for men in good farms. All horses under cover in buildings and stables, sanitation ad. no proper latrines to maintain. Men had good hot meal 7.30 pm.	
	10.2.18		Men latrines and incinerator built. Billets re-arranged and men fixed up, all the men of 139 Inf. Bde. who were carried on the march returned to their regiment with the	

WARDIARY
or
INTELLIGENCE SUMMARY.
(Erase heading not required.)

Army Form C. 2118.

Place	Date	Hour	Summary of Events and Information	Remarks and references to Appendices
AUDINCTHUN	10.2.18		with the exception of 7. who were sent to 58 CCS LILLERS. Four still fixed and remain sick in school. returned Capt. BROWN RAMC reported for duty from 1/5 Leicester Regt.	
	12.2.18.		Two men sent to RAMC school 22 CCS for course of First aid and Sanitation 4 days. Program of training drawn up. Consisting of Squad & Coy drill, Gas drill, Physical exercises route marches, Muster, rolls and First inspection, examination of Equipment, is Estuys & 2 rooms ground floor used for an R.A.P. and two places, hutting 10 stretches on rack. Medical Staff in same building arranged for morning collection of sick in my Brigade area by R.A.M.C Ambulances. Cases evacuated to 58 CCS LILLERS. + A ? min 136 Corps Rest Sc. Cars only returned on my request 3 days & reopened. 1st Lt. McCORMICK US MRC posted for duty from 40 Staffs Regt.	
	13.2.18.		Conference of SCS friends with ADMS. Visited all MOS. 136 Bde Area. Scrubbing in whole area my hour. Very fine Cleansing benches in proper Column. Bullets fine	
	16.2.18.		Car embarking from Officers RAMC. sent to RAMC School for special Lecture	
	18.2.18.		R. Seelig. taken over the Hospitals from C. Seelig. gone on Leave 7 days.	
	15.2.18		Sergt. Major Wheatey Effd. the Condr. for England to take a Commission as QM	

WAR DIARY
INTELLIGENCE SUMMARY
(Erase heading not required.)

Army Form C. 2118.

Place	Date	Hour	Summary of Events and Information	Remarks and references to Appendices
AVRINCTHUN	20.2.18		Lt. Major sent for course at RAMC School BRUAY. Capt. BROWN, RAMC to relieve Capt. Dowling RAMC as M.O. 1/5 Leics Regt. the latter proceeding to a course at the RAMC School. Conference at ADMS. — Major Trump DSO attended a lecture at HOUDAIN on "Food Economy" Capt. Donaldson 16 att 20. M.O. 1/5 Army Mustering Camp. for many sick at MATRINGHEM	
	21.2.18		The march of main ambulance cars of this divic. proved most trials sometimes needing paint, the roads will subult via paint. Very good effects and the sanitary point will attach and is easily applied. The paint must be applied warm. This method saves time in painting the cars as the water passes thro' in from 2-4 hours so that 2 coats can be put on the same day, and is cheaper than oil paint. Permission given by DDMS 1st Corps 16 evacuate cases to 39 St Hosp AIRE attached with ADMS. Return of Sergt George Wallace and Sergt Sumner Sis W. Heveringham at the opening of a course at RAMC School BRUAY.	
	25.2.18		2 NCO's & OR sent for bath test at BOMY. Lecture on Warfare in War from division by Lieut. Col. S. MILLER M.C. RAMCT. to 1/5 Leicester Regt. officers & NCOs.	
	26.		Major TURNER DSO. RAMCT proceed to England on 14 days leave.	

Army Form C. 2118.

WAR DIARY
or
INTELLIGENCE SUMMARY.
(*Erase heading not required.*)

Instructions regarding War Diaries and Intelligence Summaries are contained in F. S. Regs., Part II. and the Staff Manual respectively. Title pages will be prepared in manuscript.

Place	Date	Hour	Summary of Events and Information	Remarks and references to Appendices
N⁰ DMC THUM	27.2.18.		Warning notice from 138. Inf. Bde. of an impending mais. Conference with	
	28.2.18.		ADMS. 46 Division. Hon. Capt & QM Crow reverted sick to 59. CCS.	
			CAPT LLOYD WILLIAMS RAMC. reported from DAC 46 Div for Duty — Capt	
			DONALDSON. RAMC. to act as RMO to 1/5 Leics Regt. LIEUT JAFF RAMC, RMO	
			1/5 Leics Regt. evacuated sick to 59. CCS. BLISTERS. Ctts equipment wagons packed	
			in view of impending mais. 1 G.S.W. received from A.S.C. to carry blankets &	
			personnel whilst on the mais.	

John Challis
M.C.
LIEUT. COL. COMDG.
1/2nd North Mid. Fd. Amb. R. A. M. C.

LIEUT. COL. COMDG.
1/2nd North Mid. Fd. Amb. R. A. M. C.

140/2849.

1/2 Mtd. Mtd. F Ambulance

March
1916

Army Form C. 2118.

WAR DIARY
or
INTELLIGENCE SUMMARY.

12 N.M. 7 A Amb.

(Erase heading not required.)

Instructions regarding War Diaries and Intelligence Summaries are contained in F. S. Regs., Part II. and the Staff Manual respectively. Title pages will be prepared in manuscript.

Place	Date	Hour	Summary of Events and Information	Remarks and references to Appendices
AUDINCTHUN	1.3.18		Lieut. McCormack v.3 M.B.E. left on 14 days leave to NICE. – Left AUDINCTHUN – 6.30 am on march to CUHEM. route DENNEBROEUCQ – RECLINGHEN – BEAUMETZ-LES-AIRE to CUHEM, billets for one night. arrived 12.40 p.m. Clock hour 10 minute halt	
CUHEM	2.3.18		March. CUHEM to LE CORNET BOURDOIS. arrived 3 p.m. Started 10 a.m. Route. BEUVIN, PALFART, WESTREHEM – AUCHY – ST HILAIRE – LILLERS. billets col. wilh' Brown. Billeti (trd) at LE CORNET BOURDOIS. No horse standings in CUHEM	
LECORNET – BOURDOIS	3.3.18		March. LECORNET BOURDOIS to BETHUNE. route LILLERS, ETHOCQUES. arrived 12.45. no men fell out' during the three days march, no workshop to leave on wagons.	
BETHUNE	4.3.18	1 p.m.	Ambulance settled in the Institute. ST VAAST. Horses in standings covered over self tent. Capt. GRAHAM. with 26. O.R. took over the A.D.S. and bearer posts at CAMBRIN. relief completed 4 p.m.	
	5.3.18.		Capts. MANFIELD + BROWN. with 33 other ranks took over the A.D.S. + bearer posts at HARLEY STREET. Rest of ambulance settled in ST VAAST in rooms for own work only.	
	6.3.18		Lent post in CAMBRIN. + HARLEY STREET with A.D.M.S. 46 Div Conference A.D.M.S. office of O.C.s Fd Amb. visits with ADMS all the bear posts ADS, and route of evacuation of sick + wounded. Trenches saw condition + dry	

Army Form C. 2118.

WAR DIARY
or
INTELLIGENCE SUMMARY.
(Erase heading not required.)

Instructions regarding War Diaries and Intelligence Summaries are contained in F. S. Regs., Part II. and the Staff Manual respectively. Title pages will be prepared in manuscript.

Place	Date	Hour	Summary of Events and Information	Remarks and references to Appendices
BETHUNE.	6.3.18		There is a Motor rail from RAP. HERFORD ST. to ADS HARLEY ST. for Stretcher cases.	
			Cpl. Tinson R.A.M.S. sent to 14 Days cook at R.A.M.C. School BRUAY. Violent baths.	
			at BEUVRY, and dis jars and dirty clothing is placed much to ease the strain.	
	7.3.18		10 extra men to ADS. HARLEY ST for cleaning up and refacing ADS. 4 extra bearers to	
			CAMBRIN. ADS. for duty. at RAP. BARTS. extension of shelters case from here to VERMELLES	
			Built on earth ramp. told front and back of same. Standings for particulars of Humer	
			unable to build higher than 3 feet for want of stakes and wire.	
	8.3.18.		Visited both ADSs and posts. All quiet.	
	9.3.18.		Conducted a party of six American Senior Medical Officers round both ADSs and	
			main posts to Cambrain and Harley St. we were killed at entrance of RAILWAY	
			ALLEY, CAMBRIN end. No damage. They then inspected the hour Lines, Mess	
			and wagons of the Ambulance, also the medical equipment of our section	
	10.3.18.		Going LE PREOL in order to find a working wounded trick from Harley St. ADS	
			Infantry trucks R.11 + 1. answering the purpose. It is proposed to put one each	
			post in LE PREOL for use of the W. wounded, and as a Motor Ambulance Station	
			Church parade held in the Square of this Hospital	

WAR DIARY
or
INTELLIGENCE SUMMARY.
(Erase heading not required.)

Army Form C. 2118.

Place	Date	Hour	Summary of Events and Information	Remarks and references to Appendices
BETHUNE	12.3.18		Visit ANNEQUIN. Foss with DADMS 46 Div regarding a new ADS to take the place of the one at CAMBRIN which is heavily shelled. Tried to find a suitable crossing track from the shelling near the river. Dugouts at CAMBRIN proofed and coal stacked.	
	13.3.18		Conference of COs fld Amb. with ADMS. Visit LE PREOL with ADMS. and with one Col. Bath House for an ADS. Slipshod. Failing to be built up inside the tower sand bagged. Ambulance car to be kept at back of building.	
	14.3.18		Down from ordnance two camouflets when up and sent them to LE PREOL. R.A.P. HARFORD ST. when in observation post, no casualties. R.A.P. moved to A.20.b.8.2.	
	15.3.18		2 RAMC trans at R.A.P. Bearer post. moved to DAWSON ST A.15.c.3.3., 12 L 2 O R. Major TURNER. DSO reported from short leave. Visit LE PREOL with ADMS and wouldn't can try bathe RU Water on new field post — to be begun as soon as timber and sand bags are supplied. Arranged a weekly inspection of 452 + 453 Coys ASC at VENDIN-LEZ-BETHUNE. Capt. DONALDSON to temp. duty as MO 1/5 Leicester Regt. to relieve Lieut. JACK. Dr. CURRIE of medical treatment at BETHUNE.	
	17.3.18		Capt. LLOYD WILLIAMS for duty at ADS. HARLEY SC to relieved Capt. BROWN proceeding on 14 days leave. (to England)	

Army Form C. 2118.

WAR DIARY
or
INTELLIGENCE SUMMARY.
(Erase heading not required.)

Instructions regarding War Diaries and Intelligence Summaries are contained in F. S. Regs., Part II. and the Staff Manual respectively. Title pages will be prepared in manuscript.

Place	Date	Hour	Summary of Events and Information	Remarks and references to Appendices
BETHUNE	17.3.18		Stoled work on new ADS. LE PREOL. BETHUNE combined shell F.10.C.S.S. which will be an elephant hut sandbagged, on ground floor of the cale but about two rooms being so filled. Fed p.m. barg. 1st NCO & 12 men sent up each morning returning to HQ Coy in evening. 1st Lieut McCORMICK MORC U.S.A. reported from Evian for duty.	
	18.3.18		Visited LE PROEL. work getting on. Explored various tracks and roads round BEUVRY, for walking wounded cases.	
	19.3.19.		Visited PROEL + CAMBRIN + HARLEY ST. HARLEY ST. ADSS all satisfactory and in good condition. Rent work on others. BETHUNE shelled by 7.2 naval gun. Several casualties. 419000. S/Sgt. NEAL W.H. to be acting Q.M.S. from 15.2.18. and 419477 Q.M.S. WILLIAMS W.S. to be acting Sergt. Major from 15.2.18. inclusive. (ref. DGMS/6/1450/2184.16.3.18)	
	20.3.18		Conference A.D.M.S. BETHUNE. Shelled some casualties among Civilians and Soldiers seen in this Ambulance. Civil road through night 20-21°C. Casualties civilian and horses Singois Hon. Capt + M. AT + ROSS evacuated to ENGLAND, not struck of strength of Unit.	
	21.3.18		Visited LE PROEL, work progressing. New ADSs. and hubs at HARLEY ST + CAMBRIN. BETHUNE bombed. During evening. Some damage to roofs & civilians, one or two.	

Army Form C. 2118.

WAR DIARY
or
INTELLIGENCE SUMMARY.
(Erase heading not required.)

Instructions regarding War Diaries and Intelligence Summaries are contained in F. S. Regs., Part II. and the Staff Manual respectively. Title pages will be prepared in manuscript.

Place	Date	Hour	Summary of Events and Information	Remarks and references to Appendices
BETHUNE.	23.3.18		Took over ST VAAST from 1/3. H.M.F. Amb.	
	24.3.18		Conference at ADMS. regarding expected attack on CAMBRIN sector. Am LE PREOL post handed over as a walking wounded post to 1/1 H.M.F. Amb., and the Bearer R.U. from HARLEY ST. ADS to LE PREOL marched out; and a motor launch arranged for to carry walking wounded from LE PREOL down the LA BASSÉE canal to BETHUNE and so to G. ST VAAST. Received 100 extra stretchers from 23 C.C.S., and one Officer and 48 bearers with 160 blankets from the 1/3. H. and F.Cook.	
	26.3.18		Capt. C.H. MANFIELD. MC. promoted acting Major from 4th. 1918. Received notice of impending move.	
Pt. SAINS (FOSSE 10)	28.3.18.		Took over School at FOSSE 10 as a main dressing station, and the ADSs at FOSSE 11 CITÉ ST. PIERRE and FORT GLATZ also two bearer posts at MAROC. & BULLY GRENAY all taken over from 134 Canadian Field Ambulance. Major MANFIELD MC at 1st demi. McCORMICK MORE USA at FORT GLATZ. MAJOR TURNER DSO at C. ST PIERRE Coll. LLOYD WILLIAMS at FOSSE 11	
	29.3.18		Visit from ADMS. 46 Div at FOSSE 10. Visited ADS & Posts C. ST. PIERRE	
	30.3.18		Visited with ADMS. ADSs. FOSSE 11 and C. ST. PIERRE and bearer posts also B. GRENAY	

John Miller
Lt. Col.

160/7400

1/9 M.M. Field Ambulance.

COMMITTEE FOR THE
MEDICAL HISTORY OF THE WAR
Date 6 JUN 1918

Army Form C. 2118.

WAR DIARY
or
INTELLIGENCE SUMMARY.
(Erase heading not required.)

1/2 WM 2/4 ??? 38

Place	Date	Hour	Summary of Events and Information	Remarks and references to Appendices
P. SAINS (FOSSE 10)	1.4.18		Visited with ADMS. ADS + learn pdc at ST PIERRE.	
	2.4.18		Sited ADS + learn pdc at FORT GLATZ.	
	4.4.18		Conference of ADMS with OCs FD Amb. Said with ADMS. for GLATZ	
	6.4.18		Visits from DOMS 16c Corps.	
	8.4.18		Large number of Mustard Gas cases admitted. Symptoms Conjunctivitis Laryngitis and cough. Some blistering of skin. 3 serious cases. 2 of which died later. Also at ADS. much slyer relief.	
	9.4.18		Still large numbers of gas cases coming in. Shell gas yellow cross + blue cross cases mostly from the back areas. Report on gas cases (Shell) from 6.4.18 to 16.4.18. given in Appendix I.	appendix shell see above no I
	11.4.18		Conference ADMS. Capt: Donaldson RAMC transferred to 91st Bde RGA as RMO. En is struck off the strength of the ambulance. Relief by the 10th Canadian Field Ambulance. Parties relief in the ADSs + learn Pdc.	
	12.4.18		Relief of ADSs FORT GLATZ. Foss 11 + ST PIERRE completed by 12 midnight. Also the 10th Canadian Fd amb took over the MDS at Fosse 10.	
	13.4.18		The 1/2 North Mid FD Amb. marched away from Fosse 10 at 5am. for BARLIN.	

WAR DIARY or INTELLIGENCE SUMMARY

Army Form C. 2118.

Place	Date	Hour	Summary of Events and Information	Remarks and references to Appendices
BARLIN	13.4.18		Reached BARLIN at 10.15 am. Men billeted in huts on site of old CCS. Horses & mules in covered standings nearby, and Transport drawn in Park on Bows Road. Ambulances to be ready to move off at 4 hour notice.	
	17.4.18		Conference with ADMS. Still standing to 4 hour notice. An epidemic of PUO among the 1/5 Lincoln Regt. Symptoms. Headache, pain in back & limbs, laryngitis and in some cases pain in shins. Symptoms like Influenza.	
	18.4.18		Issued 1/5 Lincoln Regt. 150 cases of PUO. Transferred them to Lecuve and Amb. Camp to the 1/3 N.M. F Amb. at BRUAY.	
	19.4.18		45 fresh cases among 1/5 Lincoln Regt. Same symptoms. Removed them to BRUAY	
	20.4.18		49 fresh cases 1/5 Lincoln Regt. of PUO. Removed them to BRUAY.	
	21.4.18		12 new PUO 1/5 Lincoln Regt. 5 similar cases in the 1/4 Lecuve Regt and 11 cases in the 1/4 Lincoln Regt. All cases removed to BRUAY. One officer & 2, cases in 1/2 N. and 7th Cmb. PUO. Officers evacuated to 23 CCS men dealt with from camp. 3 clerks all clear cases of PUO on Influenza. In these cases the men had been in trenches 16 days, and others to in large amount of vents and in some cases concentrated hill air. The temperature varied from 99° to 103°	

Army Form C. 2118.

WAR DIARY
or
INTELLIGENCE SUMMARY.
(Erase heading not required.)

Instructions regarding War Diaries and Intelligence Summaries are contained in F. S. Regs., Part II. and the Staff Manual respectively. Title pages will be prepared in manuscript.

Place	Date	Hour	Summary of Events and Information	Remarks and references to Appendices
BARLIN	21/4/18		Lieut: McCormick evacuated to 23. CCS sick	
	22.4.18		The whole unit inspected by 46 Div Gas Officer at SBR inspected and men passed through the gas chamber. Capt. Hugh O'Curran to M.O. 45 Bmb to relieve Capt Donnelly sick. Bren in S/SD Movement L.D. Way	
LABEUVRIERE	24.4.18		Conference with ADMS. Took over 1St Corps. R.O.C. S.Cullin, 2nd Corps Col-GRAHAM and A Seanie. 16 late over 1St Corps. Services S(Ciller)	
	26.4.18		Convoy north sec CCS. Major Turner A. Blanch, Major Kingsford, C. Blanch and Capt Mann. B. Blanch	
	28.4.18		Ordered by DDMS 1St Corps 16 remove BRCS and hospital material from Aire to B section CRS at FOUQUIERES. Drs/sheets blankets etc.	

J M Miller
Lieut Col RAMC
1/2 H. M. F. Amb.

Appendix I

has been detached and filed under plans

"Rest Stations"

trenches the cavalry field ambulance in question sent a detachment to TOUR DE PAISSY to open an advanced dressing station. Thus, at this period it had begun to operate anew behind the 1st.Division, and had now withdrawn entirely from the 2nd.Divisional area, for the cavalry brigade there had been relieved by a brigade of the newly-arrived 6th.Division.

The

140/2983

1/A NZ. Med. + G.

COMMITTEE FOR THE
MEDICAL HISTORY OF THE WAR
Date 9 JUL 1918

Army Form C. 2118.

WAR DIARY
or
INTELLIGENCE SUMMARY.
(Erase heading not required.)

1/2 N.M 3rd Army 907 39

Place	Date	Hour	Summary of Events and Information	Remarks and references to Appendices
LABEUVRIERE	1/5/18		Conference ADMS 46 Div. Work at 1st Corps Rest Station. Removed all beds from stores and R.E. from B. Section 1st Corps Rest Station also all BRCS on loan. Obtained Stretcher Cxn general rest Station equipment to A Section 1st Corps Rest Station at LABEUVRIERE, after this I was able to place beds in any ward and hut.	
	4/5/18		Had then good concert for the patients during past week, free admission, and also three for which a small fee was charged for the benefit of the concert party. Received an order from DDMS 4th Div 1st Corps that Division cars to send their own cars into the C.R.S. Except from the Corps Scabies Station and 1/1 M.M 7 Camb. which were collected by my Horse Ambulance.	
	4/5/18		Two concerts given by the C.R.R. Party.	
	8/5/18		Visit from DDMS 1st Corps. Conference ADMS 46 Div. Cxn G.S wagon loaded with equipment by a W.U.S. sent to 1/3 North M.D Fd Amb, will return and Service, to remain until return (?)	
	10/5/18.		Some shelling on railway near my Horse Emic. Evacuated by classification 26 men 110 Railway Coy R.E. For rest of men see marked A	

A6945. Wt W11422/M1160 35/000. 12/16 D.D. & I. Forms/C./2118/14.

Army Form C. 2118.

WAR DIARY
or
INTELLIGENCE SUMMARY.
(Erase heading not required.)

Place	Date	Hour	Summary of Events and Information	Remarks and references to Appendices
LABEUVRIER	12/5/18		Orders from DDMS. 1st Corps. to reduce number of patients in CRS. on accounts of shelling. 40 patients to be sent to 7 Pro & 4 Stationary Hospital daily by MAC cars. Telegram 16th sent to ADMS. ST OMER. St OMER. Sorry number to be sent not to exceed 300.	
	14/5/18		Attended a lecture at 34th FA Amb. on Gas. by Colonel Horne. Subject Cylinder 1st Army Dry industry, & chlorine were attended. Got kits and refers of patients in CRS. handed over. Lecture kept under the beds in the wards in case of a sudden move in which case men CO of G. 22 CCS PARNES.	
			1st Current given by cement party of Yr. Hond. Ind. FD Amb. by Sgt. Drewn huff near of cement-park. Dr. W.N.TOOS. Cement blocks are during night, no tracks dropped near the CRS.	
	18/5/18		Saw cement gun in shelter during bombardment. Attended in Board of Revenal at HQrs 46. Division.	
	19/5/18		Colic G.S BROWN. RAMC. Refr for Embry duty. as RMO IS 1/4 Lincoln Refr in place of Colic Macpson. RAMC. Sick So W.	
	22/5/18		Capitan of W.N.TOOS. ADMS 46 + Col HOBBS DSO Attended. good show.	

Army Form C. 2118.

WAR DIARY
or
INTELLIGENCE SUMMARY.
(Erase heading not required.)

Instructions regarding War Diaries and Intelligence Summaries are contained in F. S. Regs., Part II. and the Staff Manual respectively. Title pages will be prepared in manuscript.

Place	Date	Hour	Summary of Events and Information	Remarks and references to Appendices
LABOURSE	22.5.16		Conference ADMS HQ Division. Men billets in Farbus and Adms' Relays	
			Sergt KEOGH RAMC 1/2 hr in F amb relieved (the ranks of F&CM.) by Schreibery & Scheer	
			Shells during night - with 6·8 inch Shrapnel + precs on CRS. No cas.	
	27.5.16		An advanced party of 1 Sergt and 20 O.R. sent to WAVRANS. to take over site occupied by 57 CCS. Centos standing. All beds 100 expected. Cookhouse ready for use from 10·21 feet across instead of my 17 feet expect. The something big not necessary.	
			Three lorries from 1st Corps Dris to remove CRS equipment. Lt Col E.Tyler arrived on Leave.	
	26.5.16		Col. HOUTHOUSEN RAMC. Deposed on duty. 40 Cars to No 4 SCS Horse.	
	28.5.16		Being shelling last evening. Several Odo. B Broca by billets land just close in Carrus	
			(1) WAVRANS. with orderlies behind and cooking equipment - 40 Cars to 4 SC Hosp	
	29.5.16		Remvd all the rest of patients in lorries and ambulances to WAVRANS. also sent	
			amount y. Equipment Bns Ecs. Two extra lorries supplied from Army I. Journey-	
	30.5.16		Shelled during evening no cas. Lut. Inome H.Q. Ops. G. 1st CRB ans I C. cond. 6.	
			WAVRANS. Lenning Major Turner and 20 m. o back t cond equipment	
	31		Shelled at 5 am. good deal of damage to Ridge + Church Major Cutlerran arrived	
			who now attend to y Major Turner. Can start 6" HE entered the Transport lines	

A 6915 Wt. W11422/M1160 35,000 12/16 D. D. & L. Forms/C./2118/14.

Army Form C. 2118.

WAR DIARY
or
INTELLIGENCE SUMMARY.
(Erase heading not required.)

Instructions regarding War Diaries and Intelligence Summaries are contained in F. S. Regs., Part II. and the Staff Manual respectively. Title pages will be prepared in manuscript.

Place	Date	Hour	Summary of Events and Information	Remarks and references to Appendices
WAYRANS	31.8.16		From car the Lorre attele, and horses on back from wounding Pte ALAN RAMC wagon orderly. Emptied pockets R breast and woman's bag (Hand completed) trans not injured. Shell filled with dust and pieces of briety. A certain amount of transom destroyed. All horse men and wagons got away under Cpl Graham RAMC who remained behind to bring clear away, without any further injury or loss, and arrived at WAYRANS at 2.30 p.m. in good condition. Wish two survey men at own CRS. Visit from CRA W Army who proceeded to end advance for work down, took home retains and broken stars.	
WAYRANS				

John Mullin
LIEUT. COL. COMDG
122nd North Mid. Fd. Amb. R.A.M.C.

WAR DIARY
or
INTELLIGENCE SUMMARY.

(Erase heading not required.)

Army Form C. 2118.

Instructions regarding War Diaries and Intelligence Summaries are contained in F.S. Regs., Part II and the Staff Manual respectively. Title pages will be prepared in manuscript.

Place	Date	Hour	Summary of Events and Information	Remarks and references to Appendices
			M E D I C A L. C O N F I D E N T I A L. W A R D I A R Y O F T H E 1/2. NORTH-MIDLAND. FIELD AMBULANCE. F O R J U N E 1 9 1 8.	

Army Form C. 2118.

WAR DIARY
or
INTELLIGENCE SUMMARY.
(Erase heading not required.)

Instructions regarding War Diaries and Intelligence Summaries are contained in F. S. Regs., Part II. and the Staff Manual respectively. Title pages will be prepared in manuscript.

Place	Date	Hour	Summary of Events and Information	Remarks and references to Appendices
WAVRANS	1.6.18.		Capt. H.L.E. MACKENZIE left the Conference to act as RMO to RE 46 Division in place	
			of Capt FOSTER RAMC Sick. MAJOR TURNER RAMC arrived with CCS	
			with closing party and ½ section of CCS equipment from LABEUVRIERE	
	2.6.18		CAPT A.S. BROWN R.AMC. attached RMO 4th Guards Bn a attach ed to 4th 9th Ambulance	
			4th Guards party arrived a number left. Sockage pit dug.	
	3.6.18		Water Turn put up. Some material received from RE 1 Army. Ambulance arriving also	
			Ambulances and shortage of fitments. Patent Cover slient WAVRANS 5.41 pm and on road by	
			few NCO and Rt. men any Casualties of Medical Subalterns and arranged with CCS Pernes	
			evenings & weekly on hospital rail carriage, names the nearest NCO a friends and carrier	
			WAVRANS - SIZIN would arrange pick for the R.T.O. It arrival at SIZIN to 20 cans motor cover	
			when 30 patients are collected to duty in one day. Go motor could be sent the present Ambulance	
			to TRAGNIE - PERNES Sorry number of cases (Ex Battalion)	
	4.6.18		Water laid on from water tower of South India. Visit from DDMS 1st Corps Garden being	
			planned and cultivated and flowers	
	5.6.18		Conferred with AD M.S. 46 D. Parke cards to camp forms for A D. I. Church part leaves. Begin issue	
			and hours for dinner.	

Army Form C. 2118.

WAR DIARY
or
INTELLIGENCE SUMMARY.
(Erase heading not required.)

Instructions regarding War Diaries and Intelligence Summaries are contained in F. S. Regs., Part. II. and the Staff Manual respectively. Title pages will be prepared in manuscript.

Place	Date	Hour	Summary of Events and Information	Remarks and references to Appendices
MAVRANS	6.6.18		Sgt M.G. Lloyd transport on Parade. Officers inspected kit and had usual gas alarm.	
	7.6.18		Ordinary Parades all day.	
			Cont- Fine arrangements complete. Fire Steady Alarm tests for pack animals & men.	
	8.6.18		As above until evening to pack MO [?]. Parties afoot very early but [?]	
			General inspection by Adj in [?] order (rifles & [?])	
	9.6.18		Stables & Grooming & Parade. Inspect [?] [?] [?] & [?] [?]	
			Afternoon & [?] Group Semi. Pres: Lt Col O.R. Wilmot	
	10.6.18		O.C. Coy Platoon [?] [?] [?] [?] in each troop. Relief held for O. Troop in [?]	
			and Regt from FLERES by [?] Regt Alhussain at ANKIN	
	11.6.18		1 N.C.O. and 20 OR attached to 1/8 Quid Sqnd Hy Cav. on leaves [?] and G from R [?]	
			[?] inward	
	12.6.18		1 N.C.O. and 18 O.R. arrived 1/5 Quid Sqnd MD Cav. or leave [?] Shower and gas	
	13.6.18		Return and Troop ICC Brown & Ross [?] at from RHQ DIEUSU	
			Cols HEITHOUSEN RAMC to England on 14 days leave	
	14.6.18		Next [?] [?] [?] & O.R. of [?] [?] from [?] [?] Regt [?] [?] on D. [?]	
	15.6.18		150 [?] [?] [?] [?] [?] [?] PARAS Hd Qrs	

Army Form C. 2118.

WAR DIARY
or
INTELLIGENCE SUMMARY.
(Erase heading not required.)

Instructions regarding War Diaries and Intelligence Summaries are contained in F. S. Regs., Part II. and the Staff Manual respectively. Title pages will be prepared in manuscript.

Place	Date	Hour	Summary of Events and Information	Remarks and references to Appendices
WAVRIN'S	16.6.18		Tattooed spoke for the Coats Guild the Oct 1 ACS inspection pursued Card & 180 Canadian Cas	
			Clrg Stn in attendance. Football by 1st Army Command, who followed the DMS 1st Army	
			Suger Candle Village. Lunched by ADMS 41 Div tea LIEUT COLONEL PRESTON	
	18.6.18		Witch husband soft pedal sextumore. Touring along front from Jet out	
			Oblique Catholic from CRE 18 long to Orient Cluster and miles from ROD TASHINCOURT	
			ST POL. 2 OSW trains as a rule daily	
			Card below at 1st Army RAMC School on the RAP, ADS, MDS and WW.S.	
	19.6.18		Visit from DDMS 13C Corps	
	21.6.18		Visit from ADMS 41 Div The accumulation of the CRS were increased to 720	
	22.6.18		all the annex dealt remarqué of revisitn rooms, officer and sept rooms to each time	
			and the placid at the end of the 29th Pourtgnees wards Sunday last until 6 Pourines	
			the present position roomy Club Office sand dispensary little oversee was the single ward	
			treatment in ext which is nearly done. June was alone bnt preliminary that	
			Treatment was general and even Cooker but could count	
			two tony her 2 arts marquee pitched alongside the operating but and necessarily	
			and to the officers and respectable train. Col Bruce Sy Surgeon referred as to whether	

WAR DIARY
or
INTELLIGENCE SUMMARY.

(Erase heading not required.)

Army Form C. 2118.

Place	Date	Hour	Summary of Events and Information	Remarks and references to Appendices
WAVRANS	26.6.18		Conference with ADMS 46 Div. Lieut Tyler RAMC reported for duty with the	
			50th Division to check off the strength of the Unit.	
	29.6.18		Bearer party marches all the G.S.W's it being war weeks long said mile avoiding intervals	
			Red Cross and GHQ also permit to all stretcher bearers & ambulances at the Charge Refreshment	
			Stalls. Room ample and from recorded facts a Canteen found the an essential part of the charge	
			was to the painful in wakening for stretcher bearers. 6" shells over the front	
			Large numbers of cases to RAPs 3 days duration has been admitted to the CRS during the 2 days.	
	30.6.18		Visit from ADMS & DADMS 46. Division. 6 NCOs + 2 O.R. attached to CRS for	
			instruction from the 2/1 West Lancs Fd Amb, proceeded to their Sections the Units	
			at 1st Corps Rest Station	

John Orr ??
LIEUT. COL. COMDG,
1/2nd North Midg. Fd. Amb. R.A.M.C.

Army Form C. 2118.

WAR DIARY
or
INTELLIGENCE SUMMARY.
(Erase heading not required.)

Vol 4.
140/3136

CONFIDENTIAL

WAR DIARY OF
1/2. NORTH MIDLAND FIELD AMBULANCE.

FROM 1/7/18. to 31/7/18.

July 1918

Place	Date	Hour	Summary of Events and Information	Remarks and references to Appendices

Army Form C. 2118

WAR DIARY
or
INTELLIGENCE SUMMARY.
(Erase heading not required.)

Instructions regarding War Diaries and Intelligence Summaries are contained in F. S. Regs., Part II. and the Staff Manual respectively. Title pages will be prepared in manuscript.

Place	Date	Hour	Summary of Events and Information	Remarks and references to Appendices
WAVRANS	1.7.18		Accommodation of CRS in Room 720 with the entire billets	
			Serjeants (11)stch. Received warning from DDMS 1st to proceed to Bruay & open CRS	
			to R 2/1 WEST LANCS Fld Amb on the 3-2 of July.	
	2.7.18		Received orders from MEDICAL 46 Div to report 46 Div on July 3rd 1918	
			for personal Handing Ouer to 2/1 West	
			of the 2/1 West Lancs Fld Amb arrived to take over 1st CRS	
	3.7.18		Fwd Coml Transport left WAVRANS via ST POL h BRUAY to	
			HOUDAIN BRUAY arrived at abt 10.30 CRS at 11.30 am	
			Great confusion. At 9.30 to Bruay arrived DDMS in	
			also G BRUAY arrived at 1.30 pm by Motor 11.10	
			Whole is DDMS in Cars ready for inspection Col		App 1
			R ADAMS 46 Division Pres of 1st CRS to attend Visit Inspect W.V.		Em + DDCR5
BRUAY	5.7.18		Sent 2 NCOs and 35 OR from A Sect Hygiene unit A Baker Sergeant	
			Orders on hour 15 12th July Section Bakery	
			Col GRAHAM RAMC T in charge of 1st CRS	
			Lieut Ord Smith Off. for Section Administration Dept Cols	

WAR DIARY
or
INTELLIGENCE SUMMARY.

(Erase heading not required.)

Army Form C. 2118.

Place	Date	Hour	Summary of Events and Information	Remarks and references to Appendices
BRUAY	5.7.18		Sent 34123 PTE HACKETT RAMC to HQ 350/ETM Coy RE for 28 days course of instruction in the making of the Electric Light Plant.	
	6.7.18		Inspected 13th Corps Sentry Section, inspecting a good deal of infect wearing and cleaning. The Divn. Capt. A.G. MACKENZIE RAMC attached RMO to 46 Divisional RE in charge spoke off the strength of this Unit.	Qm
	7.7.18		Pte HACKETT returned from his course of instruction in Electric light. A page of Form 57 offered for the Corporal numbers of men pulled up as a Rear in the transport lines and suitable composed About 1 picket = 13 ell at when 13½ the Total 26 of the picked up men Total from ADMS to 9 Div.	Qm
	8.7.18		17 O.R + 3 NCOs that to be attached to 1/3 W N Field for duty. In return the same number attended up the line.	Qm
	10.7.18		Inspection of 3rd Cook Transport by GOC 46 Division 11.650 am at Corps watch East Bruay 3 L that out a good satisfactory. General O.C. remarks "Horses going very well conditions had been well I have seen for a very long time". Capt Davis went up the line inspecting & protecting and repairing the present Cook on the	Qm
	11.7.18		Inspection of all SBR Infected Section S(Town) and A Section 1/2 L W 3rd Cook in full marching order. Were much smartly and performed marched out smart and clean.	Qm

M9945 Wt. W11422/M1160 35,000 12/16 D.D. & L. Forms/C/2118/14.

Army Form C. 2118.

WAR DIARY
or
INTELLIGENCE SUMMARY.
(Erase heading not required.)

Instructions regarding War Diaries and Intelligence Summaries are contained in F. S. Regs., Part II. and the Staff Manual respectively. Title pages will be prepared in manuscript.

Place	Date	Hour	Summary of Events and Information	Remarks and references to Appendices
BRAY.	12.7.18		Work parade in fore marching order. good turn out	
	13.7.18		Capt HOLTHOUSEN detached in temporary duty as RMO 1/6 Scott Sigh Br - relied 1/4 S.S.	
			Transport & horse lines begun	
	14.7.18		Church parade 11.30 a.m. One water cart sent to Ordnance workshops for repair	
			38 hands of units picked up on Ambulance right hand Transport. Cases of quiet head	
	15.7.18		Scabies infection of men of 139 Bde before BRAY on scabies	
	16.7.18		1 NCO + 12 OR to relieve them at 1/3 IM FAMB. Total 139 Bde. Scabies 3.	
	17.7.18		Conference with ADMS 46 Division	
	18.7.18		MAJOR MANFIELD leave (c England). 19th 7.18 to 18.8.18. Blanchers Sgt Cox	
			AUMAGNE obm state	
	21.7.18		2 NCOs + 18 men IC 1/3 Scott medical Field Ambulance with breakfast ration 12 at his bearers.	
			Church parade and inspection of Unit 11.30 a.m.	
	22.7.18		Inspection of 139 of Bde school for scabies now found. Lieut Mc CORMICK Returns from	
			2/2 1/6 S Stanord Fords Bn for duty.	
	23.7.18		Inspection of Transport by Major Gordon Harvey 1/6 Dorset	
			Half yearly marks for inspection of Transport and H.M. Cars 8 Class 2 H marks. 1st prize 250 Transport forms.	

Army Form C. 2118.

WAR DIARY
or
INTELLIGENCE SUMMARY.
(Erase heading not required.)

Instructions regarding War Diaries and Intelligence Summaries are contained in F. S. Regs., Part II. and the Staff Manual respectively. Title pages will be prepared in manuscript.

Place	Date	Hour	Summary of Events and Information	Remarks and references to Appendices
BRUAY	24.7.18		1 NCO 4 OR sent with ambulances and civilian employees attended 46 Divisional artillery sports. No casualties	
	25.7.18		Sent first aid squad with ambulances NO 6 & 24.7.18 attended 138 Inf Bde sports on Cornelia Ground. B-D Prize for best turned out mounted NCO and B-D prize for best saddled gelding.	
	28.7.18		2 NCOs + 10 OR to 1/3 Bedfd and 3/1 Goals for relief of lessan from 7.30p upto per bus service	
	30.7.18		Inst-ADMS 46 Div reading former Stationary returned at BRUAY. Conference with OC 66 Stationary asking injection returns of casualties. School to be constructed	
	31.7.18		Gave lecture on Evacuation of Sick + Wounded from Front Line to 1st Army N.A.M.C. Subject and afternoon to demonstration of the making arrays of improvised methods of dealing in lessons	

J. In Mullin
LIEUT. COL. COM.DG.
2nd North Mid. Fd. Amb. R. A. M. C.

Army Form C. 2118.

WAR DIARY
or
INTELLIGENCE SUMMARY.

(Erase heading not required.)

Instructions regarding War Diaries and Intelligence Summaries are contained in F. S. Regs., Part II. and the Staff Manual respectively. Title pages will be prepared in manuscript.

Place	Date	Hour	Summary of Events and Information	Remarks and references to Appendices

SECRET.

WAR DIARY

of

1/2 North Midland Field Ambulance.

From 1/8/18 to 31/8/18.

Army Form C. 2118.

WAR DIARY
or
INTELLIGENCE SUMMARY.
(Erase heading not required.)

Place	Date	Hour	Summary of Events and Information MEDICAL	Remarks and references to Appendices
BRUAY	1.8.18		Sent M.O. bearers and 4 motor ambulances to scene of railway accident between BRUAY and HOUDAIN. 16 attend wounded. 20 O.R. to shew ground to fuel Coy. for 46 Divisional Horse show.	
	2.8.18		46 Divisional Horse show. colour team consisting of 1.H.Camb. 1GSW 1GS orderlies in charge of mounted N.C.O. 1 GS limber + Pair horses, 1 Stretcher Wagon, 1 sleeping marquee, no tent only. commandeered for pair horses + orderlies. Rained hard all day.	
	4.8.18		Church service 11.30 am. Inspected XIII CSS. Relief went to 1/3 H. Fond F.A. Comb. by 20 ann no attend.	
	5.8.18		10 bearers attached to 110 46 Sanitary section. to help in construction of models for Sanitary school proposed to be held at BRUAY	
	6.8.18		Visit from ADMS. 46 Div. . QM + Hon. Lieut. T M STEVENS reported for duty from No.1. Base.	
	7.8.18		Inspection of 139. Inf. Bde School for Section, no cases. Inspected Scabies Station ALLOUAGNE	
	8.8.18		Transport. Union to celebrate the half year. transport prize officers attend.	
	10.8.18		Waliscent. returned from Wahilolo, rebound.	
	12.8.18		Inspected 13th C.S.S. every thing in good condition	

Army Form C. 2118.

WAR DIARY
or
INTELLIGENCE SUMMARY.
(Erase heading not required.)

Place	Date	Hour	Summary of Events and Information	Remarks and references to Appendices
BRUAY.	14.8.18		Scabies Inspection of 139 Inf. Bde School, no cases. Pte J. SMITH. 1/2 N. M. F. Amb. evac'd	
			to 6. CCS. from same place sexual of char. Capt. Hotchmin evacuated from 22 CCS.	
			shell son w. is charges shrink of Unit. LIEUT. McCORMICK. MORC. u.s. on	
			10 days duty 13. CCS. to relieve Capt. GRAHAM...on 14 days leave to ENGLAND	
15.8.18.			Sent funeral party to attend funeral of PTE J. SMITH. RAMC. att. 6. CCS.	
16.8.18.			Inspected 13th CCS. everything satisfactory. Capt. A/MAJOR. A.C.F TURNER DSO. RAMC.T	
			obtained Commanding Officer of 1/3. North. Mid. and Fuel Ambulance. is struck off the strength	
			of this Unit. Handed over 1/2 the transport of 1/3. N. Mid F. Amb. on	
			a decrease orders of and. at BRUAY for the 46 Division	
18.8.18			Visited 13th C.S.S. every thing in a satisfactory condition. Church parade and Inspection 11.20 am. on	
19.8.18			Major MANFIELD MC. reported for duty from one months leave in England. Capt G. AYLWARD + P.B.	
			BELANGER reported for duty from leave. and are taken on the strength of this Unit.	on
21.8.18			Inspection of 139. Inf. Bde School. no cases. Visit from ADMS 46 Divi	on
22.8.18			Conference ADMS. and DDMS 13th Corps. Visited 13. Corps Scabies Station	on
23.8.18			Much an enormous base dressing at request of DADVS. 46 Division of Clay.	
			60 parts Chalk 20 parts Shale 20 parts mixed with water and spread 4 inches thick	

Army Form C. 2118.

WAR DIARY
or
INTELLIGENCE SUMMARY.
(Erase heading not required.)

Instructions regarding War Diaries and Intelligence Summaries are contained in F. S. Regs., Part II. and the Staff Manual respectively. Title pages will be prepared in manuscript.

Place	Date	Hour	Summary of Events and Information	Remarks and references to Appendices
BRUAY	24.8.18		Visited XIII C.C.S. scabies facility. Send one 2c Cpl. and two R.O. as a burying party at the main dressing station ANNEZIN. IC take over from 16th Division : also one Sergt and two O.R. as a burying party to take over MDS at BOIS des DAMES. D.226. 9.5". Lieut. Belton comdg Pr	
	25.8.18		Sent Cpls. JUPE + HITCHCOCK for instruction at XIII Corps Gas school	Pr
	26.8.18		Visited XIII C.C.S. Attend a lecture on Gas by Col. MILLER. 1st Army. Relieved Capt. BELANGER M.C. by Capt. Duffy with 1/3. North. Mid. Fd. Coys. and Capt. AYLWARD 16 Coys. Duffy with 1/3. Shumond Fenkin. Regt -	Pr
	28.8.18		Inspection of 139 Inf. Bde. school for scabies one case.	Pr
	29.8.18		Visited burying parties at MDS ANNEZIN + BOIS des DAMES.	Pr
	31.8.18		Inspection of scabies equipment of B + C Sections. Re organized Field Ambulance Scheme. A section consisting of O.C. 1 M.O. 1 Q.M. Sergt Major. Q.M.S. all trade and duty men major in Section and G.D. men. Total 51. B + C sections increased to 66 each section full working strength. Released to 2nd Lt APM S was instructor. 1 Pair FMP. 1 pair FSP. 2. F.M.C. 12. S. Howrachs. 3. Fracture boxes.	Pr

John Miller
LIEUT. COL. C.O.M.D.S.

SECRET.
****

WAR DIARY

OF

1/2 North Midland Field Ambulance

For Month ending 30/9/18.

Army Form C. 2118.

WAR DIARY
or
INTELLIGENCE SUMMARY.
(Erase heading not required.)

Instructions regarding War Diaries and Intelligence Summaries are contained in F. S. Regs., Part II. and the Staff Manual respectively. Title pages will be prepared in manuscript.

Place	Date	Hour	Summary of Events and Information	Remarks and references to Appendices
BRUAY	1.9.18		Church parade and Induction 11.30 a.m. Visited ANNEZIN + BOIS des DAMES.	Dr.
	2.9.18		Capt. BELANGER reported for duty from 1/3. North Mid. Fd Amb.	Dr.
	3.9.18		Received warning of impending move. Lieut McCORMICK MORC v.S. Leave to Paris 4-9-18 to 13.9.18	Dr.
	4.9.18		Induction for Scabies. 139. Inf Bde School, no cases,	Dr.
	5.9.18		Visited 13th CCS and M.D.S at BOIS des DAMES. Morning Collection of sick from 139 Inf Bde.	Dr.
	7.9.18		Orders from ADMS the Bois to be ready to move, all cases to be sent to CCS: all stretcher cases to be Dr. 5th CCS, and other cases to 32 CCS.	
	8.9.18		All weapons horribly packed and ready for move. Standing by. details. and return front.	Dr.
	10.9.18		Visited A.D.M.S. received orders to entrain on Sept 12th at 12.40 pm. at CALONNE RICOUART. Inspected station for entraining at CALONNE RICOUART. all hosp. field kits returned on Sept 11th. Standing by at a line. one man known only. Standing will be shown mobs standing by. 2 trucks only at a time, the entraining arrangements. Visited HQ. 139. Inf Bde re entraining arrangements.	Dr.
	11.9.18		Visited A.D.M.S. and BOIS des DAMES. Received visit from A.D.M.S. 46. and A.D.M.S. 47. re taking on M.D.S Bruay. 13th CSS and MDS. Bois du Dames. Train wagon attached for journey. Handed over the 13th Corps Scabies Station at ALLOUAGNE to the 1/4 London Fd Amb, the M.D.S at BOIS des DAMES. to a holding party of the 1/4 London Feild Amb., and the Field ambulance site at BRUAY to a holding party of the 1/6 London Field Amb. All standing own paper and receipts for brick stores. 2 copies sent to A.D.M.S. 46 Div	Dr.

WAR DIARY or INTELLIGENCE SUMMARY

Army Form C. 2118.

(Erase heading not required.)

Instructions regarding War Diaries and Intelligence Summaries are contained in F. S. Regs., Part II. and the Staff Manual respectively. Title pages will be prepared in manuscript.

Place	Date	Hour	Summary of Events and Information	Remarks and references to Appendices
BRUAY	11.9.18		and 2 coffers left with the meconis Field Ambulance	
	12.9.18		All wagons packed sheeted and roped ready for the road by 6.30 am. hired off 7.30 am. by road. to entraining station at CALONNE RICOUART arriving there 9.30 am. Train due to leave 12.40 pm. All trains 5 hours late. Started to entrain at 1.25 pm, all wagons horses mules and men entrained by 2.40 pm. One bay grey mule injured its R fetlock severely so shot. It was left behind at 47 Divl Mobile Vet Sect.	
CORBIE.	12.9.18.		Arrived at CORBIE Station 1 pm. Detraining delayed by previous train, own detrained at once and marched to area billets at FRANVILLERS. Forestry party 40 men and 15 horses together with transport left in train. All wagons horses and mules detrained safely and reached billets at 8 am, no accidents on journey.	
FRANVILLERS	12.9.18.		Billets for NCOs and men, good in barns and houses. Officers billet good. Transport in orchard, horses in paddock under trees. Picketted by each trunks. Reported arrival to ADMS in charge of troops at FRANVILLERS	
	13.9.18		Supplies A.S.C. from 138 Inf. Bde. S.O. Formed a small hospital 12 stretchers in empty barn for use of 138 Inf Bde to which we are attached. Daily collection and evacuation of sick to units of 139 Inf Bde group. Detailed 2 NCOs in charge of billets at FRANVILLERS and at BEAUCOURT.	

Army Form C. 2118.

WAR DIARY
or
INTELLIGENCE SUMMARY.
(Erase heading not required.)

Instructions regarding War Diaries and Intelligence Summaries are contained in F. S. Regs., Part II. and the Staff Manual respectively. Title pages will be prepared in manuscript.

Place	Date	Hour	Summary of Events and Information	Remarks and references to Appendices
FRANVILLERS	14.9.18		Sick parade daily for units without R.M.O. at hospital and collection of sick from 139 Inf Bde. Grounds	
	16.9.18		Sgt Brown transferred for duty with the 2/3 South Midland Field Ambulance. Tactical Exercise with officers of 139 Inf Div. 3 M.O.s no transport or men.	
	17.9.18		14 bearers including one Sgt. obtained and sent for duty at III Corps W.W.S. at D.20.c. Central. Lieut. a.2.c. under charge of Capt. AYLWARD. R.A.M.C. Capt. BELANGER. to bomb duty as M.O. to 1/6 N. Staffs Regt. to relieve Capt. HOLMAN on leave	
	18.9.18		Conference A.D.M.S. 46 Div. Received warning notice from 139 Inf Bde to be in readiness at 2 hours notice. Lt. Col. MILLER M.C. proceeded to England a Short Leave. MAJOR G.H.H. MANFIELD Infantry Command. at 9 P.M. Unit left FRANVILLERS by motor bus to POEUILLY arriving at 9 A.M. on 19.9.18. Grand Section lorry 8 troops. CAPT AYLWARD & A. & 9 O.R.s reported back in C.W.W.S.	
POEUILLY	19.9.18		arrived at POEUILLY at 9.a.m.	
	20.9.18		Transport section arrival 1 a.m. Convoy left one intercept (damaged) on the road. Rejoined Convoy later. Ees to A.D.M.S.	
	21.9.18		Details 2 Clerks for infantry duty at left infantry transport sent by tending party to HANCOURT. Lt. E. McCORMICK reported ready on the line and proceeded to HANCOURT arriving at 9.5 a.m. MAJ. G.H.H. MANFIELD & LT E. McCORMICK & 12 O.R. proceeded to VENDELLES to establish a W.W.C.P.	
HANCOURT	23.9.18		Cavalry Brigade attached 22 Bearers & allotted apart by VENDELLES reported to a Bearer Section. 138 Brigade on HORSE AMBULANCE WAGONS PONTRUET. 19 Crew passed thro' W.W.C.P.	
VENDELLES	24.9.18		Returned to HANCOURT	
HANCOURT	25.9.18			

Army Form C. 2118.

WAR DIARY
or
INTELLIGENCE SUMMARY.

(Erase heading not required.)

Place	Date	Hour	Summary of Events and Information	Remarks and references to Appendices
VADENCOURT	28.9.18		MAJORS GRAHAM FIELD & T. GRAHAM + Lt E. McCORMICK with 23 O.Rs. proceeded to VADENCOURT to establish a W.W.C.P. + to proceed forward A.D.S. 8 O.Rs. reported for temporary duty with R.M.O. of each Bn. 85, 139 Brigades. 74 O.R's reported for temporary duty to O.C. 1/3 N.M. F.B.AMB. 30 O.Rs. & 40 stretcher bearers attached as follows: 16 Bearers & 139 Brigade, 14 Bearers Reserve Bearers.	
	29.9.18		Bearer Relay reported to O.C. 1/3 Sth & Midland attd. by 137 Bgde & by 139/138 Brigades on SIEGFRIED LINE at 11.a.m. MAJOR GRAHAM & 12 O.Rs established an A.D.S. at M 2.6. on BELLENGLISE Rd. (wounded by Capt AYLWARD. Reserve 2 O.Rs evacuated wounded at Reserve A.D.S. under MAJOR GRAHAM regained W.W.C.P. ring fenced this of crew including 10 Germans carry parties W.W.C.P. during 29th & 30th	
	30.9.18		751 (including 33 Germans) cases passed through W.W.C.P. during 29th & 30th 1 officer & 14 O.R. evacuated wounded.	

d.d. 1.10.18.

Bumfield
Major R.A.M.C
O.C. 1/2 N.M. F.L.D.AMB.

CONFIDENTIAL.

WAR DIARY OF

1/2 North Midland Field Ambulance

for the Month of

OCTOBER. 1918.

Army Form C. 2118.

WAR DIARY
or
INTELLIGENCE SUMMARY.
(Erase heading not required.)

Instructions regarding War Diaries and Intelligence Summaries are contained in F. S. Regs., Part II. and the Staff Manual respectively. Title pages will be prepared in manuscript.

Place	Date	Hour	Summary of Events and Information	Remarks and references to Appendices
Havrincourt	1.10	4:30 pm	Returned from VADENCOURT leaving a walking Party of 5 O.Rs. CAPT E.A. AYLWARD & 1st Lt. E.J. McCORMICK with 19 O.Rs. established a WOUNDED COLLECTING POST at BELLENGLISE. CAPT AYLWARD later proceeded to MAGNY LA FOSSE where he established (19 O.Rs) a W.C.P. Received a letter from O.C. 1/0 N.M.F.D.A.M.B. thanking the Personnel of 1/2 N.M.F.D.A.M.B. whom O.C. 1/3 had kept temporarily under his Command for their good work.	
VADENCOURT	2.10	11am	The Ambulance moved to VADENCOURT CHATEAU 1st Lt. E.J. McCORMICK with remaining personnel W.U.E.P. opened CAPT E A AYLWARD at MAGNY LA FOSSE.	
"	3.10		Sergt MAJOR WILLIAMS & 42 O.Rs. reported to A.D.S. BELLENGLISE 13 & 13 Buglers attached to 1/1 F.R. RAMIGOURT & MONTBREHAIN. The letter being subsequently retaken by the Enemy. Casualties at W.U.E.P. approximately 400	
"	4.10		2 O.Rs. evacuated grupd. CAPT BELLANGER reported for duty from 6 NORTH STAFFS. Bn Shaftesbury & hospital over Command of the	
"	5.10	5:35 pm	LT. COL J. MILLER returned from short leave & took over Command of the Ambulance	
"	6.10.18		Issued A.D.M.S. and received orders to stand by for a move at short notice. All wagons packed with the exception of Cooks cart. Capt GRAHAM evacuated to No 12 C.C.S. Sick sans.	R.
	8.10.18		Received orders to move to LEVERGIES. and open up an A.D.S. Rest of Personnel and transport to billet in open at H.326.N. note sheet 62.B.	Qm

Army Form C. 2118.

WAR DIARY
or
INTELLIGENCE SUMMARY.
(Erase heading not required.)

Instructions regarding War Diaries and Intelligence Summaries are contained in F. S. Regs., Part II. and the Staff Manual respectively. Title pages will be prepared in manuscript.

Place	Date	Hour	Summary of Events and Information	Remarks and references to Appendices
LEVERGIES.	9.10.18.		Moved unit to H.32.6. N sick Rd. Sending forward Capt. LOMAS with GSW femur and 20 men to open ADS at LEVERGIES. Sent Capt. BELENGER to learn Office to form relay bearer posts and get in touch with the RAP's and form Car post on the LEVERGIES – SEQUEHART Road. Ambulance car post at LEVERGIES. Supplied 8 bearers with 2 stretchers to each Inf. Batt. 135 Inf. Bde. To evacuate wounded from RAP. It meant Bearer relay post.	
		3.p.m.	Advanced ADS to SEQUEHART. Capt. ALYWARD + Capt. LOMAS MORC O.S. in charge. Capt. BELENGER came as forward learn officer at H. 30.8.5. Car stand at LEVERGIES, one ear at ADS, very few sick and wounded found in W.S. Opposite ADS Capt. LOMAS in charge.	
	10.10.18.		ADS. opened by 1/1 Sr. Med. Fd. Amb. at the Convent. FRESNOY-LE-GRAND. evacuation to 1X Corps. M.D.S. MAENY-LA-FOSSE. Hosb. B. 3. Sect 626. Capt. BELENGER as bearer officer will relay and car post. Renewed stores and extra dressings from VADEN COURT. Also Sound by 3 men.	
FRESNOY – LE-GRAND	12.10.18.		Moved Unit to FRESNOY-LE-GRAND. Officers and men billet'd in town. Transport in field. Capt. BELENGER has established bearers and Car post; in touch with the RAPs. Wounded evacuated to ADS. FRESNOY by means of relay posts without stretcher carries and Cars. The evacuation then Quite smoothly, and well. The enemy fired 40 rounds of H.V. 4.1 + 5.9 into the town during the night. Had 2 mules wounded; one evening 16 to evacuate (1), no casualties among personnel. Capt. Sullivan on day.	
	14.10.18.		2 RAPs. D23.b. 45. 70. and J4.b. 20. 40. Four bearer posts 3 with 4 bearers one with 2 bearers.	
	15.10.18		Six Car posts and six travelling stage board by Capt. BELENGER. Surgeon MERIWETHER ERA RN + Lieut SIRIS FE VSAMC reported for duty.	

Army Form C. 2118.

WAR DIARY
or
INTELLIGENCE SUMMARY.
(Erase heading not required.)

Place	Date	Hour	Summary of Events and Information	Remarks and references to Appendices
FRESNOY-LE-GRAND	16.10.18		Orders. Open up an ADS at the Convent. BOHAIN. D.22.c.6.2. with car and relay bearer posts in touch with RAPs. along the VAUX-ANDIGNY-BOHAIN and the ANDIGNY-LES-FERMES-BOHAIN Road. Capts. BELENGER + SUTTIE RAMC as liaison officers. MAJOR MANSFIELD MC in charge of ADS. and WMS. with three medical officers and 31 personnel, 2 lorries attached for WM and 11. Ambulance car. To evacuate sick and wounded to IX Corps. M.D.S. at MAGNY-LA-FOSSE. 30 bearers from the 1/3 N. M. F. Coot. To be at ADS in reserve. ADS BOHAIN 10 other ranks as b.bars. All posts marked by flags + lamps. WW route flagged out.	
BOHAIN	17.10.18.		Zero hour was 5:20 am. Jumping off line V20.c south of VAUX. ANDIGNY 17 D.6.c.80. The attack being by the 130 + 139 Infantry Bdes., the 137 hy. Bde. being the line from F.18.a. to D.14.d. As the attack progressed the bearer stretcher and ambulance cars were pushed along the BOHAIN-VAUX. ANDIGNY Road. Along which most of the casualties came. Relay bearer and Car posts were moved to D.6.c.9.5. and V.25.b.77. The wounded were very rapidly brought in by Ambulance Cars and Coord Ambulances. As the Bearer Cars secure 2 were sent up in front of the ADS. the main number of Casualties were cleared to the ADS by 12 noon. A few stretcher and walking wounded cases came in during the rest of the day. German prisoners of war. as the Corps Cases were used as stretcher bearers.	

Army Form C. 2118.

WAR DIARY
or
INTELLIGENCE SUMMARY.
(Erase heading not required.)

Instructions regarding War Diaries and Intelligence Summaries are contained in F.S. Regs., Part II. and the Staff Manual respectively. Title pages will be prepared in manuscript.

Place	Date	Hour	Summary of Events and Information	Remarks and references to Appendices
BOHAIN.	17.10.18.		27 P.O.W. were detained at the ADS. to act as bearers, and bearing parties. at one time before noon the ADS was congested with wounded owing to so many ambulance cars being up in front of the ADS, and only 2 cars used for the evacuation to the IX Corps MDS. Two lorries were attached for the W.W. The journey to the MDS and evacuation P. (being on an average 3½ to 4 hours there and back). Some men lorries were obtained. and by 4.30 pm most of the wounded were evacuated	
		11.30 pm.	The 138 and 139 Infantry Brigades were relieved from the line. Capt Sutlie and bearers relieved their field ambce. (and returned to ADS. The 137 Inf Bde. remaining in the line	
	18.10.18.		Quiet night very few casualties through. at 7am the IX Corps MDS and W.W. Post ceased to take over the Hospice BOHAIN. The ambulance returning to FRESNOY. with the relieving of Capt. BELANGER and his bearers, who evacuated any casualties to the IX Corps MDS. thus doing away with the ADS	
FRESNOY	19.10.18		The 46 Division being relieved. Capt. BELANGER and his bearers reported at the Head Quarters of the ambulance FRESNOY. Stretcher bearers. { Officers: 7, OR 247, POW 6 }	
			Number of Casualties { Officers 7, OR 102, POW 6 } W.W.Can. Total Casualties through ADS 375	

Army Form C. 2118.

WAR DIARY
or
INTELLIGENCE SUMMARY.
(Erase heading not required.)

Instructions regarding War Diaries and Intelligence Summaries are contained in F. S. Regs., Part II. and the Staff Manual respectively. Title pages will be prepared in manuscript.

Place	Date	Hour	Summary of Events and Information	Remarks and references to Appendices
FRESNOY.	20.10.18.		Sent. 2 Officers and 50 OR to Divisional Church Parade, March past D.G.O.C afterwards.	
	21.10.18.		Appointed A/ADMS. 46 Div while ADMS notes on leave. General training of Unit, and repelling of clothes + equipment.	
	23.10.18.		Lieut. SIRIS. MC.VS attached to TK EMDS. for temp duty. also 3 Clerks + 12 of nursing section.	
	25.10.18		Attended a conference of the DDMS IX Corps. 5.30 pm. Detailed 2 Officers and 50 OR to attend an American parade, and march past the French General.	
	26.10.18.		Capt. SOTTIE attached for duty as M.O. with the 1/5 Sherwood Foresters.	
	30.10.18.		Held medical Board on officer for reclassification.	
	31.10.18.		Return of ADMS. 46 Div. Hand Ambulance to BUSIGNY. Very good billets. V10.d 2.5.	

John Miller
Lt. Col. RAMC T.

Army Form C. 2118.

WAR DIARY
or
INTELLIGENCE SUMMARY.

(Erase heading not required.)

Summary of Events and Information

MEDICAL.
****

From November 1st. 1918   to   November 31st. 1918.

O.C. 1/2nd. N.M. Field Ambulance.

Place	Date	Hour	Summary of Events and Information	Remarks and references to Appendices

Army Form C. 2118

WAR DIARY
or
INTELLIGENCE SUMMARY.
(Erase heading not required.)

Place	Date	Hour	Summary of Events and Information	Remarks and references to Appendices
BUSIGNY	1.11.18		Detailed 2 Horse Ambulances to follow 138 Inf Bde. in their march to BUSIGNY and BEERVIGNY. In order to pick up men falling out on the march. The sick of the Bde. and men unable to march were collected at the church FRESNOY and conveyed by motor ambulance to their new area.	
	3.11.18		Received RAMC order No 153 regarding the attack by IX. Corps. Visited L'ARBRE DE GUISE and established an RAMC assembly post at W.6.B.8. Sheet 57.B. Ordered 2. GS Sections packed for ADS work. 2 water carts, 3 Horse limber Wagons and 1 GSW to be at RAMC post by 8 A.M. on 4.11.18. Also bearer officers, extra stretchers, blankets, together with motor tenders of the Division and 2 MOs to collect. Detailed 1 NCO + 12 OR. with 6 stretchers + 6 blankets to each of the following regiments. 1/5. Linco, + 1/4 + 1/5 Leicesters Regts. and also 1C Hussars Regt. Also 1 NCO + 4 OR. as a Dressing bay at RAMC Post. W.6.B.8.	
	4.11.18		Capt. Belanger M.C. RAMC. evacuated to 48. CCS. Influenza. Received orders from ADMS to take over the evacuation of wounded from the line, as soon as the 46. Div. came into action, after the 32 Div had taken their 2nd objective. Had attached to this Ambulance. 2 limbers + 2 water carts + 2 GSW packed to form 2 ADSs from the 1/3 North Mid Fd. Amb. Extra bearers, stretchers and blankets and Horse and motor ambulances, together with 2 lorries for walking wounded, reported to RAMC assembly post at 9 A.M.	

Army Form C. 2118.

WAR DIARY
or
INTELLIGENCE SUMMARY.
(Erase heading not required.)

Instructions regarding War Diaries and Intelligence Summaries are contained in F. S. Regs., Part II. and the Staff Manual respectively. Title pages will be prepared in manuscript.

Place	Date	Hour	Summary of Events and Information	Remarks and references to Appendices
OUSIGNY.	4.11.18		MAJOR LANE, Capt. MILLAR + Capt. REID as bearer Officers. Each A.D.S. being manned by 2 Officers 20 O.R. 1 Bearer G.S.W. already packed 165 GW with 50 Stretchers + 100 blankets + 1 water cart. Site bearers from the char fried ambulance. Band, Labour Coy + Whippet troops, made a total number of bearers 120.	
L'ARBRE DE GUISE		7. a.m.	Division taking over the line. I sent MAJOR HERGA with his complete A.D.S. party to open up at CATILLON. R 24 a.6.3. I further with Capt. MILLAR as bearer Officer with 20 bearers with wheeled Stretcher carriers. Also Capt. RICHARDS and his A.D.S. party to LA. LAURETTE. W 7. J 33. and Capt. REID + 20 bearers. Capt. RICHARDS met 16 Open up under we found Bearer Officers 16 A.D.S. party. 15 Open up under we found Brigade over Canal at M 19 b 6. We are only a small foot bridge over, making it impossible to get transport over. Formed relay posts from A.D.S. along CATILLON — MÉZIÈR road. Very few casualties.	
CATILLON	5.11.18.		Went forward at day break with Major HERGA and moved A.D.S. forward and found a site for an A.D.S. at MÉZIÈR, large small house M 21 b 8.8. Got a Ford car over canal at Embrouy about a mile south of canal. Hand carried A.D.S. material over canal to Ford car, and established the A.D.S. at MÉZIÈR. Cars were brought from A.D.S. by Ford car to Canal, and then hand carried over the canal to village of bearers. Moved my whole Field Amb. to CATILLON around 7 p.m. Capt. RICHARDS and party still at LA. LAURETTE.	

Army Form C. 2118.

WAR DIARY
or
INTELLIGENCE SUMMARY.
(Erase heading not required.)

Instructions regarding War Diaries and Intelligence Summaries are contained in F. S. Regs., Part II. and the Staff Manual respectively. Title pages will be prepared in manuscript.

Place	Date	Hour	Summary of Events and Information	Remarks and references to Appendices
CATILLON	6.11.18	4 AM	Bridge over canal repaired, and ready for transport. Sent forward field ADS party with wagon water cart, 3 Horse Ambulances + 2 Cars motor Ambulances.	
		6.30 am	Visited ADS at MÉZIER and found ADS forward 15' N19 A 8.8 a farm house. Major HERGA in command. Sent Capt. REID 16' Confr at ADS with his bearers + 2 large Ambulance Cars. Pushed forward relay bearers and car park along CATILLON – PRISCHES. Road at N19 G. 3.6. blown up. only horse transport can shell crenit craters no motor Transport during night.	
MÉZIER		7.30 a	Short artillery barrage on Squares N 24. 18 + 17. Major LANE + Capt MILLAR in forward bearer Officers found Ambulance 16 MÉZIER 16 cd ADS site at Mall-Terren. who all cars + 4 Ambs. with 2 WW Lorries. Arrived 10 am. Ohned Walking wounded station at MÉZIER. The Corps Main Dressing Station and Gas Centre at Q 36'D. Sheet 57b. The Corps WW Station at the Horhes BOHAIN.	
		9 pm.	ADS removed 16' PRICHES. N17 D. 5.6. and relay posts and and advanced ADS pushed into CARTIGNIES. Surge Culn on PRISCHES – CARTIGNIES Rd at O14 & 2.8.	
CARTIGNIES	7.11.18		found Ambulance 16' CARTIGNIES via PRISCHES. Pt. FAYT. Started 7 am arrived 10 am. ADS. at CARTIGNIES O11 a. 9.4. under Lieut Richards and his ADS party. Back in main Dust at O11 b 2.9 blown up. Pontoon bridge at O11 b 5.10	
		11 am	Pushed ADS 15' P10. a central Capt REIDs party with limber Water Cart + Cart 2.	

Army Form C. 2118.

WAR DIARY
or
INTELLIGENCE SUMMARY.
(Erase heading not required.)

Instructions regarding War Diaries and Intelligence Summaries are contained in F. S. Regs., Part II. and the Staff Manual respectively. Title pages will be prepared in manuscript.

Place	Date	Hour	Summary of Events and Information	Remarks and references to Appendices
CARTIGNIES			Ambulance cars turned the first leading to pontoon bridge and the bridge under own gun from the ADS at CARTIGNIES, to act as a temporary MDS + WWS. All rich and wounded from ADS + Div MDS to to 1/1 & 2nd Fd Amb at PRISCHES where they are transferred to MAC cars and evacuated to CMDS + CWWS. The walking wounded send down in the MAC cars and in empty ASC lorries. 15 M.19 b 0.3	
	8.11.18		ADS at P.10 a Central, & CHEVAL BLANC. Heavily shelled during evening of 7th had to move back to P.1 b 6.6. Heavy horse post at P.10 Central. Casualties light. Car posts at P.3 a 4.4 and P.16 6.6. The CWWS moved to the SUCRERIE. CATILLON R23 b 1.8 the CMDS L'ARBRE-DE-GUISE Q 35 D.	
		6pm	ADS moved forward again to P.10 a Central.	
	9.11.18	6 am	Proceeded by car to ZORES. Opened an ADS Major HERGA + Party at ZORES Q y c 4.6. Lieut RICHARDS and his ADS party moved to LE CHEVAL BLANC with 2 horse ambs to current-avans to advance.	
		11 am	Pushed on to SAINS-DU-NORD. Opened Major HERGA then Rectaing bridge on main road in SAINS-DU-NORD blown up. Pushed Major HERGA on with one car. and Opened a temporary ADS at LIESSIES. Had little ADS party + cars over fields and railway in reconnect of blown upo & along road. The Ambulance cars went across onto their own power.	

Army Form C. 2118.

WAR DIARY
or
INTELLIGENCE SUMMARY.
(Erase heading not required.)

Instructions regarding War Diaries and Intelligence Summaries are contained in F.S. Regs., Part II. and the Staff Manual respectively. Title pages will be prepared in manuscript.

Place	Date	Hour	Summary of Events and Information	Remarks and references to Appendices
SAINS DU NORD	9.11.18		Found Ambulance at SAINS-DU-NORD which carried on 6 p.m. Traffic on roads very heavy and roads bad. often blocked by ditched lorries.	
		9 pm	Sent whole of Major Hogg's ADS part with Lumber, GSW, and wounded east of 2 Comb Cars and one Lorry down to LIESSIES. Main road between AVESNES + SAINS DU NORD blown up in three places. Picked up 7 French wounded men who had been wounded by bombs in SAINS DU NORD about 2 pm. and sent them to CMDS.	
	10.11.18		Visited ADS at LIESSIES at daybreak. No casualties during night. A mobile bone consisting of Cavalry and eyelids hospital [General]; they have a convalescent field Ambulance with them. Spent some way into FORET de TRELON. No casualties found; large amount of German equipment; haversacks rifles etc. blown away.	
		2 p.m.	Received orders to withdraw ADS from LIESSIES to SAINS DU NORD.	
	11.11.18		Opened a Divisional Hospital at SAINS DU NORD under MAJOR MANFIELD. Had one MO and team. 4 OR allotted for Surgical emergencies, in case to avoid evacuation of wounded at night owing to bad state of roads and congestion of traffic. All wounded that were able but 16 battalions returned with stretchers and blankets. 15 Ambulances, 10 other lorries from 16 + 13 Field Amb. Bde. Band. Labour Coy & Wilts Regt. returned to their units.	
		11 AM	Hostilities temporarily ceased, re. Armistice.	

WAR DIARY
or
INTELLIGENCE SUMMARY.

Army Form C. 2118.

Place	Date	Hour	Summary of Events and Information	Remarks and references to Appendices
SAINS DU NORD	11.11.18		Reformed Ambulance with proper medium again, and packed all equipment in usual manner.	
	12.11.18		Lieut. J.W. STEPHEN R.A.M.C. transferred from 1/3 & and 3rd Amb. to this Amb. for duty.	
	13.11.18		Received orders to march with 138 Bde. Group to AVESNES. Dumped all extra equipment, excess- at 2.00 (Stretchers) as per G.R.O. on to the attached personnel of CMDS. — Moved off well transport- at 14.00 hour. Carried AVESNES 16.30 hour. Two horse Ambulances followed the Inf. Batts to pick up men fallen out on march. Total number of men picked up 12. No of men unable to march and carried by motor Ambulances to AVESNES 32. Accidents. Wheel off one large Car. and one hole broken in Water Cart.	
AVESNES.	14.11.18		Marched in 138 Bde Group to BOUSIES. Scout Wagon Lorry arrived BOUSIES. 18.00 hour. on lorries. Fell out mid day. No ambulance men fell out. Horse Ambulances followed this Batts as before. Picked up 9 men. Men unable to march and carried by motor Ambulances 62. Ambulance billeted in School. Lieut. MERRYWEATHER left on 14 days special leave	
	15.11.18		Opened a ward in School as Rest Field. 15 stretcher for men of 138 Bde., General clean up of wagons and equipment; and horses + mules.	
	16.11.18		All men and five SIROS who were attached to the CMDS + C.VI.V.V.E.P. returned for duty with Ambulance. By order of # 46 Div. transferred 2 n.c.os Corps to 151 Division	

WAR DIARY
or
INTELLIGENCE SUMMARY.
(Erase heading not required.)

Army Form C. 2118.

Place	Date	Hour	Summary of Events and Information	Remarks and references to Appendices
BOUSIES.	18.11.18		Arranged baths for the 138 Inf Bde. and burnt in ovens, consisting of 17 huts and other baths in own Gadey. Wells fitted in salved German boilers. Fired on own grid. 6 boilers in all arranged with Bde for fuel + clean clothing. 1 Sgt + 6 O.R. RAMC in charge. Able to bath 650 men a day.	
	19.11.18		Visited ADMS. at Conference at Bde HQ was given duty of cleaning up villages. Visited 40 men + 4 wagons + hookers for this work. Freed to remunerate all baths + troughs. Arranged for Field Amb Concert Party. 1C Combine with 138 Bde. under Lieut CASTLE for myself entertainment in Convent School Room. Visited all RMO's in my area.	
	21.11.18		Prepared Inspection of Horse Transport by ADMS 46 Div.	
	23.11.18		Inspected British Cavalier and underneath C/O 46 Div MG Coy. Visited him. Traller overcrowded Lieut SIRIS MC USA. detailed as temp RMO 1/5 N. Staffs + Derby Regt	
	25.11.18		Inspection of Transport by Major General BOYD 46 Div. Wagon lines. Horses in own lines and all Reserve lined out in Saddle blankets in front of animals. Driver by animals head. Result very satisfactory.	
	28.11.18		Attended Lecture at LANDRECIES on Demobilisation + Reconstruction.	
	30		Visited RMO's + RAPs in area. General health of 138 Bde satisfactory. Baths everything well	

Signed John Mulley
Lieut North Mid Fd Amb R.A.M.C

Army Form C. 2118.

WAR DIARY
or
INTELLIGENCE SUMMARY.

(Erase heading not required.)

Summary of Events and Information

Instructions regarding War Diaries and Intelligence Summaries are contained in F. S. Regs., Part II. and the Staff Manual respectively. Title pages will be prepared in manuscript.

Place	Date	Hour

CONFIDENTIAL.

MEDICAL.

WAR DIARY

OF

1/2nd N.M. Field Ambulance.

1st December 1918 to 31st December 1918.

COMMITTEE FOR THE
MEDICAL HISTORY OF THE WAR
6 MAR 1919
Date

WAR DIARY
or
INTELLIGENCE SUMMARY.
(Erase heading not required.)

Army Form C. 2118.

Instructions regarding War Diaries and Intelligence Summaries are contained in F. S. Regs., Part II. and the Staff Manual respectively. Title pages will be prepared in manuscript.

Place	Date	Hour	Summary of Events and Information	Remarks and references to Appendices
BOUSIES	1.12.18		Visit from DDMS XIII Corps + ADMS 46 Div. Inspected Hospital area, medical Inspection room kitchen and the 130 Bde Baths, rivulet sales factory.	
	2.12.18	1pm	Marched a party of 74 men to LANDRECIES in connection with H.M. the KING'S visit to the area. Whole formed in horseshoe manner. The KING walked through LANDRECIES and was cheered to the echo by the troops.	
	3.12.18		Released from Q-3 GSW daily for personal sedative work, and a further GSW with 3 NCOs + 30 OR for sanitary work in village. Two men of 1st Oxon Regt admitted with Hospital suffering from an ulceration of forehead + chest, the other from paraphimosis. Due to an infected bullet wound sustained Oct. Prevailing had by a Sar Abdul. 3-4 weeks ago. Held bullet-bone wounds including flores and Orga fin est in centre in men late. Also ADMS German masters in a billet. Civilian child. Troops reviewed and inspected. Water placed out of bounds.	
	5.12.15		Two french claims formed, advanced and plumbing in the Unit's toilet well attended. Sent the QM to meeting at Div HQ regarding ordnance supply. The SOLESMES people of CASC to be used to for evacuation of sick + wounded	
	6.12.18		Attended a meeting at Q Branch regarding the Lomas Service for the troops	
	11.12.18		Classes in English. English History, Geography. Arithmetic started from 9-11am each day. Classes also includes the 2 french classes also.	

WAR DIARY
or
INTELLIGENCE SUMMARY

Army Form C. 2118.

Place	Date	Hour	Summary of Events and Information	Remarks and references to Appendices
BOUSIES	12.12.18		Inspected the Ambulance horse transport, wagons on the lines, horses in stables, all harness hard and on saddle blankets. Wagons, harness and horses all in good condition.	
	13.12.18		1st Lieut McCORMICK detailed for temporary duty as RMO. 1/c the RE Coys and HQ Rs at PREUX le at RE Coys and HQ Rs at PREUX Capt AYLWARD reported for duty with Ambulance from 1/5 Leinster Regt.	G.J.
	18.12.18		All loaned cases in Ambulance paraded for inspection of PADVS 46 Divn. One man to be evacuated for lumbar puncture.	G.J.
	19.12.18		Received instruction 15 inches for 3rd blanket per man.	G.J.
	21.12.18		Issued ADMS 46 Divn.	
	24.12.18		Xmas dinners to the men messes. Delayed till 6 pm owing to transport breakdown. The dinner consisted of turkey, beef & plum pudding. Fellers were decorated with flags and green stuff. An addit- dinner took place in afternoon and an informal sing song in evening. The men were agreeable on by the Sergeants. During the afternoon Major General BOYD CGM DSO DCM presented the Ambulance, and an evening each billet, wished the men a merry Xmas.	G.J.
	26.12.18		The Regimental mess had their Xmas dinner in afternoon. The officers of the Ambulance had dinner in the evening. Their Guest being Major General Boyd, GOC 46 Divn.	G.J.
	29.12.18		Major Mansfield on 14 days UK England. Lt MILLS R.17. Leaving ADAMS 46 Dn. John Muth During Col Ray DSO leave to England.	G.J.

Army Form C. 2118.

WAR DIARY
or
INTELLIGENCE SUMMARY.
(Erase heading not required.)

Instructions regarding War Diaries and Intelligence Summaries are contained in F. S. Regs., Part II. and the Staff Manual respectively. Title pages will be prepared in manuscript.

Place	Date	Hour	Summary of Events and Information	Remarks and references to Appendices
BOUSIES	27.12.18		Received orden from ADMS. 46 Division to go to BOHAIN and arrange with Town Commandant to have the Hospice there as a billet and hospital for ambulance, also had interview with re to move to BOHAIN on Jan 2. 1919.	
	24.12.18		Lt-Col J MILLIE R.A.M.C. to be A/ADMS 46 Div. during the period of Col Wags leave to England.	J.C. Millie Lt-Col

46

2 NM 7d Aut
Vol XIII

WAR DIARY OF

1/2nd NORTH MIDLAND FIELD AMBULANCE (T.F.)

Jan 1st to Jan 31st 1919.

Army Form C. 2118.

WAR DIARY
or
INTELLIGENCE SUMMARY.
(Erase heading not required.)

Instructions regarding War Diaries and Intelligence Summaries are contained in F. S. Regs., Part II. and the Staff Manual respectively. Title pages will be prepared in manuscript.

Place	Date	Hour	Summary of Events and Information	Remarks and references to Appendices
BOUSIES.	1919 Jan. 5		R. & Q.M. Stevens returned from leave to the U.K.	
	" 9		D.D.M.S. XIII Corps accompanied by A/A.D.M.S. inspected hospital — all correct.	My
	" 10.		Brigadier General Commanding 138 Infantry Brigade visited unit to enquire of number of sick from Brigade admitted to hospital, figures shewed improvement.	My
	22.1.19.		Lt Col J Miller rejoined ambulance from A/A.D.M.S. 46 Div. during his absence in England. Visited Welcken 11/5 Gunaun rept.	On
	23.1.19.		Attended meet A.D.M.S. 46 Div. at a conference of A.D.M.S.s with D.D.M.S. 13 Corps.	Q.
	29.1.19.		Inspected R.A.M.C. Personnel in full marching order, my senr hun adt visited Welcken & 4 fusiliers & 116 Linc Rgts. Educational Classes in the Unit are started every tc all schoolmasters and instructors being demobilized. All sports - football and some trials, cross-country and the army games & being encouraged.	Q. On J.E.Miller Lt Col

CONFIDENTIAL.

WAR DIARY

OF

1/2nd N.M.Field Ambulance.

1/2/19. to 25/2/19.

Army Form C. 2118.

WAR DIARY
or
INTELLIGENCE SUMMARY.
(Erase heading not required.)

Instructions regarding War Diaries and Intelligence Summaries are contained in F. S. Regs., Part II. and the Staff Manual respectively. Title pages will be prepared in manuscript

Place	Date	Hour	Summary of Events and Information	Remarks and references to Appendices
BOUSIES	1.2.19		Visited ADMS 46 Div. Orders received that no men over 10th. December enlist in Civil Pop.	
	4.2.19		Lieut C.G. Coombes reported for duty from RAMC base and was enlist in the Strength of Unit.	
	5.2.19		The final educational scheme inspected by Major General Boyd, result rales factory Animals and wagons inspected on this occas. Sergt Major Wiseman demobilized. Three cases of measles in BOUSIES among civilian Population taken.	
	7.2.19		Visited ADMS 46 Div.	
	10.2.19		Capt. AYLWARD. RAMC Demobilized. 2 Sergts + 7 O.R.	
	16.2.19		Five O.R. demobilized today.	
	18.2.19		1st Lieut The Comndt M.C.U.S. left for 14 days leave to ROME. The rest of R.E. allowed 15 %	
			Own M.O. sent men from Ambulance in a Car.. 3 O.R. demobilized	
	20.2.19		Acting Sergt Major 1 Staff Sergt 1 Sergt 1 O.R. Demobilized. Ration Strength 177 Horses 50	
	21.2.19		Lt. C.G. Coombes transferred as MO 35 Labour Group, and is struck off strength of Amb.	
	22.2.19		3 Drivers RASC HT Demobilized	
	23.2.19		46 Divs until exception Conf. moved to CAUDRY 4 O.R. Demobilized	
SOLESMES	24.2.19		Opened MD Amb. at SOLESMES. No Enfield, only a central aid post. Cases 10 ood R	

Army Form C. 2118.

WAR DIARY
or
INTELLIGENCE SUMMARY.
(Erase heading not required.)

Instructions regarding War Diaries and Intelligence Summaries are contained in F. S. Regs., Part II. and the Staff Manual respectively. Title pages will be prepared in manuscript.

Place	Date	Hour	Summary of Events and Information	Remarks and references to Appendices
SOLESMES	26.9.19		1 Driver RASC HT demobilized	
			Noted ADMS. 1 Ofcr + 4 O.R. Demobilized, and 3 O.R. sent to GBD (Jan. 16.) transferring	
			15 58 ees and are struck off the strength of the Unit	

John Miller

149/3001

1/3rd North Midlands F.A.

17 JUL 1919

May 1919

WAR DIARY
or
INTELLIGENCE SUMMARY.

(Erase heading not required.)

Army Form C. 2118.

Instructions regarding War Diaries and Intelligence Summaries are contained in F. S. Regs., Part II. and the Staff Manual respectively. Title pages will be prepared in manuscript.

Place	Date	Hour	Summary of Events and Information	Remarks and references to Appendices
SOLESMES	1.3.19		Pte POLLARD W. 416405 Res Corn awarded the Military Medal	R
	2.3.19		Summer time came into force. Cks moved fwd on the 1.3.19. 2 O.R. demob'd	R
	8.3.19		1 Sergt + 4 O.R. demob'd. Equipment surplus to new War Establishment of Field Ambulance sent to DADOS 46 Divn. + Surplus Wagons to ROD Quartery.	R
	9.3.19		Capt Lloyd Williams reports for Duty from 1/4 Line Regt	R
ST HILAIRE	10.3.19		Grand Ambulance to ST HILAIRE. Transport had 16 00 hrs journey. Owing to reduction of Animals Cpls Pattersen & RAMC reported for Duty from 1/3 Lincoln Regt and taken on Strength of Amb. Dno Brigham Ken. Only a Colonel and Post. for the whole of the 138 Inf Bde. & O.C. as this was cut (& must study ck 46 Div Artillery as they are now not to be other villages.	R
	13.3.19		1 Sergt 4 O.R. Demob'd. Major One Kenneth MC US left for S.C.C. Should be shortly sent R.	R
	14.3.19		1 O.R. demob'd also 1 Driver R.A.S.C.	R
	16.3.19		1 O.R. + 1 R.A.S.C. Driver demob'd. Return of Col Ray A.D.M.S. from leave.	R
	18.3.19		Sent MO to inspect a body of French soldiers from'd by the French Authorities Dnd to Wounds bug very decomposed. No identification.	
	19.3.19		Capt A.L.C. Mc Kenzie reported for duty from leave. Taken on the strength of the unit	

Army Form C. 2118.

WAR DIARY
or
INTELLIGENCE SUMMARY.
(Erase heading not required.)

Instructions regarding War Diaries and Intelligence Summaries are contained in F. S. Regs., Part II. and the Staff Manual respectively. Title pages will be prepared in manuscript.

Place	Date	Hour	Summary of Events and Information	Remarks and references to Appendices
ST. HILAIRE	19.3.19		Took over the oil engine and pumps for water supply. Secured 2 men for this duty. Capt Pallensky R.A.M.C. left for duty with 67 Labour group, and is struck off the strength of Unit.	
			1 Sergt, 1 Cpl + 4 O.R. sent for duty at 43 CCS. and 5 O.R. to 58 CCS. Men are struck off the strength of the Unit. Prior to farewell of Major General Boyd to Unit-	
	21.3.19		Departure of Col Day from Division. Lt. Col J. Miller acting A.D.M.S. The Officer i/c A.D.M.S. presumed 12 1/2 gr on 7 Army	R
			at ST HILAIRE Lt. Col J. Miller acting A.D.M.S.	R
	22.3.19		Capt A.C. McKenzie. egl. Unit for duty DDMS BOULONG. and is struck off strength	R
	23.3.19		Instructor proposed killed to D.H.Q. presence at Cambay. will say sorry, Jan 1915, may rate in it. Unfit for hauls in its present state	R
	26.3.19		1 Capt + 4 O.R. sent R.A.M.C. unit. 5 Cr R.A.S.C. demobilized.	R
	27.3.19		Rev. J. Cameron R.C. C.F. left unit for H.Q. Tank Corps, 3rd Army. Conference with DDMS re Sanitary Districts & Medical Officers. Only O.C. + Q.M. Fld Amb. in base, remaining M.O. in Area Stengt. Return as usual to DDMS	

Army Form C. 2118.

Army Form C. 2118.

WAR DIARY
or
INTELLIGENCE SUMMARY.
(Erase heading not required.)

Place	Date	Hour	Summary of Events and Information	Remarks and references to Appendices
ST HILAIRE	28.3.18		3. O.R. transferred to No 43 CCS and 7. O.R. to No 12 CCS. A nursing sister from 16/72 Army Bde R.G.A. at SAULZOIR while thus nursing evac'd to No 12 days leave.	
	29.3.18		One Casy. Ambulance Car and one Ford Ambulance sent to No 46 Div M.T. Coy went towards SOMS R. No A92/210. 2.3.15. Ambulance and man struck by shrapnel. 6. O.R. transferred to No 58 CCS. 1.O.R. to 46 CCS and 1 O.R. to 19 CCS. Capt Rev'd Williams still acting R.C. at No 56 CCS TINCOURT	
	31.3.18		19 O.R. + 1 Sergt. Servatoris admd to Casls from AD.M.S. office returning to W.R. Rodgers R.	

John Graham
[signature]

14/3000

1/2 Ath. Med. F.a.

Apl. 1918.

WAR DIARY
or
INTELLIGENCE SUMMARY.

Army Form C. 2118.

Place	Date	Hour	Summary of Events and Information	Remarks and references to Appendices
ST HILAIRE	3.4.19		Visited DDMS. Cavalry.	
	7.4.19		Ambulance moved to its new billets at INCHY.	
INCHY.			Guards billet.	
	8.4.19		Capt. + QM - Stevens proceeded to England for demobilization.	
	10.4.19		Lt. Col J Millen to England on 14 days leave. Major Manfred 1/3 & 2nd 2nd came in charge & 1/1 & on 7 lends as well as the 1/3 & & 7 lends.	
	25.4.19		Lt. Col J Millen returned from leave.	

J. Millen

1/2 oz North Med 4/6

WAR DIARY
or
INTELLIGENCE SUMMARY.
(Erase heading not required.)

Army Form C. 2118.

Place	Date	Hour	Summary of Events and Information	Remarks and references to Appendices
INCHY	6.5.19		1 Driver R.A.S.C. and 5 R.A.S.C. M.T. including 2 Sergt + Cpl. demobilized. Also two Large motor Ambulances and one Ford Ambulance transferred to 46 Div M.T. Coy, leaving but one Ford Ambulance with this Field Ambulance.	
	13.5.19		3 Driver R.A.S.C. and 5 privates R.A.M.C. demobilized.	
	14.5.19		3 Driver R.A.S.C. demobilized.	
	17.5.19		Pte. WRIGHT W. 408396 demobilized in England.	
	21.5.19		Pte Prusloin 12714 demobilized attached R.A.S.C.	
	31.5.19		Sergt. S. Pilby A.C. Cpl. Johnson. E. + Pte Atkinson B. R.A.S.C. demobilized.	

J.C.Mulen
LIEUT. COL. COMDG.
1/2nd North Mid. Fd Amb. R.A.M.C.